D1177722

Operation Utah
The Die is Cast

Hubert Yoshida

Luna Blue—Morgan Hil, CA
Paperback ISBN: 979-8-9853432-0-5
Hardcover ISBN: 979-8-9853432-1-2
Library of Congress Control Number: 2022907986
Title: *Operation Utah: The Die is Cast*
Author: Hubert Yoshida
Digital distribution | 2022
Paperback | 2022

Dedication

To the Loved Ones and Families
of the Veterans of Operation Utah

Laura Tayeko Okamoto Yoshida

My wife Laura represents the loved ones and families of the veterans of Operation Utah who supported us and shared our uncertainties and fears, not knowing what was happening from day to day.

Their Prayers and letters helped to keep us sane during the carnage of war, the long hours on patrol and night watch, and the occasional hours of down time when we would reflect on our lives and our connection to one another.

To the many who lost a loved one, I send my deepest condolences, my gratefulness for your support during trying times, and the dedication of this book to honor you and your loved ones.

Foreword
By Henry (Hank) Barnett

Hubert Yoshida was a platoon commander in H Company, 2nd Battalion, 7th Marine Regiment (2/7) in 1966. After 55 years, he has written this book about Operation Utah – the first battle that US Marines and South Vietnamese forces fought against the North Vietnamese Army (NVA), March 4-7, 1966 during the Vietnam War.

My name is Hank Barnett. Hu Yoshida and I became close friends while we were in the Marine Corps and have remained so since. Both of us were infantry officers in 2/7. At the start of Operation Utah, I was the executive officer of G Company, 2/7. I was wounded late in the afternoon on March 4 and was evacuated from the battle by helicopter later that day. I did not return to Vietnam after being evacuated. I have read the final draft of the book and can say with confidence that anyone who reads the book will learn about what transpired on Operation Utah from beginning to end. The reader will also learn about some of the young Marines who fought the battle.

On March 4, Companies F, G, and H of 2/7 along with a South Vietnamese Airborne battalion, made contact with the NVA in an area near Quang Ngai City in South Vietnam. It didn't take long for us to realize that we were greatly outnumbered by the enemy. Thanks to infantry reinforcements, air, and artillery support, we were victorious, but paid a high price – Marine casualties were 98 killed in action (KIA) and 278 wounded in action (WIA). South Vietnamese casualties were 30 KIA and 120 WIA. NVA casualties were 600 KIA.

Hu's book tells the story of Operation Utah as described by Marines and Corpsmen who fought the battle:

– There is the account of a Marine fire team – three Marines, none of whom should have been there- who were killed together along with a US Navy corpsman who died trying to save them.

– There was a Marine – an immigrant from Poland – who, in spite of losing the use of an arm and suffering a sucking chest wound, was able to assist in carrying a wounded officer to a medevac helicopter. After all that, he was killed by a mortar explosion just as he was being evacuated.

– There was a young man who was an at-risk teenager. He joined the Navy in order to be able to sleep in a clean bed and eat three square meals a day. He became a Corpsman and served with the Marines on Operation Utah. After leaving the Marine Corps, he turned his life around and earned two Master's degrees.

– There was a Japanese American (Hubert Yoshida) who, as a child, spent time with his family in an internment camp in Arizona during World War II. Later, he enlisted in the Marine Corps and overcame discrimination to become a Marine officer and was a platoon leader in H Company, 2/7. On Operation Utah, he led an assault that successfully rescued another platoon which had been overrun by the NVA and cut off from its company.

– There was an unlikely pair of Marines: a Mexican American Marine sergeant and a maverick cowboy from The Dalles, Oregon who was a Marine officer and platoon leader in H Company, 2/7. The two men worked together to save a company of Marines that were overrun and, as a result, became lifelong friends.

– There was a Marine lieutenant who assumed command of a company and led his men through an ambush and came face-to-face with an NVA soldier in a bomb crater. With one hand holding down the enemy soldier, he had to decide how he could kill him at close quarters.

– There is the diary of an NVA soldier – it tells how he made the trek from North Vietnam to the area where Operation Utah occurred. His diary discloses his thoughts and his dedication to the cause he was fighting for. He was killed one month after Operation Utah ended.

Reading this book caused me to think again about war. Wars have been around forever and will, no doubt, continue to be fought in the future. Wars have been fought for many reasons – to fight evil; to defend a territory or way of life; to invade and conquer an enemy; to defend those who cannot defend themselves. Throughout history, and continuing today, the decision to go to war is made at the highest levels of political and military leadership. No matter the weapons or technology used, young men in their teens and 20's have carried the brunt of fighting wars.

Many of us who fought during the early years of the Vietnam War grew up as children during World War II and the Korean conflict. When our country's leaders decided to go to war in Vietnam—this was to "stop the spread of communism in southeast Asia." I remember feeling that I was doing something worthwhile and was willing to do my duty to defend against the spread of communism and protect freedom as a way of life. I think that most of the other young men felt as I did. I felt that way even after returning from Vietnam in 1967. But, as the years wore on, dissension against the war grew and led to a decision by the president of the United States to pull out of Vietnam instead of continuing to fight the North Vietnamese. South Vietnam was conquered by the North Vietnamese and became a communist country. Today, the decision to go to war in Vietnam is widely believed to have been a bad decision. 58,000+ American men and women lost their lives for no good reason other than they unselfishly responded to the call to serve their country. For those thousands who survived, many suffered physically and/or mentally after returning to the United States.

Today, our country finds itself in the same predicament as we found ourselves in the Vietnam War. A gallant response to the attack on the World Trade Center and Pentagon in 2011 began with early military victories against those who attacked us, culminating with the killing of Osama bin Laden. Then we found ourselves in Afghanistan, fighting a war to defeat terrorism. Once again, after years of fighting and suffering casualties, politicians in Washington made the decision to quickly pull our troops out of Afghanistan. I ask myself, "Why did we commit to fight in the first place?"

My hope is that senior political leaders and military leaders will be more careful in the future before making decisions to go to war – decisions that will affect the lives of young men and women who serve in the military. They, at the very least, need to know that their service will be worth the risk they are ordered to take by fighting in a war.

NOTE TO THE READER: The last chapter of the book, Chapter 23 is a memorial to the Marines and Navy Corpsmen who were killed in action on Operation Utah. They paid the highest price for doing their duty as a Marine or Corpsman – their lives ended much too soon. I could have easily been listed in that chapter rather than writing this Foreword. During Operation Utah, I was shot in the chest, triaged, and finally medevac'd to a hospital ship where an amazing Naval doctor was able to save my life. I am thankful each and every day that my life did not end when I was wounded. I am now 81 years old and have had a good life – my wife and I have raised three children, and have enjoyed watching the growth of six grandchildren, two of whom are now in college. These are the types of blessings that were denied these 98 young men as well as all the many other men and women who were killed during the Vietnam War. I am always mindful of the price these men paid for serving their country and their fellow Marines and Corpsmen. Please take the time to look at their photos and read what is said about them. **THEY DESERVE TO BE RECOGNIZED AND REMEMBERED FOR WHAT THEY DID.**

Henry (Hank) Barnett

Acknowledgements

During the research and writing of this book I was helped by many people who generously gave of their time and effort. Some contributed to the words that went into this book and I have extensively quoted from their contributions. There were others who were also experienced in writing their own books or online blogs and were helpful in helping me craft and edit this story.

Peter Amish, FAC Attached to Fox Company 2/7
William Asbury, Plt Cmdr Echo Company 2/7
Clay Asbury, Son of William Asbury Echo Company 2/7
Jack Archer, Plt Cmdr 81mm Mortar Plt 2/7
Hank Barnett, executive officer Golf Company 2/7
Ed Bonham, Plt Cmdr 3rd Plt Fox Company 2/7
Mark Bradley, Son of Lance Corporal James Bradley Lima Company 3/1
Herman Busse, Sergeant 2nd Plt Hotel Company 2/7
Bill Campbell, GySergeant Hotel Company 7
Thomas Ciccariella, Pfc. Fox Company 2/7
Stephen Cone, Hotel Company 2/7
Ralph Edwards, Brother of Lance Corporal Jay Edwards Hotel Company 2/7
Ralph Good, Sergeant 1st Plt Hotel Company
Simon Gregory, CO Lima Company 3/1
Nick Grosz, CO H&S Company 2/7
Gary Harlan Pfc. Lima Company 3/1
Michael W. Hastriter, Corpsman India Company 3/1
Danny Hernandez, Pfc. Mike Company 3/1
Bob Hodges, Pfc. Golf Company 2/4
Bob Ingraham, Corpsman Lima Company 3/1
Roland and Jeanne Johnson, Plt Cmdr 2nd Plt Fox Company 2/7
Hank Ketchum, Plt Cmdr 3rd Plt Hotel Company 2/7
Gil Litton, Pfc. Golf Company 2/4

C. R. Peterson, Raider Plt Cmdr 2/4
Frank Picon, Plt Sergeant 3rd Plt 2/7
Raymond Potter, Pfc. H&S Company 2/7
Donald Reyerson, Corpsman Lima Company 3/1
Gary Rood, Pfc. Fox Company 2/7
Bill Seymour, CO Golf Company 2/7
Dave Shelton, Pfc. Bravo Company 1/7
Dick Thatcher, Artillery FO 2/7
John Turk, Fire Team Leader 1st Plt Hotel Company 2/7
Gary Watkins, Corpsman Hotel Company 2/7
Edward H. Wetzel, Jr Brother of Chuck Wetzel Hotel Company 2/7
Mario Ybarra Jr, Son of Pfc. Mario Ybarra Sr India Company 3/1
Elizabeth Yoshida, Daughter of Hubert Yoshida

Preface

"As Caesar said when he crossed the Rubicon, 'Alea jacta est.' The die has been cast."

1st Lieutenant Simon Gregory

When Caesar crossed the Rubicon, the die was cast; It meant that war with Rome was inevitable. In the same way, Operation Utah signaled that we were committed to be a principal combatant in the Vietnam War and not just a supporter to the South Vietnamese Army. For the Marine Corps, Vietnam was the bloodiest war in Marine Corps history. The total Marine Corps casualties, killed and wounded, in Vietnam was 101,685 which exceeded the 87.940 Marine Corps casualties in World War II. Operation Utah was the first battle of the Vietnam War between the U. S. Marine Corps and the regular forces of the North Vietnamese Army. It was one of the bloodiest battles of the war and set the tone for many subsequent engagements. It Occurred on March 4 to 7, 1966 in Quang Ngai Province of Vietnam. It pitted three understaffed Marine battalions and one South Vietnamese Airborne battalion against the newly arrived 21st (also known as the 36th) Regiment of the NVA (The NVA was officially known as the People's Army of Vietnam, or PAVN, but was most commonly referred to as the NVA) and a Regiment of local Viet Cong (VC) forces. During Operation Utah, the allied forces killed 600 North Vietnamese and VC soldiers and destroyed the regimental headquarters that was located in a series of underground tunnels and bunkers near Quang Ngai city. However, the Marines paid a high price for this victory with some of the worst casualties suffered in a battle during the Vietnam War. American casualties were 98 killed in action and 278 wounded in action. The battle was hard-fought and won by Marines who stood their ground and carried the battle against overwhelming odds compounded by inept decisions made by their task force commanders and the failure of South Vietnamese forces (Army of the Republic of Vietnam) to support the battle and provide accurate intelligence of enemy positions. Every veteran who participated in Operation Utah—no matter how many combat tours they had in Vietnam—will say that Operation Utah sticks in their mind over all the rest. What distinguishes it from all other battles in which they participated was the intensity and length of the fighting. While other battles lasted an hour or so, the battles in Utah seemed to go on forever.

The number of U. S. casualties in Operation Utah was only second to the Army's battle in the Ia Drang Valley which occurred November 14 to 18, 1965 and was documented by Hal Moore and Joseph L. Galloway in the book, *We Were Soldiers Once...and Young*. The Ia Drang Valley battle had many of the same elements of Operation Utah. Three Army battalions fought an estimated two regiments of NVA. They both landed in hot landing zones and each had a platoon that was cut off. Ia Drang saw the army suffer 96 killed and 121 wounded at LZ (Landing Zone) X-Ray and 155 killed and 124 wounded at LZ Albany. Estimates for North Vietnamese losses are around 800 killed at X-Ray and minimum of 403 killed at Albany. The fighting at Ia Drang relied on air mobility and heavy artillery support to achieve victory. Conversely, the North Vietnamese learned that the latter could be neutralized by quickly closing with the enemy and fighting at close range.

While Operation Utah was a tactical victory, it opened up a hornets' nest of NVA and VC activity. The month of March 1966 was one of the bloodiest months of the war. Shortly after Operation Utah, on the night of March 18/19, the VC and NVA attacked and destroyed an ARVN outpost just north of the site of Operation Utah and the Marines were called in to help recapture the outpost. This turned into Operation Texas, followed by Operation Indiana, in which 110 Marines were killed. The mistakes of Operation Utah seemed to be repeated in Texas and Indiana, mainly the piecemeal commitment of understaffed battalions against a numerically superior force. In April, Marines were again called in on Operation Nevada, which was fought south of the Utah area and Operation Hot Springs which covered the same area as Operation Utah.

I was the Platoon Commander for 1st Platoon, Hotel Company, 2nd Battalion, 7th Marines during Operation Utah. In 1967, I left active duty to join the corporate world and raise a family. Aside from two reunions of my Marine Officers' Basic School class I had very little interaction with the veterans of that battle due to the demands of my work and family schedule. Like many combat veterans, I had little motivation to talk about my experiences in Vietnam with people who did not experience it themselves, even though a night does not go by when I do not think about what I did or didn't do. Many of those thoughts go back to Operation Utah.

When I was on a business trip in Vietnam in 2016, I took a few days off to visit the location of Operation Utah and posted a blog about that visit which generated some inquiries from people whose relatives had died in that battle. I realized these relatives and friends had a real need to know about what their brothers and fathers, husbands and fiancés had experienced in their last few hours. When I had a casualty in my platoon, I would write to the parents expressing my regrets, describe what I could about the circumstances of their death, express my gratitude for their son's sacrifice and the honor I had to have served with them.

One parent wrote back to me describing how his son had been while he was growing up, and how proud he was that his son had been a Marine and died for what he believed. I reread that letter some 50 years later. After having raised a son and seeing him grow into manhood and having a family of his own, only then did I understand how important it was for a parent to know all he could about a son's life and death. All the parents of these Marines have passed away with very little knowledge of what happened in their son's last battle. However, I believe there are many more who would want to know about these young men.

That caused me to want to learn more about that battle and document as much as I could from the perspective of those who fought there. Although I was a participant in Operation Utah, I realized that I only saw and experienced a very small part of the battle and so I have been researching it primarily to find the stories that these men could not tell. I have read some published accounts and recognized that there were some errors which I thought needed to be corrected and recognition for things that were not published. More importantly, connecting with other veterans and hearing their stories has helped me to come to terms with some of the issues that I have struggled with in my personal journey after Vietnam. Although official After Action Reports and historical publications were helpful, I often found them at odds with the recollections of the Marines who were there. For instance, many documents had Hotel Company 2/7 fighting on Hill 85 when they were actually on a small ridge that participants identified as Hill 37. Where discrepancies were found I usually went with the eyewitness accounts. Thanks to the Internet, GPS, and Google Maps, I had an advantage over earlier writers who documented this battle in the 1960s and 1970s. I am sure that this work contains some errors as I was not an eyewitness to every event, but at least it might provide another perspective and provide a clearer overall picture of Operation Utah. I regret that so much time has passed and so much has been lost and not everyone remembers what happened in the same way.

This book is dedicated to the Marines and Navy corpsmen who fought in Operation Utah. This book was primarily written for the veterans who fought in Operation Utah and their friends and relatives. I hope to give the veterans a broader picture of Operation Utah and explain some of the decisions that went into the way the battle was carried out. I also want to describe for those who are not familiar with the Marine Corps how the organization, tactics, and weapons were used at that time, so they can better appreciate what these Marines went through.

Operation Utah occurred over 55 years ago. 79% of the United States population was born after that date, so very few today can relate to what these young men felt or believed in back then. Their lives were quite different from what we know and experience today. I hope to communicate some of that time in history so that following generations can understand what these young men believed in and what motivated them to risk their lives so unselfishly. I also try to capture some of the stories of young men in combat, and how it has affected their lives after Vietnam as we head now into our twilight years. As Veterans, the die was cast in our favor and we survived. How did we spend this good fortune during our life times?

The Narrative

This book is organized chronologically in the order in which the different Marine units were committed to battle and is presented in eight parts to describe the different phases. The first part describes the buildup to Operation Utah. The next three parts describe the battle from the perspective of the three Marine Battalions that were directly involved. This is followed by parts that describe the activities of the Supporting Units, the Home Front, the Aftermath, and finally the Tribute to all the Marines and Corpsmen that were killed in Opertion Utah.

The map below shows the overall disposition of forces in Operation Utah. The upper right of the map shows the location of the artillery at Binh Son. The lower right shows the location of Buddha Mountain where the Commanders of Task Force Delta positioned themselves to view and manage the operation from Hill 101. 2nd Battalion 7th Marines and the ARVN 1st Airborne were located south of the line between Hill 50 and Hill 37. 3rd Battalion 1st Marines was located just north of Hill 50. 2nd Battalion 4th Marines and Bravo Company 7th Marines were located near An Tuyet. Other ARVN units were located around the area for blocking purposes but were not directly involved in the battle.

Operation Utah Area 4-7 March 1966

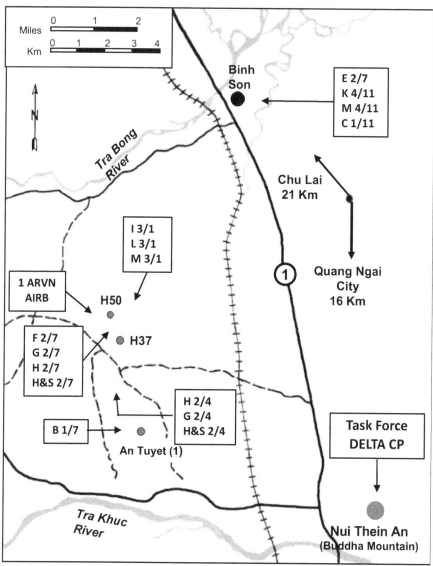

The narrative for a battle with so many moving parts is hard to follow without an outline. The following description of the parts and chapters in this book is intended to provide such an outline.

Part 1: The Buildup

Chapter 1 The Marine Buildup to Operation Utah: Since the organization of the Marine units is important to understanding how the different actions play out, this chapter describes the organization of a Marine battalion, and an introduction to the three Marine battalions that were involved in Operation Utah. It also tries to describe the young men who made up the Navy and Marine Corps at the beginning of the Vietnam War.

Chapter 2 Get On Your Horse And Go!: The second chapter describes the intelligence that triggered Operation Utah and the hasty decisions that were made by the generals of Task Force Delta that planned the operation.

Part 2: Operation Utah - Phase One

Chapters 3 - 9: The next seven chapters describe phase 1 and the activities of the different companies in 2nd Battalion, 7th Marine Regiment who were engaged on the first day of Operation Utah, starting with Fox Company, then Golf Company, H&S Company, and Hotel Company, who suffered the most casualties on the first day of the battle.
Chapter 3 Fox Company Leads The Attack
Chapter 4 Retrieving Fox Company's Lost Platoon
Chapter 5 Golf Company Holds the Center
Chapter 6 H&S Company: The Command Center
Chapter 7 Dueling Mortars
Chapter 8 Hotel Company Takes The High Ground
Chapter 9 Above and Beyond

Part 3: Operation Utah - Phase Two

Chapter 10 - 12. The next three chapters describe the second phase of Operation Utah in which 3rd Battalion 1st Marine Regiment battles the North Vietnamese who were entrenched in their regimental command post on Hill 50 as the Marines attempt to encircle the NVA.

Chapter 10 Mike Company 3/1 A Tiger by The Tail
Chapter 11 India Company 3/1 In The Killing Zone
Chapter 12 Lima Company 3/1 takes Hill 50

Part 4: Operation Utah - Phase Three

Chapter 13 - 14. The next two chapters describe the third phase of Operation Utah which occurs in the southern sector of the encirclement. Two companies from 2nd Battalion 4th Marine Regiment, joined by Bravo Company 1st Battalion 7th Marine Regiment were ambushed in a hot LZ.
Chapter 13 2/4 Ambushed in the LZ
Chapter 14 Bravo 1/7 In No Man's Land

Part 5: Supporting Units

Chapter 15 The Indestructible UH-34 And The Men Who Flew Them: This chapter describes the heroic support of the Helicopter crews that flew the Marines into hot landing zones, supplied them with ammunition and evacuated their dead and wounded.

Chapter 16 Fire For Effect
This chapter describes the support of the Marine Artillery unit 4/11 that provided a significant role in ensuring victory for the Marines and contributed to most of the enemy casualties.

Chapter 17 Corpsman Up! is dedicated to the Corpsmen, many of whom gave their lives to save so many Marines.

Chapter 18 "Ski, The Bastard Shot Me! This describes what it feels like to be wounded in combat and the process of retrieval and recovery of a wounded Corpsman.

Part 6: The Home Front

Chapter 19 Family bonds: Parents and siblings were important to these young men as many went directly from high school into the Marine Corp or Navy and had no opportunity to start their own families. This chapter describes one of the families that lost a son and brother and describes how they coped with his death.

Chapter 20 The NVA Perspective: This is a series of excerpts from the Diary of Vu Dinh Duan who was an NVA who participated in Operation Utah. Vu Dinh Duan was killed in Operation Indiana a few weeks after Operation Utah. The NVA also had close family bonds. His story helps to understand who the Marines were fighting so many years ago.

Part 7: The Aftermath

Chapter 21 Lessons Learned From Operation Utah: There were some obvious lessons that were learned in Operation Utah. Whether or not we learned from these lessons can be debated.

Chapter 22 Connecting the Dots: This chapter tries to make sense of what these young men experienced, and how it is affecting their later lives.

Part 8: The Tribute

Chapter 23 Gone But Not Forgotten: This is a photo gallery and brief bio of the men who were killed on Operation Utah. This chapter lists each of these Marines and includes their pictures which often speak more than words can describe as we look into their youthful faces. Since Operation Utah occurred over 55 years ago, very few today can relate to what these young men felt or believed in back then. Their lives were quite different from what we know and experience today. I hope to communicate some of that time in history so that following generations can understand what these young men believed in and what motivated them to risk their lives so unselfishly.

Postlude

Visiting the Operation Utah Area in 2016.

Appendix A

Award Addendum: This describes the types of awards and the process for nominating soldiers for these awards. There were many heroes who were not properly recognized. While there is a two year limitation on award nominations, several of the veterans have been recognized many years after Operation Utah. I describe some examples and include the process for award nominations in the hopes that some more heroes will be recognized.

The main sources that I used were:

˙ US Marines In Vietnam: An Expanding War, 1966
By Dr. Jack Shulimson 1982

Utter's Battalion 2/7 Marines in Vietnam, 1965-66
By Alex Lee · 2000

Loss of Innocence
A History of Hotel Company, 2nd Battalion, 7th Marines in Vietnam
by Stephen Cone Oct 30, 2012

"Fix Bayonets"
Bravo Company on Operation Utah
Robert C. Prewitt, LtCol., USMC (Ret)
February 12, 2004
http://www.hmm-364.org/1965/fix-bayonets.html

Operation Utah — US Marines battle the People's Vietnam Army
Bob Ingraham Nov 5, 2013
https://www.ephemeraltreasures.net/operation-utah.html

Silver Star: An American Story
Danny Hernandez April 17, 2018

Always Faithful: Returning to Vietnam
Gary Harlan July 19, 2020

ECHO 1-2-7
W.C. "Bill" Asbury, Dr. December 16, 2018

Texas Tech University The Vietnam Center and Sam Johnson
Vietnam Archive
For Command Chronologies and After Action Reports
https://www.vietnam.ttu.edu/

Part 1
The Buildup

Chapter 1
The Marine Buildup to Operation Utah

O peration Utah was the first engagement between the US Marine Corps and the North Vietnamese regular forces. This chapter describes the early, constrained, buildup of Marine Corps forces in the Vietnam War that left the Marines without adequate supplies and logistics. Since a lot of the action in this book revolves around the activity of different combat units, a description is provided on how a Marine Battalion was organized and operated in 1966. I also provide a description of the young Marines and Corpsmen of that time to help you understand the type of young men who fought and died in that battle. I end with some background on the three Marine Battalions that were involved in this operation.

Up until 1965, the Vietnam War was fought primarily by the South Vietnamese Army, known as the ARVN (Army of the Republic of Vietnam) with support from the United States. In 1964, the ARVN suffered some major defeats, and the North Vietnamese were reported to have attacked US ships in the Bay of Tonkin. The United States was reluctant to commit combat forces for fear that the South Vietnamese would lose interest and further relax their efforts to defend their country. The United States responded by increasing bombing raids on North Vietnamese targets. The VC retaliated by attacking US air bases at Pleiku and Qui Nhon, killing US personnel.

In an effort to provide greater security for these installations, President Johnson sanctioned the dispatch of two Marine battalion landing teams—2nd Battalion 9th Marines (2/9) and 3rd Battalion 9th Marines (3/9)—to Danang in early March, 1965. Marine battalions are self-contained combat units and are designated by two numbers. The first being the number of the battalion and the second number, separated by a slash, designates the Marine regiment to which the battalion belongs. So 2/7 would be recognized as 2nd Battalion, 7th Marine Regiment. A battalion landing team (BLT) is the basic Marine unit in an assault landing. It is composed of an infantry battalion reinforced by necessary combat and service elements. The reinforcements are usually a battery of artillery; a platoon each of trucks (motor transport), tanks, amphibian tractors, reconnaissance, and engineers; and detachments of communications, shore party, beachmasters, medical, and logistical support. BLTs are tailored to meet specific needs and the average strength of a BLT is about 1,500 men. The first Marines arrived on 8 March 1965, and this marked the beginning of the use of Marine combat units in the Vietnam War.

Marines Land in S. Viet
To Defend Key Air Base

Left Wing Laborites in Britain Join Voices Assailing U.S. Viet Landings

U.S. Fleet, Air Force Join In Operation

London (P) — Leaders of the left wing of Britain's Labor Party joined with the Communists today in assailing the U. S. Marine landing in South Vietnam.

The landings amount to "systematic and deliberate escalation" of the war, said Konni Zilliacus, leader of a group of House of Commons members who had demanded that Prime Minister Harold Wilson end his support of American policy in Vietnam. "This is just straight international aggression and nothing else," said Zilliacus.

"Unless the United States government is stopped by opposition from Britain, added to the opposition which already exists in large measure in the United States, we shall be dragged into another Korean War, or possibly an international war."

The 45 Leftist laborites who signed the motion be-

"THE TROOPS ARE EXHILARATED"—Men of the 9th U, S, Marine Expeditionary Force scramble ashore at Da Nang, South Vietnam today. Brig. Gen. Frederick Joseph Karch of

said in a front-page editorial that the Marine landing "accentuates the Indo-chinese crisis to the brink.

Carmi, Ill., said he imagined "the troops are exhilarated. There's a sense of relief at the prospect of getting some action." (AP Wirephoto. Other Picture on Page 23)

Agency (NCNA) saying the need to bring in more troops "provides further proof of the utter bank-

Da Nang, Vietnam (P)—The U.S. Marines landed by sea and air in South Vietnam today to strengthen the defense of the key Da Nang Air Base against attack by the Communist Viet Cong.

One battalion of 1,400 Marines came ashore from four 7th Fleet transport ships standing half a mile off the coast 380 miles north of Saigon.

3,500 More Expected

A second battalion began arriving without fanfare aboard C130 Air Force transports from Okinawa at the air base.

By early afternoon an estimated 2,000 marines were taking up positions at the base.

About 3,500 in all from the 3rd Marine Division at Okinawa were expected by tomorrow night, including a helicopter squadron. But the landing of the helicopter group was reported delayed by heavy surf which also

ed States from its desperate predicament on the South Vietnam battlefield."

Soviet comment was de-

Marine BLTs were chosen to be the first combat units, instead of the Army since the Marine Corps is considered to be a mission-oriented force, and would not be considered to be a permanent commitment. A BLT travels light and has 15 days of supplies. It is not designed with the logistics and engineering support for protracted land warfare. At this time in the war, the United States viewed this as a Vietnamese war in which we had a limited supporting role. Choosing a Marine BLT over an Army combat unit was intended to send the message that US combat troops were not intended to be a long-term commitment.

Another important element of the Marine buildup was Marine Air Group 36, MAG-36, whose mission was to provide combat-ready assault support vehicles. At this time, it consisted of UH-34 helicopters which were used in the Korean Conflict. Mag-36 arrived in Vietnam in August 1965. They were transported by sea and arrived in a combat zone when it launched from the decks of the USS Princeton for Chu Lai Base on 1 September 1965. Upon arrival, they provided resupply, troop lifts, air strikes, medical evacuation, and recon inserts/extracts for troops in the Southern I Corps area of operations.

The Marine intervention in Vietnam was at first very proscribed. The Joint Chiefs of Staff made this very clear in their landing order of 7 March 1965, which directed that "the US Marine Force will not—repeat—will not engage in day-to-day actions against the Viet Cong." General Westmoreland gave the 9th MEB (Marine Expeditionary Brigade) the responsibility to protect the vital Da Nang Airbase from enemy attack but declared that the overall responsibility for the defense of Da Nang area remains a RVNAF (Republic of Vietnam National Armed Forces) responsibility.

However, this changed as the South Vietnamese continued to struggle against the Viet Cong and were beset by internal political problems. By the end of 1965, more than 38,000 Marines made up the Marine Amphibious Force (III MAF) under the command of Major General Lewis W. Walt, and were fully engaged in combat operations. The Marines were the first of the U. S. Armed Services to deploy large numbers of ground combat units to South Vietnam. The Marines had responsibility for the area known as I Corps which extended from the DMZ with North Vietnam to the province of Quang Ngai.

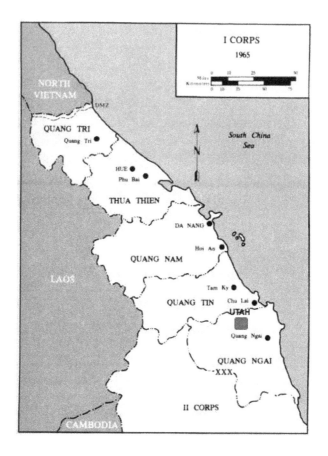

Logistics was a major challenge as the mission of the Marine units transitioned from being an assault force to being a permanent land force. In the first two to six months the first Marines to land had no logistic support. Unlike the Army, the Marines who landed in 1965 did not have adequate shelter or food or supplies to sustain them for more than 3 months in-country. If we wanted a hot meal, we bought chickens and pigs from the local farmers and cooked them ourselves. Fortunately there were enough farm boys who knew how to butcher hogs and roast them on a spit. Although the Army had facilities in major South Vietnamese cities and military installations, the Marines initial deployment was temporary and so they set up command posts in tactical areas where no facilities existed. They slept on the ground and ate two C-rations a day. They drank water from rivers and rice paddies purified by iodine tablets, and bathed in rivers. The first Marines arrived in cotton utilities and leather boots. After two

4

months their cotton clothes and leather boots were rotting away or causing their skin and feet to rot. Although the Army had jungle utilities and jungle boots that were lightweight and quicker to dry, the Marines didn't get them until late in 1965. The only shelter they had from the sun and rain was their poncho. If you wore your poncho to ward off the rain, you were drenched with sweat on the inside since the ponchos didn't breathe. The best use of the poncho was for hauling your dead and wounded. It wasn't until the end of 1965 when the Marines finally settled in base camps around Phu Bai, Danang, and Chu Lai that we had adequate supply and logistics.

The Marine Corps still used the old web gear from previous wars, which consisted of a cartridge belt and suspenders to carry pouches of ammunition, grenades, canteens, and first aid kit. The suspenders on this web gear were thin straps which cut into your shoulders and added to the many cuts and sores that you sustained when struggling through brush and leach filled rice paddies. The rifle they had was the M14 which weighed around 11 lbs. and fired a 7.62 NATO round which was fed from a 20 round magazine. Initially a rifleman carried 5 magazines with another in the rifle for 120 rounds. After their first firefight, most Marines added a few more magazines especially after they saw the volume of fire that the communist AK-47 with its 30 round magazine could put out. Marines could also take along a few bandoliers that carried 60 rounds in 5 round chargers. The chargers would fit on the open chamber of an M14 and the rounds could be pushed down through the chamber into the attached magazine below for fast reloading.

The M14 could be set to full automatic where the rifle will continue to fire as long as the trigger was depressed and there were rounds in the magazine. A full magazine of 20 rounds can be fired in about 2 or 3 seconds. Many Marines did not like to use an M14 in full automatic mode since the recoil from multiple rounds would tend to cause the barrel to rise when you were firing from the shoulder. Experienced riflemen countered that by holding the M14 under the arm of their trigger hand and placing their other hand over the plastic hand guard on the top of the barrel to control the direction of fire. That way the recoil went straight back and they could keep the weapon on target. The disadvantage of this position was that more of your body was exposed to enemy fire. The full automatic M14 could be accurately fired from the shoulder when targeting one or two rounds or firing from a prone position. Later in the war, the M14 was replaced with the M16 which was 2 lbs. lighter, and fired a smaller 5.56mm round in a 20 round magazine that allowed Marines to carry almost twice as much ammo. While the M14 was ideal for the battlefields of NATO countries, the M16 was better suited for the jungles and close in battles of Vietnam where the volume of fire was more important than long range accuracy. However, the M14 served the Marines well on Operation Utah since the Marines were familiar with this weapon and early adopters of the M16 suffered many malfunction problems due to corrosion and inadequate cleaning procedures.

The Marine Corps Rifle Battalion

The rifle battalion is the heart and soul of the Marine Corps. The rifle battalion attacks by land, air or sea and maneuvers by foot as it pursues its mission of locating, closing with, and destroying the enemy. An Infantry Marine identifies himself with a particular battalion throughout his career, although the Vietnam deployment did a lot to destroy that identity.

The battalion's primary weapon is the rifleman, and the fireteam that supports him. The U. S. Marine Corp is organized around a "rule of three." The rule of three assumes that one person can efficiently organize and lead a team of three people and every person on that team can cover for each other. It also facilitates the transmission of orders when you only need to tell three people who in turn tell their three people, etc. The rule of three applies to the number of fireteams, squads, and platoons in the rifle company. The fireteam is the basic unit in a battalion and consists of a fire team leader, an automatic rifle man whose rifle is set for full automatic fire, an assistant automatic rifleman, and a rifleman. Three fireteams make up a rifle squad which is led by a squad leader. Three rifle squads combine to make up a rifle platoon and three rifle platoons make up a rifle company. The rifle company also has a weapons platoon which consists of a squad of machine guns, a squad of rockets, and a section of 60mm mortars. The M60 machine gun and rocket squads consist of three teams of two men each, a gunner and assistant gunner. During combat operations a two man M60 machine gun team and a two man rocket team would be assigned to each rifle platoon. The section of 60mm mortars would consist of an eight-man squad with two 60mm mortars tubes and would usually deploy with the company command group in support of the company mission. During the Vietnam War, four rifle companies, a weapons company, and a headquarters and services (H&S) company would make up a battalion.

The rifle squad would be led by a corporal or sergeant. In addition to the three fireteams, a rifle squad would have a grenadier who was armed with an M79 grenade launcher, a single-shot, shoulder-fired, break-action, grenade launcher that fires a 40x46mm grenade. It has a distinctive *blooping* sound when it is fired and has a range of 150 to 300 yards. When fired, a grenade would have to travel about 20 meters before it would be armed. During Operation Utah, where the fighting was at such close quarters, the grenadiers would fire into the air, using the trajectory like a mortar to arm the grenade and bring the rounds in closer. Otherwise, they had to rely on their side arm, usually a .45 cal pistol. Squad leaders would often use the M79 to mark targets for their fireteams.

The grenadier also acted as the squad radio man with the handheld PRC 6 radio (a "Prick 6") that would be set to a platoon net for communication between the squad leaders and platoon leader. Maintaining contact with three squads, some 50 men, especially in rugged terrain where visible contact is not possible is a major challenge. The battery life of a PRC 6 was very limited in the heat and humidity of Vietnam and the durability of the handheld two-way radios was subject to the care of a Marine whose primary mission was to be a grenadier or rifleman, who had the radio dangling off his shoulder while he moved through the jungle and rice paddies, dodging bullets and mortar fire. When one of our NCOs went on R&R (Rest and Recreation) to Bangkok, he returned with some small transistor radios which could fit in a shirt pocket and were great for handling this type of communication. However, they were confiscated since they were unauthorized and were considered a security risk. Today we look with envy at the individual headsets that our modern combat troops are wearing as they go into combat.

Three 14-men squads would make up a platoon that would be led by a 1st or 2nd lieutenant, assisted by a platoon staff sergeant and a sergeant platoon guide. There would also be a platoon radio man with the larger PRC 10, backpack radio which was used to communicate with the company commander. This would bring the full-strength of a rifle platoon to 46 Marines. During combat deployment a reinforced rifle platoon would have a two-man M60 machine gun team and a two-man rocket team assigned from the company weapons platoon, and one or two Corpsman assigned from the battalion H&S company, for a total of 52 men. In some instances, forward controller teams consisting of an officer or senior NCO and a radio operator were assigned for air control (close air support and helicopters), artillery, and 81mm Mortar support. The forward air controller was a pilot who was assigned temporary duty with the infantry battalion. He was familiar with close air support tactics and could converse with the pilots in their technical language for calling in airstrikes and helicopter evacuations and resupply.

Although a reinforced rifle platoon at full strength would be about 50 to 52 men, after a few months in country, most reinforced Marine rifle platoons were less than 45 men, and as the months of attrition progressed, most were less than 40 men. In addition to combat casualties, there was attrition due to malaria, heatstroke, immersion foot, festering sores due to insect bites and cuts that did not heal, leave rotations, discipline problems, and a host of other problems that occur when men live under stressful, unsanitary conditions, with poor quality food and water. For combat troops, we slept on the ground in the open for most of the time in 1965. When we moved to the more permanent Marine bases like Chu Lai, the battalion H&S company would build temporary shelters. Oftentimes, when we were in an area for a while, we would chip in our own money and hire a local Vietnamese to build a bamboo hut for platoon use and acquire cots and air mattresses from nearby sources. (Our NCOs were very good at finding sources of supply which we did not question, usually at the expense of nearby Army units). Unknown to us at that time was the use of Agent Orange which has left a mark on many of us today. Despite the warnings, troops would often stand outside when the planes flew overhead to apply the agent just to enjoy the cooling effects of the toxic mist.

A rifle company is led by a captain and an executive officer, so, with the addition of the four platoon commanders, there were a total of six officers in a rifle company. In addition, there would be a 1st sergeant—responsible for the morale, welfare, and conduct of all the enlisted members in a company and the main bridge between enlisted Marines and their company commander—and a gunnery sergeant serving as the unit's operations chief and works with the executive officer to plan and coordinate unit training and operations. A full rifle company would be about 200 men with M60 machine guns, rockets, and 60mm mortars. At the time of Operation Utah, the rockets were being transitioned from the 3.5in bazookas of WWII and Korea, to the M72 LAW (Light Anti-Armor Weapon, a portable one-shot 66-mm rocket used to destroy fortifications like machine gun nests and armored vehicles). At the same time, the Marine Corps was phasing in the 60mm mortars into the company weapons platoon in order to provide coverage in the range between the M79 grenade launcher and the heavier 81mm mortars which were used by the battalion. Mortars also provided another assault dimension with its high trajectory which could be lobbed behind barriers and up hills where the rockets and M60 machine guns were not as effective due to their straight-line trajectory. During combat operations, companies could be reinforced with teams of forward observers with their radiomen for air support, artillery, and 81mm mortar support. A senior corpsman would also be attached.

A Marine rifle company in an online formation is an imposing sight. Imagine 200+ men in battle gear, helmets and weapons, spaced one to two meters apart. That is a span of about 400 meters or a quarter mile. They would also be spaced forward and back by several meters, usually with two up and one back. To actually see this in person is an impressive and imposing sight.

At the battalion level, four rifle companies along with a weapons company and a H&S company report to a battalion commander who is a lieutenant colonel. The weapons company had 82mm mortars, .50 cal machine guns, 106 recoilless rifles, and flamethrowers. However, during the Vietnam War, the heavier weapons like the .50 cal machine guns and the 106RR were too bulky to load in helicopters or carry out on mobile operations where there are no roads for wheeled vehicles so they were usually left behind. Flamethrowers were also left behind because of their bulk and the men were converted to a mini rifle platoon to support the battalion commander and H&S company. I would also like to think that our company and battalion officers did not use flamethrowers for humanitarian reasons. If you have ever seen the horrors and smell of men dying from napalm or flamethrowers you would never wish it on any human being.

The Young Marines of 1966

Although many of the Senior Officers and NCOs had participated in World War II and the Korean Conflict, all the rest of the young men had been born during World War II, had grown up during the Cold War, and started high school in the beginning of the 1960s. In the United States, the 1960s began with a wave of optimism. There was a young, new president who ushered in the age of Camelot. Who stood up to the Russians and proclaimed that we would land on the moon by the end of the decade, and told us to ask not what our country could do for us, but what we could do for our country. The generation of young men who served in the Marine Corps in 1966 were very idealistic. They grew up with war and the rumors of war. They all had fathers or uncles or other relatives who served in World War II or Korea, and were aware of the ultimate sacrifice which some of them made to keep our country safe. Communism was a real threat and many had done the school drill where they crawled under their desk in the event of a nuclear attack.

They had all seen the movies like *Sands of Iwo Jima* and *Battle Cry* and played at War or Cowboys-and-Indians with their cap pistols and BB guns. Television came along in the 1950's and their ideals were shaped by heroic westerns and idyllic families like *Leave it to Beaver*. Although some came from broken homes, most grew up in nuclear families where they ate dinner together every evening and were very close to their families. Many came from small towns and farm communities and were used to working at hard chores from a young age. Most had experience hunting and handling rifles and shotguns. Many had played sports in high school like football and baseball and enjoyed the feeling of being part of a team, especially a winning team. Many had never travelled beyond their hometown and never met people outside of their social group. Few if any had ever met an Asian person, or knew anything about Asian cultures. At this time in the war, these young men were all volunteers, most of them joining the Marine Corps as soon as they graduated from high school. These were the first young men to fight in the Vietnam War and were younger than the others that followed. The average age of a Marine that was killed in Operation Utah was 21.5 years and nearly a third of them were still in their teens. These were tough young men, who believed in their country and were volunteering to risk their lives for the cause of democracy.

However, life was not ideal for everyone. Everything was not perfect. There was still racial discrimination and segregation in the 1960s for people of color, Blacks, Latinos, and also Asians. Many of the Latinos were 1st generation immigrants whose parents labored in the field for less than minimum wage. As a Japanese American, I spent part of my childhood in a prison camp and remember being turned away from barber shops and not being served in some restaurants after we were released. Blacks were more severely discriminated against and could only sit in the back of the bus in some states. Black Americans and Japanese Americans had to serve in segregated units during World War II. It wasn't until the Vietnam War that the Marine Corps was fully integrated. The 2nd Battalion 7th Marines was unique in that it had two Asian American officers: 1st Lieutenant James Lau, who was a West Point graduate and the Hotel company commander on Operation Utah and myself, 1st Lieutenant Hubert (Yosh) Yoshida, who was the Platoon Commander for Hotel Company's 1st Platoon. Otherwise, there were very few Asian Americans in the Marine Corps at that time.

Black Marines who trained in the South, suffered discrimination. Often, when they went off base they had to go their separate ways. Latino Marines sent money home to families who lived in farm labor camps or city ghettos. Even with the level of discrimination during this period, Marines of color signed up with the same dedication and commitment as their fellow Marines. What distinguished these

Marines was their individualism and their commitment to serve their country. They would often be the only non-white in very stressful situations. 22% of the Marines who were killed during Operation Utah were Marines of color.

In 1966, the Vietnam War was still a noble cause, and the problems of anti-war protests, race-riots, and drugs had not touched these young men. However, Operation Utah was a traumatic event that was about to change many of their lives.

The Three Marine Rifle Battalions in Operation Utah

Three Marine Rifle Battalions were involved in Operation Utah and each was involved in the three different phases around which this book is organized. 2nd Battalion 7th Marines was involved in the initial phase which occurred on D-Day when they were inserted into the battle area on the morning of 4 March 1966 with a Battalion of the South Vietnamese 1st ARVN (Army of the Republic of Vietnam) Airborne Battalion. 3rd Battalion 1st Marines was involved in the second phase when they were quickly inserted into a blocking position north of the battle area by 1800 hours that evening in an attempt to encircle the NVA forces. 2nd Battalion 4th Marines was involved in the third phase when they were inserted into a blocking position south of the battle area on the next morning, 5 March. Attached to 2/4 was Bravo Company of 1st Battalion 7th Marines. What follows is a description of the combat capabilities of these Marine rifle battalions and their readiness as they joined Operation Utah.

2nd Battalion 7th Marines

2nd Battalion, 7th Marines, (2/7) consisted of four rifle companies which were designated by letters, E, F, G, and H (Echo, Fox, Golf, and Hotel). With H&S company, 2/7 was about 1000 men strong when it left Camp Pendleton for Vietnam in May 1965. The regimental commander for the 7th Marines was Colonel Oscar Peatross, who was a legend in the Marine Corps for leading the first raid against the Japanese on Makin Island, as a 2nd lieutenant in World War II. The battalion commander was Lieutenant Colonel Leon Utter who was an enlisted Marine at Guadalcanal and a platoon leader in Korea. Lieutenant Colonel Utter was highly respected by his men at all levels. Officers who have worked up the rank from private are known as *mustangs*. Lieutenant Colonel Utter was especially respected since he knew what it was like to be a private in combat and he took care of his troops.

2/7 was formed in July of 1964 at Camp Pulgas, in Camp Pendleton, California. The core of the troops had rotated in from the 3rd Battalion, 9th Marine Regiment which had just completed a tour of duty in Okinawa. Many of the junior NCOs (non-commissioned officers) were from 3/9 and most of the corporals and lance corporals had two to three years of field experience. And were considered to be the *old salts* by the privates and privates first class who had just completed their boot camp and Infantry training at Parris Island or San Diego. This core of junior NCOs were the squad leaders and fire team leaders who were key to the survival of 2/7 during Operation Utah. There was also a cadre of junior officers who had been platoon leaders in the old 3/9 and were now in different staff or executive officer positions as 1st lieutenants. All the new 2nd lieutenant platoon leaders had just graduated in June from the same Basic School Class, and so they were a very tight knit group. The captains and staff NCOs were brought in from other units across the Corps.

2/7 had a year of intense training at Camp Pendleton and had a short stopover in Okinawa before making an amphibious landing in Vietnam on July 8, 1965. 2/7 landed first in Qui Nhon to provide security for the Army supply depot and civilian construction company located there. They participated in several search and destroy operations with the 101st Airborne and Korean Tiger Division including Operation Stomp. During Operation Blue Marlin in November 1965, they made an amphibious landing by armored vehicles at Tam key and moved from Qui Nhon to rejoin the 7th Marines in Chu Lai. Their heaviest casualties occurred on Harvest Moon in December of 1965 which caused them to redefine some of their tactics. There were a number of other smaller operations and nightly patrols and ambushes. By March of 1966, they had been in-country for 8 months and they were suffering from the wear and tear of attrition with most rifle platoons down to about 38 men from their normal strength of 46 men. However, the remaining men were experienced combat veterans, with proven unit leaders. Having survived 8 months in-country, the men were growing used to the routine of almost daily patrols and nightly ambushes interspersed with larger sweep and destroy operations like Harvest Moon. The battalion had just been assigned to provide security for the Chu Lai Marine base and life promised to be more settled with a mess line for hot meals, showers and latrines, and even some tent squad bays. The men were beginning to feel confident that they were going to survive and were starting to count the days till June when many of them expected to be going home. A few new men were joining the units and some of the men were being promoted and given new assignments.

As part of the rotation plan for the Marines in Vietnam, the higher command decided to switch rifle companies within the battalions so that there would be a mix of companies with different rotation dates. This rotation plan was known as *Mix Master* and was strongly criticized by the unit leaders and the men who preferred to keep their battalion identity and continue to fight with men that they had trained with and trusted in combat. In late November 1964, Echo Company was replaced en masse by a company from another battalion just in time for Operation Harvest Moon. The new Echo Company under Captain Theer had three months prior to Operation Utah to learn how to work with the Marines in 2/7 as well as their supporting arms in the artillery battery from the 11th Marines. However, Echo Company was placed on security duty for an artillery unit during Operation Utah and was not committed to combat with the rest of 2/7. Fox Company was replaced at the end of February and the new Fox Company had only a few days before orders were issued for Operation Utah. The new Fox Company arrived in Vietnam in November 1965 as Hotel Company 2nd Battalion, 1st Marine Regiment under the command of Captain Jerry Lindauer.

2/7 was an experienced combat unit with a strong core of senior and junior officers and NCOs. However, they would be going into Operation Utah with only two of their original rifle companies, Golf and Hotel Companies, and a third rifle company, Fox Company, that they had not worked with before. 2/7 was down to about 600 men when they were committed to Operation Utah with Fox Company being closest to full strength with 230 men.

3rd Battalion 1st Marine Regiment

The 3rd Battalion 1st Marine Regiment was commanded by Lieutenant Colonel James R. Young who was a decorated veteran of the Korean War and an experienced combat leader who had been severely wounded on the Pusan Perimeter. The core of 3/1 came from the Marines who had served together in Okinawa as 1/9. In April 1965, 1/9 returned from Okinawa and became the new 3/1. Having just arrived from Okinawa the troops were eligible to stay in the states for 6 months. However, it was becoming obvious that the Marines were going to be committed to Vietnam, and over half the men from 1/9, about 700, signed waivers to stay with 3/1 so that they could go to combat with the men that they had trained with for almost 2 years. Some had their 4 year enlistments extended to join 3/1. They were joined by newly enlisted Marines who had graduated from Infantry Training Regiment and junior officers who had just graduated from Quantico's Basic School. Some of the former Platoon leaders from 1/9 like 1st Lieutenant Simon Gregory stayed with 3/1 and some of the Senior NCOs who had experienced combat in Korea, and WWII provided a solid base for training the new Marines. All the training was focused on Vietnam. The new 3/1 landed in Okinawa on 12 September and was assigned to Camp Schwab where they commenced an aggressive training program for the new personnel that had just joined prior to departure in order to transform them into an effective combat unit in the shortest possible time. A lot of the training was in the northern jungles of Okinawa. In mid-October they were assigned another 70 basic Marines who received accelerated training in their primary MOS (Military Occupational Specialty). 3/1 consisted of four rifle companies: I, K, L, and M (India, Kilo, Lima, and Mike) and an H&S company. 1st Lieutenant Gregory took over as the company commander of Lima Company during Operation Utah.

3/1 was designated a battalion landing team, or BLT, which meant that they would be a battalion aboard ship that would be ready to land in any combat emergency. At one time, they were on alert to evacuate US personnel from Indonesia, but that did not occur. On 7 January, 3/1 embarked for Vietnam and after an amphibious landing exercise at Subic Bay in the Philippines, landed in Vietnam on 28 January with an amphibious landing during Operation Double Eagle

I. Operation Double Eagle I was conducted in Quang Ngai province and Binh Dinh province until February 19. On 17 February, 3/1 officially disembarked at Chu Lai but immediately began planning for Double Eagle II which began on 19 February which kept them busy until Double Eagle II ended on 28 February. Just four days later on 4 March, 3/1 was called out to helicopter into Operation Utah with only three of their four rifle companies.

3/1 was under a lot of pressure with the hurry up training of new troops, and the non-stop schedule of boarding ship, amphibious assaults, and two months of search and destroy activities during operation Double Eagle I and II. Double Eagle I and II provided valuable on the job, combat training for the men in 3/1. They suffered some casualties and learned to work as a team and adjusted to the heat and humidity. It is a wonder that they were able to do so well during Operation Utah. Although 3/1 had trained in Okinawa for four months, Vietnam is much further south and the weather is even hotter and more humid than Okinawa. The first few days in Vietnam, especially after being aboard ship for a few weeks, takes a lot of adjustment. Just acclimatizing to the heat and humidity in Vietnam, let alone being thrown into combat with an enemy who was used to the weather and the countryside, was challenging. I have a lot of respect for what 3/1 was able to accomplish on Operation Utah.

3/1 was originally scheduled to go into Operation Utah with two rifle companies, Lima and Mike Companies. Fortunately, Lieutenant Colonel Young requested and was approved to include India Company. The rifle companies were reinforced with two sections of 81mm mortars and two squads of engineers who were used to clear booby traps and destroy caves and tunnels. Having just arrived in Vietnam in January, 3/1's rifle companies were nearly at full strength. The After Action Report for 3/1 does not indicate how many men were deployed for Operation Utah. My estimate would be that, with reinforcements, 3/1 was about 800 men.

2nd Battalion 4th Marine Regiment.

The 2nd Battalion 4th Marines, 2/4, was part of the first Marine brigade that was stationed in Hawaii prior to Vietnam. 2/4 was one of the first Marine Battalions in Vietnam. They landed in May of

16

1965 near Chu Lai. They participated in major engagements like Starlight, Harvest Moon, and Double Eagle I and II and were a battle tested unit when they were called to support Operation Utah. Many of the original members were short-timers, looking forward to going back to the states. The commanding officer was Lieutenant Colonel P. X. Kelly who would later become the Commandant of the Marine Corps from 1983 to 1987. 2/4 was called to helicopter into a blocking position to the south of Lieutenant Colonel Utter's 2/7's position on the morning of 5 March. The unit that Lieutenant Colonel Kelly commanded in Operation Utah seemed to be scraped together. 2/4 went in with two rifle companies, Hotel and Golf, and one platoon from Fox Company. 2/4. They were joined by Bravo Company from 1st Battalion 7th Marines. Bravo Company1/7 arrived in Vietnam on 18 November 1965 from Okinawa as Alpha Company 1/3. As part of the Mix Master program, Alpha Company was transferred to 1/7 and became their new Bravo Company 1/7 on 22 January. Although 1/7 had arrived in Vietnam in July of 1965 and participated in Operations like Starlight. Bravo 1/7 was a relatively new unit commanded by Captain Robert C. Prewitt. Mixing a company from another battalion presents some coordination problems as the radio frequencies have to be adjusted. And the battalion staff, the forward observers for air, artillery and mortars, as well as Corpsmen would be working with new people. Lieutenant Colonel Kelly's "battalion" that he led into Operation Utah was a little over 400 men, less than half the men that would normally be in a 1000 man battalion.

These Were the Finest

The Marines who were committed to Operation Utah were the finest that we had. They were trained, experienced and motivated to close with the enemy. However, they would be vastly outnumbered by the NVA and VC forces that they went up against. Their piecemeal commitment to battle, lack of good intelligence and the lack of support and false information from our South Vietnamese allies, led to some of the highest casualties that these battalions suffered during the Vietnam War. This is their story.

Chapter 2
"Get On Your Horse and Go!"

On 2 March, ARVN (Army Republic of Vietnam) units made contact with VC in the hill area 7 miles north-northwest of Quang Ngai and captured two VC. They stated that they were members of the demolition company of the 36th NVA Regiment and that their regimental command post was located in the hamlet of Chau Nhai (4). (There were a number of hamlets in the area with the name Chau Nhai followed by a number in parenthesis). On 3 March another intelligence report was received indicating the possibility of a regimental command post in the same area. Armed with this information, Colonel Bruce Jones, USA Senior Advisor to the 2nd ARVN Division, visited Brigadier General Platt on 3 March, just after Platt returned to his command post at Chu Lai following Operation Double Eagle II. Jones told Platt that the ARVN division had obtained intelligence that the 21st NVA Regiment had recently moved into the area northwest of Quang Ngai City 22 KM (13 mi) south of the Marine base at Chu Lai. This Regiment was known by both its 36th and 21st designations. This was not unusual, since giving a unit two or more designations was commonly practiced by the VC and the NVA. The analysts came to believe that the NVA were massing for a possible offensive action against Quang Ngai city where the 2nd ARVN Division was headquartered or against the Chu Lai Enclave which was a Marine Corps air base. This conclusion made things happen very quickly. The general officers had just come off of Double Eagle I and II,   large scale, joint Marine Corps and ARVN operation that began in January and had just concluded at the end of February. That operation was inconclusive as the People's Army of Vietnam and the Viet Cong had largely slipped away. As a result, the commanders were anxious to bring the enemy to battle, nose-to-nose with the superior power of our ground forces and supporting arms.

With the concurrence of both Generals McCutheon and English who were acting CG III MAF and CG 3rd Marine Division, respectively, Brigadier General. Platt, CG Task Force Delta decided to mount a coordinated attack with the 2nd ARVN Division. Platt ordered his senior regimental commander, Colonel Peatross, commanding officer of the 7th Marine Regiment, to meet with General Lam, CG 2nd ARVN Division. Colonel Peatross had worked closely with General Lam during previous operations. Peatross and Platt flew that evening with Colonel William G. Johnson, CO MAG-36 to the ARVN 2nd Division HQ at Quang Ngai City. Although the intelligence reports indicated that there might be two enemy regiments in the area, the 21st NVA regiment, plus a large regiment size, local Viet Cong presence, the American and South Vietnamese commanders agreed to launch a combined operation using 1 ARVN and 1 Marine battalion. A regiment would normally be three battalions, with 3000 men while a full battalion would be 900 to 1000 men. Pitting two battalions against a regiment, let alone two regiments, would put the Marines at a numerical disadvantage. If there were two regiments against two battalions that would give the enemy a 3 to 1 advantage. As it turned out, the combined strength of the two battalions would only amount to a little more than 1000 men—400 ARVN and 600 Marines, essentially the strength of only one battalion—that increased the enemy advantage to 6 to 1. There was also no contingency plan for any reserve force. This imbalance of forces was surprising since they had just concluded Double Eagle I and II where they deployed two Marine regiments (six battalions) and a division of ARVN against an estimated two regiments of NVA and 1 VC regiment.

Any time you fight an enemy on their home turf, you are at a disadvantage. They know the lay of the land, they have the support of the people. They have fortifications and booby traps, and large stores of ammunition. As the invader, you have to carry everything in with you and you have to navigate through terrain that you had never seen before. Going into Operation Utah there was no intelligence briefing given to the men expected to fight the battle. No recon was done of the area. I doubt if there was even an aerial reconnaissance done of the area. The troops going into this battle were expecting a continuation of Double Eagle II where they got on line and swept through rice paddies and villages with occasional fire fights which lasted a few minutes. The planning of these generals may have been influenced by the lack of contact during the previous Operations Double Eagle I and II, but having been forewarned of the possibility of a regimental command post in the area, they should have spent more time gathering intelligence and planning the appropriate force that would be required for success

Colonel Peatross chose his 2nd Battalion, 7th Marines which was commanded by Lieutenant Colonel Leon Utter. The planning period was very brief. Arriving back at Chu Lai late on the night of 3 March, Colonel Peatross and Colonel Johnson, who had been designated tactical air commander, met with Lieutenant Colonel Leon N. Utter, and told him about the forthcoming operation. Captain Alex Lee, the battalion's assistant operations officer, characterized the preparations as "nothing more than get on your horse and go."

Colonel Peatross and Lieutenant Colonel Utter

The odds became even worse on D-day, March 4, when the high command decided to assign one of 2/7's rifle companies, Echo Company, to a separate mission of providing route and perimeter security for M Battery 4/11. This was the direct support artillery battery for this operation which would be located in Binh Son, about 6 miles northeast of the operational area. This assignment meant Echo Company would not be directly involved in the operation with the rest of 2/7. This left 2/7 with only three rifle companies with about 600 Marines to face a fresh NVA regiment. Although the 1st ARVN Airborne Battalion of 400 men, from Quang Ngai was to join 2/7 in the assault, its presence proved to be more of a liability than a help due to their refusal to support the Marines at critical times and their misinformation regarding the disposition of their troops.

In previous operations like Double Eagle I and II, there would be an initial intense engagement and then the VC would quickly melt away, before the full power of the supporting arms and reinforcements could be deployed. The military planners for Operation Utah were probably guided by their recent past experience and possibly viewed this as just an extension of the previous operation. This may explain their haste in trying to close with the enemy and committing such a small force, two under-staffed battalions against a possible regiment or two of VC and NVA regulars. They also failed to warn the first line unit leaders of the possible dangers of the forces that would be aligned against them. The first line company and platoon leaders might have been more cautious in pressing their attack across open fields and villages if they knew they were facing a regiment of regular NVA soldiers dug into well prepared fortifications surrounded by booby traps and armed with heavy machine guns and recoilless rifles. The fact that the NVA and VC were so numerous and so well entrenched within 10 miles of a major city like Quang Ngai and a major Marine base like Chu Lai was not expected. It was later learned that there were thousands of NVA in the vicinity, building fortifications and stocking supplies in what appeared to be open farmlands for months. Having thousands of people in such a small area should have been detectable by reconnaissance units. They were well armed with heavy weapons, with plenty of ammunition cached nearby and fortifications that could withstand the heaviest aerial and artillery bombardments. After Action Reports reported that the shell casings of the NVA's spent ammunition were still shiny, indicating that these were fresh supplies and the fortifications appeared to be freshly dug in the past few weeks. This would not be another walk in the sun like previous operations. If the strength of the NVA presence in this area were better appreciated, more care should have gone into the planning and briefing of the troops.

The plan for this operation was to have the Marine battalion and the ARVN airborne battalion land inland by helicopter and sweep toward the coast, hoping to trap the enemy against the sea. According to the concept of operations, the two battalions were to land near the hamlet of Chau Nhai (5), 15 kilometers northwest of Quang Ngai City. The ARVN battalion was to land first at LZ (landing zone) Alpha, and secure the landing zone, followed by the Marine battalion. Then both battalions were to advance southeastward to the sea, paralleling Route 527 toward Chau Nhai 4, the reported location of the NVA regimental command post, and then due east to Route 1, a distance of seven miles. The ARVN battalion was to operate north of Route 527, while the Marines were to deploy south of the road. The Artillery battery from the 11th Marines would support them from the Binh Son located to the north, where they could provide enfilade fire across the front of the advance. It sounded like a typical search and destroy operation where the Marines and ARVN would land inland, get online and sweep east toward Highway 1 and the coast. This is a portion of a topology map at that time.

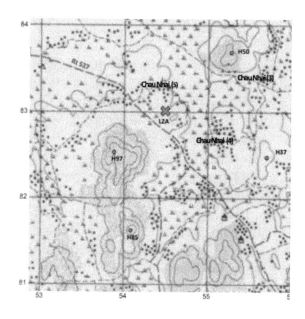

The objective area consisted of paddy lands and the hamlets of the Chau Nhai village complex. Hills 97 and 85 overlooked the landing zone from the southwest. Doughnut-shaped Hill 50 was the dominant terrain feature 800 meters to the northeast of the landing zone. The hamlet of Chau Nhai (5), was the first objective of the ARVN battalion. The area southeast of Hill 50 was to be the scene of extensive fighting during the next few days. Hill 37 was also a scene of heavy fighting on 4 March.

On the morning of 4 March, Marine A4s from MAG-12, F4s from MAG-11, reinforced by USAF Martin B-57 Canberra bombers, strafed and bombed the objective area to prepare for the helicopter landings. Despite this aerial bombardment, the MAG-36 helicopters carrying the first elements of the 1st ARVN Airborne Battalion were taken under 12.7mm (.50 cal) anti-aircraft fire as they began to land at 0900. Accompanying the slower UH-34 troop carrying helicopters were four of the new Huey, turbine powered, armed helicopter escorts, equipped with rocket launchers, grenade launchers, and Gatling guns. Within 10 minutes, all four of the accompanying armed Hueys from VMO-6 were hit. One made an emergency landing, 1600 meters southwest of LZ Alpha, between Hills 97 and 85. The crew was safely evacuated by a UH-34. Despite the intensity of the anti-aircraft fire, the MAG-36 helicopters continued landing. Ten of the 20 UH-34s from HMM-261 and HMM-264 in the first lift were hit. The presence of 12.7mm, equivalent to US 50 cal heavy machine guns, was an indication that this was a well-equipped regular force.

When hearing of the heavy resistance encountered in the landing zone, Colonel Johnson ordered by radio, all MAG-36 helicopters to report to Quang Ngai for a briefing. This order caused an interruption of all planned missions and "consternation in air command and control agencies, but was effective." Sixteen UH-34s from MAG-36's remaining transport squadron, HMM-363, soon joined HMM-261 and HMM-364 to lift the remaining ARVN troops from Quang Ngai to LZ Alpha. Thirty minutes after the first ARVN troops were on the ground, enemy ground fire shot down an F4 Phantom Jet from VMFA-531 while making a napalm run. The pilot and radar intercept officer were forced to eject over the South China Sea where they were picked up. Marine jets overhead attacked, while the tactical air commander increased the landing interval between successive helicopter waves.

By 1030 that morning, the last elements of the 1st ARVN Airborne Battalion had landed. The Marine helicopter group had completed the lift of more than 400 men of the battalion under most adverse circumstances. However, once they had landed, the ARVN troops met little resistance as they attacked northeast, crossing 500 meters to reach the base of Hill 50.

By now, intelligence reports were trickling into the 3/1 command post, back at Chu Lai, of the enemy resistance at LZ Alpha. The 1st Marines Operations Officer advised 3/1 to place two companies and a command group on immediate standby, for possible helilift to the Task Force Delta area of operations to a landing zone to be determined. Lima and Mike Companies of 3/1, 2 sections of 81mm mortars, two squads of engineers and a command group were alerted. Lieutenant Colonel Young requested and got permission to increase his force with one more rifle company, India 3/1. Things were moving in quick order. The action appeared to be shifting to the north around Hill 50 rather than to the East as per the original plan. Within 30 minutes, 3/1 was advised to establish a helicopter landing zone at Chu Lai, where they would lift off before dark to establish a blocking position in the area north of 2/7. The planners were still more concerned about preventing the NVA from escaping to the north while 2/7 was more concerned about surviving the night.

The Task Force Delta planners saw the resistance that Lieutenant Colonel Utter was experiencing and saw the opportunity to fix the NVA in position for annihilation, a goal that had eluded them on Operation Double Eagle. Using Utter's battalion as the pivot point, (some Marines described this as being the bait rather than the pivot point) 3/1 was to be deployed immediately to the north of Utter's battalion to cut off any escape in that direction, while 2/4 would be deployed to the south of Utter's battalion and Chau Nhai (4) where the NVA's regimental HQ had been previously reported. As it turned out, this intelligence was wrong. It was discovered later by Lieutenant Colonel Young's 3/1 that the NVA Regimental HQ was located at Chau Nhai (3) and Hill 50 which was heavily fortified.

3/1 was lifted into position by the evening of 4 March with three rifle companies: India, Lima, and Mike, minus one platoon from India Company who would join them in the morning. Their fourth rifle company, Kilo, was left behind to provide security for the Chu Lai base.

Lieutenant Colonel Kelly's 2nd Battalion 4th Marines was alerted to lift off in the morning of 5 March. Lieutenant Colonel Kelly was given Hotel and Golf Companies and one platoon from Fox Company from 2/4 and was augmented by Bravo Company 1st Battalion 7th Marines. Why a rifle company from a different battalion was assigned to 2/4 was not explained. It might have been done since the other companies in 2/4 were already committed to providing security for the Chu Lai perimeter. (2/4 had originally replaced 2/7 on the Chu Lai perimeter when 2/7 was assigned to lead the assault on Operation Utah on 3 March.) Additional ARVN units were deployed to the east and west of Utter's battalion to complete the encirclement. The encirclement would be in place by the morning of 5 March, although the battalions were still understaffed. After all the casualties that 2/7 suffered on 4 March they were down to about 480 men. 2/4 plus Bravo 1/7 was about 498, and 3/1 was in the best shape with about 800 men. They would still be out-numbered by 2 to 1. The pieces were all in place to bottle up the NVA 21st Regiment. Now was the time to execute.

Part 2
Operation Utah
Phase One

Chapter 3
Fox Company Leads the Attack in Operation Utah

Prior to Operation Utah, 2/7 had just returned to Chu Lai on February 28 after nine days of hard field operations in Double Eagle II and had just taken over part of the defensive perimeter for the Chu Lai Enclave. A new Fox Company under Captain Lindauer had just been rotated into 2/7 and its first assignment was to provide security duty around Tam Key, which was north of Chu Lai. Fox Company did not return to Chu Lai until noon of March 3, the day before Operation Utah. Fox Company had only twelve hours to acquaint themselves with a new battalion and prepare for a major engagement. The rest of 2/7 had no knowledge of the new Fox Company. Most of 2/7 thought they were going into combat with the Fox Company that we trained with in Pendleton and fought side by side with, in major operations like Harvest Moon and Double Eagle. This was not the best way to introduce a new rifle company to a battalion that was headed into a major combat operation. What follows is a description of Fox Company's actions during Operation Utah.

Although Fox Company was new to the battalion, it was chosen to lead the helicopter assault for 2/7 since it was the closest to being at full strength as a rifle company with over 230 men and 4 Officers. The other rifle companies in 2/7 had been in country for 8 months and were down to between 120 to 150 men with three to four officers instead of the normal 6 officers.

A helicopter assault is one of the riskiest types of assaults due to the type of vehicle that is used. At the time of Operation Utah, the helicopter assault vehicle used by the Marine Corps for the insertion of troops was the UH-34, a piston engine helicopter that was used in Korea. During our training at Pendleton, 2/7 had practiced assaults in Amphibious Landing Crafts (LST) and Armored Personnel Carriers (APC). The keyword is *armored*. The UH-34 Helicopter has no armor. Unlike the steel ramp in the front of an LST or the steel shell of an APC, the UH 34 is sheathed in a thin skin of magnesium, which provides no protection from incoming rounds. When an LST or APC is disabled, you can survive by swimming, when a helicopter is disabled you fall out of the sky. Helicopters also make a very tempting target especially as they hover and come in for a landing. The landing area is usually a large clear area with very little cover to avoid entanglement with the rotor blades. The UH-34 also has minimal fire power to suppress enemy fire. The platform is too fragile to mount rockets or Gatling guns. Their only weapon is a manually operated M60 machine gun mounted on a swivel on the side of the open door to suppress enemy fire. The newer turbo powered Huey helicopters with 20mm machine guns and rockets were often used as gunships to support the UH 34 troop carriers. While Hueys were used as gunships in the helicopter lift on Operation Utah, they were disabled after the first two waves by enemy heavy machine gun fire. The UH-34s with their thin skins seemed to be able to absorb the incoming fire and continue operating.

Fox Company's plan was to lead with 3nd Platoon under 1st Lieutenant Ed Bonham, followed by 2nd Lieutenant Don Lumley's 1st Platoon, and 1st Lieutenant Roland Johnson's 2nd Platoon. Fox 2/7 was scheduled to be picked up from Chu Lai at 0930 by approximately 20 MAG-36 helicopters. Because of the damage done to the helicopters during the landing of the ARVN battalion earlier in the morning, plans had to be altered. After some confusion in obtaining the right number of helicopters. A group of eight copters finally lifted off at 1040 from Chu Lai, carrying most of Lieutenant Bonham's 3rd Platoon and Captain Lindauer and his two radio men. There were no Huey gunships to support the landing since they had all been damaged during the previous ARVN landing. This was not the optimal plan that they had hoped for.

The plan was to land four helicopters first with Lieutenant Bonham and his machine gun and rockets followed by the other four helicopters if the landing zone was clear. LZ Alpha was reported to be secured by the ARVN, but they were greeted by sniper fire which caused the fourth helicopter to abort and the other four helicopters to delay landing. There were no ARVN there to secure the landing zone. They had apparently moved on to Hill 50. The three helicopters in the first wave were carrying seven to eight men each.

Lieutenant Bonham's helicopter landed with one fire team, two radio operators and a machine gun team. The other two helicopters landed a rifle squad, and the rocket team, for a total of about twenty to twenty-two Marines. Lieutenant Bonham was engaged in a fire fight immediately for about forty-five minutes. This small group suffered two WIA who were evacuated on the next wave of helicopters. They uncovered two machine gun nests and captured 2 NVA who quickly surrendered. If the NVA had been more aggressive, Lieutenant Bonham's small contingent could have been easily overrun, but the NVA did not act on their advantage. The prisoners were sent back on the next wave of copters. The other five helicopters with Captain Lindauer's command group were able to land and discharge their troops before heading back to Chu Lai for the rest of Fox Company.

A further delay in landing troops was caused by confusion at the heli-lift site. Although the pickup zone was marked with yellow panels, and a controller was present at each point, there was some confusion on the part of the copter pilots as to where loading sites were located in the pickup zone. Once oriented, and with the arrival of the remaining twelve helicopters, the lift progressed gradually, but with considerable shifting and reorganizing of heli-teams. From start to finish the lift took almost three hours to move 2/7's troops to LZ Alpha. Hotel Company was the last company of 2/7 to land and did not arrive at the landing zone until 1340. 2/7 had three reinforced rifle companies—Fox, Golf, and Hotel—and H&S company, consisting of 665 Marines. Echo Company did not make the assault since they were at Binh Son providing security for the artillery battery.

During the landing two Helicopters were disabled. One helicopter went down on the south side of Hill 85 and another was disabled and in need of repair at LZ Alpha. Lieutenant Colonel Utter was instructed to send a platoon to each site to protect the helicopters and crews. There are three rifle platoons in a company so taking a rifle platoon out of a company would reduce its force by a third. Golf Company assigned 1st Platoon under 1st Lieutenant Joe Lloyd to protect the helicopter near Hill 85 and Hotel Company assigned 1st Lieutenant Hubert Yoshida's 1st Platoon to provide security for the downed helicopter at LZ Alpha.

The ARVN battalion that landed earlier was located to the northwest and was starting to be heavily engaged in a fire fight with the NVA on the south slope of Hill 50. Initially 2/7 proceeded to move southeast as per the original plan. However, at 1330 the Senior ARVN Advisor, *Red Hat One*, Captain Pete Dawkins, reported by radio that they were meeting stiff resistance and requested help. 2/7 then received permission to alter the plan and move north to support the ARVN battalion. New orders were issued at 1342 to pivot 2/7 to the north with Fox Company on the left flank with instructions to tie in with the ARVN battalion, Golf Company on the right flank, followed by H&S company and Hotel Company in reserve. Since Lieutenant Bonham had already taken some casualties, his platoon was moved into reserve and Fox Company's formation was led by Lieutenant Lumley's, 1st Platoon on the left flank, and Lieutenant Johnson's 2nd Platoon on the right.

Lieutenant Colonel Utter recalled later that they had gotten off to a good start as they changed directions.

> We got off to a good start. It was fairly even ground, we had a nice even line with good contact, there was enough excitement to keep everyone on his toes, air was on station and artillery was within range and in position. I wasn't too concerned about being minus one company and short a platoon in each of the others.

When the order was given to pivot direction from southeast to north, this meant that the Artillery at Binh Son would be directly in front of 2/7 and this would restrict any fire on any NVA activity between 2/7 and Binh Son. Unfortunately, artillery shells do not come down vertically, especially when they are fired from 6 miles away. That means that the over-splash from the artillery fire could fall on 2/7. In the original plan the artillery would have been firing obliquely to the direction of 2/7's as it headed southeast. This new direction would restrict the support that could be provided by the artillery from Binh Son.

Sporadic long-range sniper fire and occasional automatic weapons fire met the lead elements of Fox Company as they crossed a patchwork of open rice paddies to join up with the elements of the ARVN battalion who were still firmly engaged on the southern slope of Hill 50. The ARVN advisor then notified 2/7 that they were going to work around the hill where they were at and Fox Company was directed to continue to move on the ARVN right flank until they were oriented to the north and to hold their line until Golf Company moved abreast. This seemed like many of the other search and destroy missions that they had been on. That was about to change.

Fox Company was maneuvering into position at about 1450, when they came under intense small arms fire, heavy .50 cal machine guns, and 81mm mortars on the left flank. The ARVN battalion did not move as they had indicated which left Fox Company exposed on that flank. Fox Company was caught in a crossfire with intense enfilade fire from the left flank and increasing fire from the front which prevented them from maneuvering to face the flanking fire. They were also caught in flat open rice paddies with fire raining down from Hill 50 which was supposed to be neutralized by the ARVN battalion. Lieutenant Lumley's 1st Platoon bore the brunt of the attack. Golf Company was also being hit and lost contact with Fox Company. Supporting arms in the form of air and artillery was being utilized to the west but the fighting around Fox Company was fierce, at ranges of 50 meters or less. This contact was different from any that they had experienced before. On other operations like Double Eagle, after the initial contact, the VC would quickly break off and avoid further contact. It was clear that the enemy they were facing were wearing North Vietnamese green uniforms and were not VC. These North Vietnamese regulars were different. They were dug in and were staying to make a fight of it. They also had heavier weapons like .50 cal Machine guns and 81MM mortars. Fox Company was in a nose to nose firefight!

A firefight is pure chaos. The noise is intense with the cracking noise of rifles and the thumping of heavy machine guns, the explosion of grenades and mortars, the ricocheting of bullets and the yelling and screaming of men who are wounded. There was also the roaring sound of close air support and the explosion of bombs and napalm, mixed with the smell of gunpowder, smoke, blood, dust, and sweat. Some men experience fear, especially if they were wounded. Others describe an out of body experience, where time seems to slow down. Others feel an adrenaline rush and they see things rushing by a mile a minute. The fire team and squad leaders are busy getting their men to fire back. Targets are darting back and forth. Unlike the firing range where you have time to line up your sights and squeeze the trigger, you point and fire as quickly as you can before they

31

shoot at you. The objective in a fire fight is to gain fire superiority, where the enemy is pinned down until you can close and destroy them. As you can see in the photograph below, you don't have time to line up your sights.

The growing gap between Fox Company's left flank and the ARVN battalion posed the greatest danger to the Marines. Lieutenant Colonel Utter requested Captain Dawkins, the U. S. Army advisor, to ask the ARVN battalion commander to attempt to close this gap between the two battalions but the Vietnamese commander "refused to do so." After the Marines altered their plans to assist the ARVN when they requested help, the ARVN failed to support their part of the agreement.

Personal account from Lieutenant Colonel Utter:

> This meant our left flank was wide open, with nothing to put there. But the People's Army of Vietnam (PAVN) had plenty of people, so they poured through… And back to the south the enemy was going at it again with Hotel Company. And there we were, taking it from 3 sides, the front, both flanks, and from an enemy who was literally hugging us so we wouldn't use our supporting arms.

32

Pfc. Emmett D. Westbrook, ammunition carrier, 1st Platoon, was wounded during the initial enemy attack. As the fighting continued, several heavily armed NVA attempted to envelop the platoon's left flank. Ignoring his wound and refusing evacuation he ran up the trail toward the NVA. He engaged them with rifle fire and throwing grenades which killed seven. Completely exposed to hostile fire, he rushed across the trail and succeeded in securing the left flank. Pfc. Emmett Westbrook would be awarded the Silver Star Medal for his actions.

Lieutenant Bonham attempted to close the exposure on their left flank, by giving his squad leader, Corporal Bruce Davis the mission of assisting Lumley's platoon in holding off an enemy assault and evacuating wounded Marines. Corporal Davis led his squad through intense fire against the enemy unit that was attempting to envelop the company's left flank. Through his aggressive leadership and skilled deployment of his squad, his squad was able to repulse the enemy assault without a single friendly casualty. His men succeeded in killing twenty NVA in the process. While he was maneuvering his squad in order to contact the left flank platoon, one of his men was seriously wounded. When he attempted to reach the wounded Marine, he was met by a large volume of fire. Corporal Davis, continued to move through the intense fire to the side of his comrade and gave him aid. While attempting to remove the wounded Marine, Corporal Davis was mortally wounded Corporal Davis was 20 years old and was posthumously awarded the Silver Star.

Personal account from Lance Corporal Guillermo "Bill" Castro, 1st Squad 3rd Platoon:

> I was with Corporal Davis and Corporal Robert Quigley on that trail on our right flank. We were getting heavy fire from that side and lost one of our machine gunners when we charged it. In that trail over the bushes, Corporal Davis got shot twice thru his chest and when he knelt down to help the machine gunner, he got one through his right eye. I was right behind him and when I started to pull him back, I almost took a burst of AK. That's where Bob Quigley got shrapnel in his leg from a grenade that the NVA were throwing at us over the bushes that lined the other side of

that trail. Me and Bob started throwing our grenades back at them.

The NVA then struck F Company with a heavy volume of fire; causing the entire Company to take heavy casualties and cutting off Lieutenant Lumley's platoon from the rest of the Company, clearly the enemy wanted to cut through the unit and reduce its combined strength. Captain Lindauer, was 200 meters behind his lead platoons, the 1st and the 2nd, when the enemy struck. He moved forward "...to get a firmer grasp of the situation." He managed to reach the 2nd Platoon on his right, but, 1st Platoon, further north, was cut off from the rest of the company, and the entire company was under heavy fire. Lindauer was hit by an AK-47 and suffered a badly shattered arm but he was still lucid and calling in air and artillery. However, his requests for supporting arms on the left flank were denied because they were too close to the ARVN battalion. Captain Lindauer reported his situation to the battalion command post. That is when Lieutenant Colonel Utter contacted the ARVN Advisor and requested that their battalion move forward to close the gap with Fox Company, but the ARVN commander refused to move, leaving 2/7's left flank fully exposed.

Personal account from Captain Jerry Lindauer, Fox Company CO:

Other than the fact that I was damned mad about the situation, I was lucid and able to make decisions. I radioed the battalion executive officer, Major Gentry, reported the situation, and remonstrated about delays in artillery and medical evacuation helicopters. I later apologized, explaining that I was somewhat distraught with all the dead and wounded around me and that I expected miracles in that field, but now realized that the battalion was doing all that was possible, under the circumstances. In fact, shortly after speaking to the executive officer, Air came up on the battalion tactical net and asked me to mark the target. I had a yellow smoke thrown and told him to take a 90-degree azimuth 100-200 meters from it and keep hitting it. Simultaneously Arty said they were ready to fire, so I told air to stand by until completion of the fire mission, and if Arty was on, to hit the same area. You can tell Jim Black

(Captain James O. Black, Commander, Battery M, 4/11) he was right on the money, and then the air started a continual attack which took a lot of pressure off us...

Lieutenant Johnson's 2nd Platoon deployed with two squads on line facing the objective and one squad in reserve. Coming on line, the chatter by these Marines was quite loud. But once in position, all talk stopped. Several minutes later, 2nd Platoon secured the left flank with 1st Platoon and Golf Company coming on the right. The 2nd Platoon then moved forward when an NVA in a spider trap threw off the trap door, not realizing that 2nd Platoon was behind them, rather than in front. Pfc. Haygood shot and killed two or three of the enemy.

The advance stalled as men sought cover behind the low paddy dikes. Realizing that this would not protect them for long due to the heavy machine guns that were chewing up the paddy dikes in huge chunks, Sergeant Donnell Dean McMillin, an eight-year veteran, age 25, sprang into action. With complete disregard for his own personal safety, he made his way through intense enemy fire to some of his men who could not advance. Ignoring the vicious fire, he led these men out of their covered position and across a fire-swept rice paddy to rout the enemy. Immediately after this movement, the leader of the 3rd Platoon, Lieutenant Johnson, was seriously wounded and Sergeant McMillin, with full knowledge of the hazard involved, went to his aid. In doing so, he was mortally wounded. However, his bold initiative and uncommon courage inspired his men to continue the offensive and avoided being picked off by the heavy machine guns. Sergeant McMillin was posthumously awarded the Silver Star. He was one of the few enlisted men who was married. He was the husband of Dorothy L. McMillin of Mena, AR.

Lance Corporal Michael Shands was the gunner on a rocket team with Pfc. Gary Rood that was assigned to 2nd Platoon. While they were waiting for the helicopters to take them into the landing zone, Shands made the comment that he would like to get shot in the leg if he was to be wounded in the coming battle. Unfortunately, he was killed in the early part of the battle. His assistant gunner, Rood, picked up his four LAW (Light Anti-armor Weapon) rockets and continued the advance with the rest of the platoon. Rood fired off 7 of the rockets until the last LAW failed to fire as he was attempting to take out a .50 cal machine gun nest. Rood ran back through a hail of fire to get grenades, then ran back to within thirty feet of the .50 cal machine gun nest, where he was able to take out the nest with his grenades, eliminating a serious threat which had prevented the advance of Lieutenant Johnson's 2nd Platoon. The Marines used the captured machine guns on the enemy, until the ammunition ran out. Efforts by the NVA to maneuver between Fox and Golf Companies were thwarted by the use of those enemy weapons. Pfc. Gary Rood would be awarded the Silver Star Medal for his actions.

In a matter of minutes, all of the officers except Lieutenant Bonham became casualties. In addition to Captain Lindauer, their Forward Air Controller, Lieutenant Pete Amish, was wounded and his radio man was killed while trying to locate a landing zone for medevacs. 1st Platoon's Lieutenant Lumley was killed and 2nd Platoon's Lieutenant Johnson was severely wounded while advancing through a rice paddy. Lieutenant Johnson's radioman Pfc. Alfred Smith and a rocket man were killed around him. Lieutenant Johnson was hit by an AK round that went through his flak jacket and lodged in his left lung. At the same time two grenades landed around him, but fortunately did not detonate. Lieutenant Johnson's first thought when he was shot was for his mother whom he was supporting. He wondered how she would survive without his support. Lieutenant Johnson lay there in the open for some time, an hour or more, before the corpsmen were able to move him behind a rice paddy dike. Breathing was difficult and they had to prop him up in order to breathe. It took several hours before he could be evacuated. Lieutenant Johnson was also the acting executive officer until he was evacuated. This left Lieutenant Bonham as the only officer to lead the company. His first task was to assess where everyone was. With so many key people down, it was difficult to know who was still operable and where everyone was. Many of the radio men were also down as their radio antennas and bulky gear made them prime targets. In order to get information, Lieutenant Bonham used Pfc. Thomas Ciccariella as his runner to help assess the situation and find the few leaders who were left.

1st Lieutenant Peter Amish, the Forward Air Controller and his Radio Operator, Pfc. Thomas Wardrop III, were assigned to Fox Company from H&S company and were working under the most adverse conditions, initiating airstrikes and medical evacuations.

While simultaneously requesting close air support and maneuvering across the fire-swept terrain to locate a helicopter landing zone, Lieutenant Amish was seriously wounded by a sniper. A firefight erupted around Amish as he lay on the ground alone and exposed. Pfc. Wardrop heard his cries for help. Pfc. Wardrop, while still carrying his heavy radio equipment and with complete disregard for his own safety, exposed himself, without hesitation, to enemy fire, and went to aid the wounded officer. Pfc. Wardrop was mortally wounded attempting to shield the wounded officer from the unrelenting fusillade. His heroic action was directly responsible for saving the officer's life. A third Marine, Pfc. Frank Lopez Jr., another communicator, tried to reach them.

"Get out of here!" Amish warned Lopez as he approached. An instant later, Pfc. Lopez was fatally wounded. His body also fell on Amish, who was eventually rescued by Marine reinforcements.

Pfc. Ronald William Goddard was the son of a widowed mother Mildred A. Goddard of Seattle, WA, was one of the youngest Marines with 2/7, having enlisted at 17. Now at the age of 18, he was a Marine anti-tank assaultman, carrying an M20 bazooka. He was also in Lumley's left flank platoon, bearing the brunt of vicious enemy automatic weapons and small arms fire. When his platoon became pinned down and sustained several casualties. Pfc. Goddard, seeing one casualty lying in an exposed position, immediately ran through the fierce enemy fire to the aid of his comrade. In doing so he was mortally wounded. For his initiative and courageous actions, Pfc. Goddard was posthumously awarded a Bronze Star for valor.

Ammunition was running low in all companies and the issue was still in doubt. Fox Company had neither the combat power to move forward in its widely spread formation, nor did it have the flexibility of movement to consolidate for further action. The wounded could not be abandoned and they had to be moved before any maneuver was possible. Marines were scrounging ammunition and grenades from the dead and wounded. Some Marines were trying to learn how to use the Russian made AK-47s taken from dead enemy soldiers.

Lance Corporal William F. Costello, attached to Fox Company as an informational service representative, was traveling with the Company HQ group. After the company became engaged in an intense firefight with the well organized and entrenched enemy, rather than reporting from a concealed position, exposed himself to enemy fire, and calmly helped Marines load magazines. As casualties continued to mount, Costello, seeing a Marine burned by white phosphorus, ignored enemy fire and went to his aide. Since phosphorus ignites in contact with air. Lance Corporal Costello made a mudpack and applied it to the man who was severely burned, undoubtedly saving a fellow Marine's life. Lance Corporal William Costello would be awarded the Silver Star Medal for his actions.

Ammunition was finally brought in by two helicopters, which swooped in under fire, and jettisoned their badly needed cargo, from 50-100 feet in the air. The battalion S4, Captain Martin E. O'Connor, had organized a group of 81mm mortarmen to distribute ammunition to the frontline elements from the battalion landing zone. At the moment Captain O'Connor and his men arrived in the Fox Company area, after crossing several hundred meters of open rice paddies, the enemy fire slackened. They dropped off the ammunition boxes and cases of grenades, then the H&S company mortarmen moved forward, to gather the wounded Marines and evacuate them to the rear. The wounded had been concentrated as much as possible into low places, where they would be partially sheltered from enemy fire.

Personal account from Daniel Anderson, H&S 81mm Mortars FO radioman:

> I was Comm. I was usually the radio half of a two-man FO team for our battalion's 81mm mortars. But I was assigned to Bob Gentry, battalion executive officer that day. Did make a couple of trips to Fox Company's position bringing ammo and grenades up and wounded back. Freaking hot that day... I also caught the staff meeting the night before due to just being on radio watch when the staff meeting went down. Time compresses and skews memory but I think there was supposed to be one NVA battalion. Turns out we ran into three. And they weren't alone either. Lindauer was just following orders. Leon Utter sorely missed not having Echo company with us that day. ARVN commander not supporting our left didn't help either.

By this time, 1st Lieutenant Yoshida's platoon from Hotel Company that had been providing security for a helicopter that was downed at LZ Alpha, was sent to Fox Company by Lieutenant Colonel Utter to assist Lieutenant Bonham in recovering the Fox Company platoon that was cut off. According to Utter, "although the situation was dire. . . the decision was made for me—they [the H Company platoon] had to go to that open left flank." Lieutenant Bonham recognized Lieutenant Yoshida, coming across the open fields of fire, having worked with him briefly at Camp Pendleton. He quickly briefed Lieutenant Yoshida on the situation with Lumley's platoon. He had lost communications with the platoon and assigned Pfc. Glen Hensely to Lieutenant Yoshida as a radioman to provide communication with the Fox Company net.

Lieutenant Yoshida's platoon headed down the path that the previous Fox Company Platoon was last seen on before they were cut off. The thought was to work through the hedgerows to gain some cover and retain some element of surprise. Fortunately, Lance Corporal George Kabeller spotted an NVA bunker and was able to sneak up behind them and drop in some grenades. This caused the other NVA in the area to panic and break cover, attempting to escape up the path. The hedgerows worked to the Marines' advantage and Sergeant Good's squad quickly chased them down and was able to kill all the NVA, some 15 to 20 men.

They found the Fox Company platoon in a small clearing surrounded by dead NVA. Sergeant August O. Miller had taken charge of the platoon and reported that Lieutenant Lumley was further ahead and was pinned down in an open field with two other men. Any attempt to recover the men in the open field would result in more casualties as they were well covered by enemy fire. Radio contact was established with the men that were pinned down and it was determined that Lieutenant Lumley was dead, but the other two men were mobile. Lieutenant Yoshida advised them that the only way out was for them to make a break to our side when they laid down a volley of covering fire on the opposite hedgerow. On signal, the Marines opened up with everything they had, including 3.5 rocket launchers and the two men were able to make it back to safety. Unfortunately, Lieutenant Lumley's body had to be left behind since it could not be retrieved without risking further casualties. The NVA were caught by surprise thanks to the aggressiveness of Lance Corporal George Kabeller and Corporal Ralph Good and his squad. The platoon from Hotel Company suffered only 1 KIA, Lance Corporal Robert Lee Smith, their

Machine Gunner, and two WIA, Corporal Moore and Lance Corporal McClung. After retrieving the two men who were pinned down with Lieutenant Lumley, the Hotel Platoon then helped evacuate the wounded from Fox Company and made their way to consolidate back to the battalion command post at Chau Nhai (4). Fox Company had put up a tremendous fight as the area was littered with dead NVA. You could not walk around the hedgerows without stepping on dead NVA bodies.

In the meantime, Lieutenant Colonel Utter sent his assistant operations officer, Captain Alex Lee to relieve Captain Lindauer and assist Lieutenant Bonham who was keeping Fox Company together. The runner, Pfc. Thomas Ciccariella was sent to guide Captain Lee to the Fox Company command post. Captain Lee asked "Can you get me to Fox Company without getting shot?" Ciccariella confidently responded that he had gotten here without getting shot and if he followed him and stayed low he would get him back without either of them getting shot and he did. Captain Lee was met by Lieutenant Bonham and 1st Sergeant Gene Mills who helped him assess the situation and reorganize what was left of the company. After Lumley's 1st Platoon was successfully recovered by the Hotel Company platoon. Fox Company withdrew on orders to the battalion command post which was consolidating at Chau Nhai (4).

Before consolidating to Chau Nhai (4) where the 2/7 command post was located, the 2/7 companies were situated as shown on the following map. Fox Company was located at the base of Hill 50. Hotel Company was fighting for their life on Hill 37 and Golf Company was between Fox Company and Hotel Company maintaining the center of the formation from a hedgerow.

Disposition of 2/7 Forces On 4 March 1966

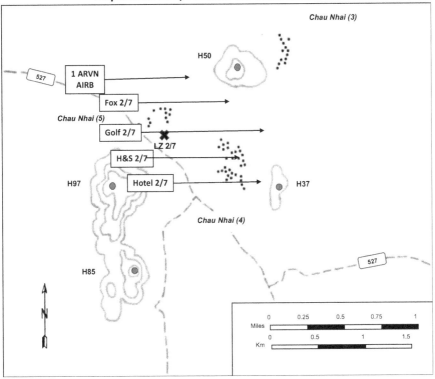

The next day, Lieutenant Bonham led the remaining Fox Company survivors to recover the remaining bodies of Marines that were left behind, including that of Lieutenant Lumley. They also found a lot of NVA KIA and a few who were wounded. The NVA had not returned to the battle area to recover their dead as they normally did. The NVA may have been spooked by the assault by the Hotel Company platoon and thought it was a counter attack which prevented them from going back to police up their dead and wounded. These NVA wore new uniforms and were obviously new troops who had travelled a long way from their home villages in North Vietnam. They were young men who had probably never been far from home and they had just experienced bombardment with napalm and 500 pound bombs, as well as strafing from close jet air support and helicopter gunships with their 6000 rpm gatling guns. It was understandable if they were shaken up.

The first helicopters that were slated to arrive the next morning, 5 March, were supply helicopters with much needed ammunition and water. However, the first helicopter was filled with press correspondents and camera men. They descended on the Fox Company area like vultures and one of the cameramen began to remove the ponchos which were covering the dead Marines in order to take pictures. The dead were still in the area since priority was given to evacuation of the wounded during the night. According to Captain Alex Lee, who had replaced Captain Lindauer, as commanding officer of Fox Company:

> A violent rage ripped through us all at the thought that he would do such a thing. Physical violence followed within seconds, and both the cameraman and his camera were harmed... The incident could have been followed by the murder of the cameramen had not Lieutenant Colonel Utter arrived. His hatred for the indignity being done to his dead Marines was obvious, but he held his blazing temper and separated the unhurt newsmen and camera men from the out-of-control Fox Company command group.

This was the first engagement between the US Marine Corps and regular North Vietnamese troops. They were well-equipped, well-disciplined and ready to stand and fight. Lieutenant Colonel Utter characterized the NVA enemy by saying, "They're not supermen. But they can fight. And they will fight when cornered or when they think they have you cornered."

****

Captain Lindauer recovered from his wounds and retired as a Lieutenant Colonel after 20 years in the Marine Corps. He later became a lawyer and worked in the US Secretary of Defense Office for James Schlesinger and Donald Rumsfeld. He also became a well-known executive in the telecommunications industry.

Lieutenant Roland Johnson returned to Vietnam after recovering from his wounds in Guam. He left the Marine Corps and retired from the Texas Workforce Commission while teaching sociology and psychology at Kilgore College. He lives with his wife Jeanne in Kilgore Texas.

Lieutenant Bonham who played such a key role in keeping Fox Company together during the attack, was also the youngest officer in the battalion, having just turned 22 at the time of Utah. Lieutenant Bonham had a successful corporate career and recently retired from Bank of America. He lives with his wife, Barbara, in upstate New York.

Sergeant August O. Miller, whose leadership kept Fox Company's 1st Platoon together when they were cut off, was awarded a battlefield commission and later trained new officers at Quantico.

Pfc. Thomas Ciccariella left the Marine Corps and after 7 years joined the Army and retired as a Colonel. Colonel Ciccariella publishes a Fox Company newsletter and is active in organizing Fox Company Reunions.

As of March 2020, Julio Schnars, who was the Marine who was burned by the WP Grenade visited Gary Rood and appeared to be doing well.

Chapter 4
Retrieving Fox Company's Lost Platoon

The following is my account of the actions of the 2/7 Hotel Company platoon that was called up to aid Fox Company in the recovery of their 1st Platoon that had been cut off during Operation Utah. My name is Hubert Yoshida, and I was a 1st Lieutenant in charge of 1st Platoon Hotel Company during this operation.

I received a heads up call that we would be going on an operation toward the late afternoon of March 3. I called up my squad leaders and told them to call in their patrols and get their men ready to mount out in the early morning. Our perimeter would be turned over to a platoon from 2/4. We would not get the details of the plan until late that night. It was about 0400 when I was finally briefed by 1st Lieutenant Lau who had just been promoted to company commander from executive officer. Captain Marty O'Conner who had been our CO since we formed up at Camp Pendleton had just been promoted to Battalion S4. 1st Lieutenant Bill Peters from 2nd Platoon was promoted to take Jim Lau's old position as executive officer and Bill's Platoon was assigned to his platoon sergeant, Staff Sergeant McDermitt. McDermitt was a tall, lanky Marine who was a Korean War veteran and well-respected by the troops. I had 1st Platoon and 1st Lieutenant Harry Ketchum had 3rd Platoon. Bill Peters, Harry Ketchum and I had been classmates in Officer Candidate School and Basic School and had been with Hotel Company since its formation in 1964.

Someone said that steak was being served that evening in the chow line. I had too much to do so I skipped dinner and ate some leftover C-rations. After seeing that the men were getting supplied with ammo and had their gear ready for the next day, I left to take a shower since I did not know how long we would be in the field. I also changed into a clean set of jungle utilities. The showers were out in the open and gravity fed by a large water tank. Someone had painted *Class of 1966* on the water tank.

When we were on watch, we lived in small bunkers or foxholes on the perimeter. Our platoon NCOs, Staff Sergeant Bedwell and platoon guide Sergeant Jack Holmes had hired a local workman to build a bamboo hut for our platoon gear. It slept about twenty-five men, so when the men were not on patrol or perimeter duty we had a place to relax that was near our tactical area. The night before an operation the bamboo hut was where we all prepared ourselves in different ways. We didn't know whether tomorrow would be another walk in the sun like Double Eagle, dodging VC snipers, or another bloodbath like Harvest Moon. After cleaning their weapons and loading their magazines these young men had time to prepare mentally for tomorrow.

Every Marine thinks about the odds of returning home alive before each operation. Most of the Marines who were still in 1st Platoon since it shipped out in June of 1965, had survived 6 or 7 operations, numerous patrols and fire fights, and were looking forward to rotating home by the end of June. Each new operation was a roll of the dice. How many times could we roll the dice before our number comes up or we seven out. Will our luck hold out until the end of June? Has the die already been cast regarding our fate?

Some of the men took time to write a letter, others played cards, some gathered in small groups to shoot the breeze or just stayed by themselves trying to sleep and not think of the next day or the memories of back home. Some of the Marines had ordered 11-inch, Randall Bowie Knives from a mail order company and were honing them to a razor's edge. Many sorted through their gear to see what they would take with them, a lucky piece, a picture, or letter. I carried a small Korean bible that had been given to me by a South Korean chaplain that I befriended when we were in Qui Nhon with the Korean Tiger Division. I couldn't read it but I always took it with me since I had gifted him my bible which my brother-in-law, George Suda, had given me. The rest of our gear we piled in our corner of the hut, in designated areas, so that it could be picked up and sent home in case we didn't make it back. We usually had a company clerk or someone who was not going on the operation to watch our gear. I went back to the hut and wrote a letter to my wife, Laura. I don't remember what I wrote or whether I even mailed it.

The turn-around time to send a letter and receive a reply was about a two week overlap. Most of the Marines wrote to their parents, other family members, or their friends from high school. Most of the Marines at that time were 19 to 21 years old and had been in intensive training for the last two years so very few had close girlfriends. I was the only one in my platoon who was married. The long turn around for mail might have been a blessing. You had time to think about what to write and messages were usually uplifting and you only had time to write to a few people at a time. Today with the internet and international networks, you could be talking to your wife about the bills that needed to be paid, or the kid's behavior problems. Or you could get ensnared in the social media frenzy of posting likes and dislikes. You could be talking to your wife or mother just before you headed out on an operation and she could hear the emotions that she could not read in your letters. Getting letters was something to look forward to. It was a connection from home that we could hold in our hands and carry in our breast pocket. My wife and family were very supportive in their letter writing and care packages. I was especially fortunate since my brother, Victor Yoshida, was a pharmacist who able to supply me and my platoon with simple first aid products like Bacitracin which helped heal leach bite wounds, something the Marine Corps did not have.

We were on the last wave of helicopters that were scheduled to fly out of our base in Chu Lai. We were scheduled to lift off at 0900 so we hustled to gather up our gear and head to the landing zone and assign the teams for the helicopter flights, but it wasn't until 1300 that we saw the helicopters return to pick us up. When the choppers landed, we noticed bullet holes in many of the fuselages and the chopper crews unloading some bodies wrapped in ponchos. When we boarded the choppers, the floor was slick with blood. We knew that we were headed into a hot landing zone.

On the flight in, I sat next to the door and saw the lush green countryside below that looked so beautiful and peaceful. As we neared the landing zone we caught a few rounds through the fuselage. Because of the noise of the choppers we could not hear them hit but we could see the holes open up and the sunlight shining through like blossoms of light. We held on tight as the pilot took some evasive action and the door gunner sprayed some rounds from his machine gun. As we came in for the landing, I tried to orient myself to the perimeter of the landing zone to see where we needed to go. From the angle of the sun, it looked like we were facing east, although it was hard to tell since it was about noon. As soon as we got close to the ground, we started jumping out and headed straight out to the edge of the landing zone. I could see the rest of the platoon landing to either side of us and it looked like we were in the right position. Fortunately, the helicopter dropped us where we were supposed to be. Except for the noise of the helicopters and the roar of jets flying overhead, the landing zone seemed to be quiet with no incoming. One helicopter was down and seemed to be having engine trouble. There was a swirl of debris that was kicked up by the helicopters and there was smoke in the air and the smell of napalm. We set up a perimeter and were about to join up with the rest of the battalion, when I was told to have my platoon stay and provide security for the landing zone and a downed helicopter until it could be retrieved. Since it was about lunch time, and most of us had not had time for breakfast, some of the troops broke out their C-rations and ate while the others kept watch.

My platoon was assigned a two-man M60 machine gun team as well as a two men rocket team that was carrying the older bazooka style rocket launcher. I remember my machine gunner, Smitty, eating a tin of peanut butter and crackers. Robert Lee Smith, was usually assigned to our platoon along with an assistant gunner. He was a big, husky Marine who carried his heavy M60 with ease and we always knew he would be in the right position to support us. Although as a platoon commander, I had responsibility for the control of the weapons in my command, Smitty seemed to know where he was needed before I did. Machine gunners were in a high risk position. When we got in a fire fight, the first thing we tried to take out were the enemy machine guns, and the enemy did the same to us. Every 5th round is a tracer round which helps the gunner zero in on his target, but it also helps the enemy locate the machine gun.

We began to hear the increasing sound of rifles, mortars and heavy machine guns coming from the direction of the battalion. We could hear the distinctive, thump, thump, thump of 12.7mm (.50 cal) heavy machine guns, and we knew our battalion did not have any .50 cal guns, so we knew we were out-gunned. This was not an engagement with a local VC force. We were facing a well-equipped force with the fire power to bring down our helicopters. We heard later that they had shot down an F4 Phantom jet during a napalm run.

The company radio traffic came alive and I knew that Hotel Company was caught up in some activity to the northeast of us as we also heard the sounds of gunfire and mortars increase. Suddenly, my radio man told me that Lieutenant Colonel Utter wanted to talk to me on the radio. Normally, Colonels don't talk directly to Lieutenants so I knew it was important. Lieutenant Colonel Utter told me that Fox Company was being chewed up and I had to come to their relief as soon as possible. Apparently, the ARVN had fallen back and Fox Company's left flank was exposed. This allowed the NVA to roll up their flank and drive a wedge through Fox Company, cutting off one of their platoons. I was the only reserve force that Lieutenant Colonel Utter had left and so I was his only hope to support Fox Company and save their platoon. I gathered up my platoon and since we did not see any activity around the area I told the downed helicopter crew, who were nearly done with their repairs, that they would have to fend for themselves. Fox Company was somewhere to the south of Hill 50. We had to move across several hundred meters of open rice paddies to get to their command post. We were under fire from heavy machine guns and mortars, but my platoon made it to the Fox Company command post without any casualties.

Corporal Ralph Good, our 1st Squad leader was the first to reach the Fox Company command post where they were sheltering behind a grove of trees. There were several dead and wounded Marines lying behind a paddy dyke. A Fox Company sergeant, approached Sergeant Good and asked if he had some spare ammo. Sergeant Good was surprised to see his old drill instructor from Paris Island, Sergeant Donnell McMillin, as we did not know that this Fox Company had replaced the Fox Company that we had worked with since Camp Pendleton. Sergeant Good gave him three bandoleers of ammo and reminded him that he had been one of his recruits in boot camp. Sergeant McMillen smiled and said, "I'm glad you finally made something of yourself" and returned to his troops. Sergeant McMillen was later killed and was posthumously awarded a Silver Star.

When I arrived I found the Company Commander as well as many others badly wounded and learned that they had lost contact with their 1st platoon. Their Executive Officer and 2nd Platoon commander, Lieutenant Johnson was also severely wounded. The only officer who was not wounded was Lieutenant Bonham of 3rd Platoon who quickly briefed me on the situation. He was cool and calm under the circumstances with all the dead and wounded around us and bullets whipping overhead. He explained that their 1st Platoon had been in the lead when they were cut off from the left flank. They had lost radio contact with the platoon and were not sure where they were. Lieutenant Bonham gave me one of their radio men that I could use to communicate on the Fox Company net and pointed me in their 1st Platoon's last known direction. My mission was to recover their 1st Platoon and bring them in so that Fox Company could consolidate with the rest of the Battalion at Chau Nhai (4). It was about 1700 hours and there wouldn't be much daylight left.

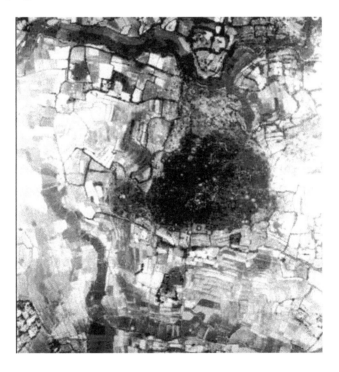

This is a photo of the area around the south part of Hill 50. You can see the type of terrain that we fought over. The patchwork of open rice paddies and the darker patches of manioc, a leafy plant that had tubers similar to yams. The little lines between them are the paddy dikes which were the only cover that you could find while crossing the rice paddies. The rice paddies were slightly terraced and the paddy dykes offered about two feet of cover. The heavier lines are the hedgerows along which there were pathways that created a maze. The hedgerows consisted of barb wire fencing with thorny bushes growing in them. Approaching this from the ground, the hedgerows seemed randomly placed and it was difficult to know where they would eventually lead or who was hiding behind them.

The situation was filled with unknowns. There was no radio contact with the cut off Platoon and there was no time to do a reconnaissance since it was getting dark and we needed to consolidate back to the battalion CP.

We didn't know where they were, and how many NVA were between us and them. All we knew was that these were North Vietnamese since we saw that their dead were wearing green khaki uniforms. These were not VC in pajamas with rusty, old mauser rifles who were more likely to run than stand and fight. They had the latest AK-47s and heavy machine guns and mortars. They were everywhere to our front and our flanks and we had no reserves to bail us out if we ran into trouble. Ahead of us were a series of hedgerows which would channel our movement and provide cover for enemy ambushes. The alternative was to maneuver across the open rice and manioc fields and expose ourselves to view. We decided to follow the hedgerows to have some level of cover.

I don't remember how I briefed the men on our mission. All that is a blur to me now. We moved out with Corporal Ralph Good's squad in the lead. As we moved forward, we could hear sporadic gunfire which we presumed were from Fox Company's 1st Platoon. We followed a sunken path which had hedgerows growing on both sides, the worst place to be in an ambush. This was the path Fox's 1st Platoon had followed. Lance Corporal Kabeller's fire team was in the lead. As they were coming around a corner Kabeller spotted three rifle barrels sticking out of the hedgerow not more than ten feet away. It was too close to throw a grenade so he signaled his team to back off while he circled around behind the VC and threw a grenade in the bunker. After the grenade went off he ran up to the entrance and emptied his magazine into the bunker. It was one of those moments where battles are lost or won. Another fifteen to twenty

NVA apparently panicked and popped out of their holes and began scurrying up the hill. The squad opened fire and cut them all down. The alert action of Lance Corporal Kabeller and the aggressive action by Corporal Ralph Good's squad destroyed the NVA. There the hedgerows worked to our advantage making it difficult for the NVA to escape. The action was over in less than a minute and there were no prisoners. If the NVA had not panicked and stood and fought we would have had a tough time digging them out of their bunkers and we would have suffered a lot of casualties.

There was silence at first while we listened, expecting to see more NVA coming after us. But there was nothing. Apparently this was it, although we expected a hoard of NVA to appear any minute. The men checked the NVA to make sure they were dead. There was a feeling of relief and even jubilation over our victory until someone noticed that Smitty, our machine gunner, was dead. My machine gunner who had been eating peanut butter and crackers just a few hours ago was dead. His assistant gunner had tears running down his face and was visibly shaken. My platoon sergeant, Sergeant Bedwell went over to him, put a hand on his shoulder and said a few words to him. The young Marine pulled himself together, picked up the machine gun and moved forward with us, leaving his teammate and good friend behind. While I didn't give it much thought at the time, the image of Sergeant Bedwell comforting the assistant gunner and getting him back into the fight sticks in my mind. It showed compassion under a stressful situation. We don't give medals for compassion but I wish I had said something to Sergeant Bedwell to thank him for what he did.

As we moved forward we found the remnants of the Fox Company platoon. They were scattered around a small clearing behind some hedgerows. There were dead and wounded lying around and the rest were hugging the ground, some with terror in their eyes. Discarded backpacks, bandages and other gear littered the area. A sergeant—August O. Miller—and a corpsman were the only ones who seemed to be functioning.

Sergeant Miller said the platoon commander and two others were pinned down in an open rice paddy to our front. One of them had a radio but it may have been on another frequency since the third man was an artillery FO. This would explain why we could not contact them on the company frequency. The sergeant asked for help in moving his wounded back to the rear. I assigned Corporal Charles Moore, my second squad leader, to help the sergeant with the evacuation. A corpsman was busy tending to a Marine, who had taken a round on a phosphorous grenade that he had been carrying on his belt. It exploded and he was screaming in pain as the phosphorus ignited on contact with air and burned into his flesh. The corpsman suggested that we pack his wound in mud to keep the air from igniting the phosphorus. As I emptied my canteens into the dirt to make mud, the thought flicked through my mind that I might need that water for my own use and I held back about a half of a canteen. His screaming was adding to the chaos and fear around us. Although I was sorry for his condition, I wanted to move him out as soon as we could so that we could get the rest of the men focused.

Sergeant Miller was able to get his men moving again to gather up the wounded and check the dead. There were NVA dead bodies scattered all around as the fighting had been so close. My 2nd Squad stayed behind to help move the wounded and the remnants of the Fox Company platoon while I led my other two squads to try to rescue the three men who were pinned down in an open field to our front. I realized that I now had only two squads, which was about twenty men. I had second thoughts about leaving Corporal Moore's eight-man squad behind when I didn't know what we were going to face ahead of us.

When we reached the edge of the rice paddy, we could see three men taking cover behind a paddy dyke. In front of them, about fifty meters was a hedgerow, from which they were receiving fire. One of them seemed to be dead and the others were wounded. One of my fireteams attempted to crawl out to them but they were driven back by machine gun fire and one rifleman, Lance Corporal McClung, was wounded in the arm. Sergeant Bedwell was able to bring back our wounded Marine. In order to reach the men pinned down in the open, we would have to assault across an open field. There wasn't any cover on either side for us to work around. Any attempt to do so would result in more casualties. In the meantime, my company network was exploding with activity and my radioman reported that the rest of our Hotel Company was heavily engaged.

By shouting and hand signals, we were finally able to make radio contact with the men who were pinned down, over the Fox Company radio frequency. We determined that the platoon commander was dead and the two wounded men, a forward artillery observer and a radio man were wounded but were mobile. I asked them if they would be able to come back to us if we laid down some suppressing fire. They said they would give it a try, since there didn't seem to be any other option. So, I gave the signal and we poured everything we had on the hedgerows on the other side. This enabled the two men to make it to our side. They reported that the platoon commander, 2nd Lieutenant Lumley was dead and we had to leave him where he lay.

After I reported the situation to Lieutenant Bonham, we were told that the battalion was withdrawing to consolidate around Chau Nhai (4). It was getting dark by now. We took a head count and had one dead, and two wounded in our platoon. In addition to Smith and McClung, Corporal Moore was shot in the hand while he was assisting Fox Company evacuate their wounded.

Corporal Moore's squad had previously moved the wounded from the Fox Company platoon back to their medivac site. They were given some ponchos and were asked to retrieve the dead Marines that had been left on the battlefield. As his squad was heading back to find the bodies, they came under machine gun fire. His squad took cover behind a stone wall and began to return fire. Several NVA had returned to the area that we had recently cleared and set up a machine gun bunker. As Corporal Moore leveled his rifle over the wall to return fire, another machine gun opened up from the other direction, shattering his rifle and injuring both his hands. Fortunately, other Marines from Fox Company opened up on the NVA machine guns which caused them to divert their fire. Lance Corporal John Turk, was next to Corporal Moore. He assumed command of the eight-man squad, applied a battle dressing to Corporal Moore's hands, and led the squad back to link up with the rest of 1st Platoon Hotel Company.

With the return of the NVA to the area we had cleared earlier, we were now the cut-off platoon. As platoon commander, I decided to leave the dead and not risk any more contact with the NVA by trying to link up with the Fox Company command post. I could see the clump of trees and huts that was Chau Nhai (4) about 400 meters to my southeast across a patch work of open rice paddies and manioc fields. We were not taking any direct fire so I gave the order to retreat directly across the open fields to Chau Nhai (4) where the 2/7 command post was located.

Just as Sergeant Bedwell and I were rounding up the last of our platoon, one of our Marines came running up to me, saying that he had been pinned down and was only now able to free himself. I suspect that he had been hiding during the fight, but I reserved my judgement and told him to join his squad.

We left the cover of the hedgerows and trees and began to cross the open fields. We could hear some firing behind us but no rounds were coming our way. After we covered about 100 meters the NVA began to   pepper us with long range sniper fire and mortars. The NVA had the high ground and were firing down on us from Hill 50. Heavy .50 caliber machine gun rounds were chewing up chunks of paddy dykes around us. Your first instinct when you see incoming fire is to dive into the closest depression you can find and stay there. But my squad leaders and I urged everyone to keep moving. It's a lot harder to hit a moving target from that distance, so we kept moving. We didn't want anyone stopping and getting pinned down in the open rice paddies. The gathering dusk was to our advantage. At times like this everything seems to move in slow motion. You can see the tracer rounds coming at you and you feel like you can reach up and grab them. The stream of tracers was like a stream of water from a garden hose. It undulated across the paddies as the gunner tried to target our movement. The mortars that were impacting around us were the smaller 60 mm mortars which didn't bother us since the rice fields were muddy and absorbing much of the impact and explosion. The stream of machine gun tracers and the flash of mortars was like a light show. A full moon was overhead, having risen in the early afternoon, and the scene was almost beautiful until you realized they were trying to kill us. We all made it back without any further casualties.

We brought all our wounded, but we had to leave our dead behind. Marines in combat have a personal commitment to leaving no man behind. That also applies to our dead. The fear is that the dead could be mutilated, booby trapped or missing so that they would never be found. However, under the circumstances of that day, I made the unpopular decision to leave them behind. Although the dead I left behind were recovered by 1st Lieutenant Bonham, the next day, that is a decision which haunts me to this day.

When we reached the battalion perimeter, Lieutenant Colonel Utter began to call airstrikes down on our position since we were running out of ammo and the supply copters could not come in to resupply us. Hotel Company was assigned a section of the perimeter to defend and when we were moving into that section, which was in a drainage ditch, an enemy grenade exploded as we crossed an open area and my point man, Lance Corporal John Edwards was killed in a burst of automatic fire. We took cover. Ralph Good had an M79 grenade launcher but the NVA were too close for the M79 grenades to arm in flight. He was finally able to lob one in the air like a mortar and he was able to get it to detonate near the NVA. Although there was almost a full moon, the area we were in was overhung with trees and it was pitch black. We could hear the NVA calling to one another. After a little while we were joined by Hotel Company's 3rd Platoon and prepared to move forward again. Whoever had shot at us was gone and we occupied the drainage ditch. Later we surmised that the group that had ambushed us was a forward observation post for their mortars, because after they left the mortars stopped. At about 2130, some copters finally came in to evacuate the wounded and resupply us. During the night several fire fights broke out around the perimeter but the close air support prevented any major assault which was fortunate since we were almost out of ammunition.

The next day we were reinforced by two battalions of Marines and two ARVN battalions. 3rd Battalion 1st Marines landed to the north of us where the fighting was the heaviest and 2nd Battalion 4th Marines landed to the South of us to protect our flank and the ARVN battalions landed to the east and west. The powers that be were trying to encircle the NVA now that they had fixed their position thanks to our sacrifices the day before. What remained of our 2/7 Battalion was held in reserve.

On the morning of March 5, I realized how lucky my platoon had been. The 2nd and 3rd Platoons of Hotel Company suffered heavy casualties when they were overrun on Hill 37. Since my platoon had the least casualties, I was assigned the task to go back up Hill 37 to see if there were any NVA left after the heavy bombing and napalm that had plastered the hill during the night. The Hill was deserted so the task was now to recover the dead that 2nd and 3rd Platoons had to leave behind when they were overrun. I will always remember the smell of blood, death and decaying flesh as we went up that hill. We found the dead Marines in different positions where they fell. We were able to account for every man who did not make it back. I remember seeing one Marine from 3rd Platoon who had been pulled partially out of a fighting hole. His wallet was tossed to one side and the contents were scattered about. A picture of a young lady that I took to be his wife had been torn apart and left in the dirt. Killing a man in combat is what we are taught to do and it is not personal. But to take the picture of the dead man's wife and rip it up seemed like an act of desecration. I believe the dead man was Corpsman Lawrence Everett Johnson, the husband of Shirley Hayes Johnson and the father of Corinna Marie Johnson of Binghamton, New York.

I also found the body of a Marine from 3rd Platoon, Pfc. Franz Joseph Kolbeck, who I had helped to find boots before we shipped out of Camp Pendleton to Vietnam. Although he was not in my platoon, I was the duty officer on our last day at Camp Pendleton when his squad leader informed me that this Marine would fail his last inspection since he did not have an extra pair of boots. He was a big Marine, well over 200 pounds and he had large feet which needed special size boots which we did not have in our supply. I drove him all around Camp Pendleton in my car until we found him a pair of boots in a PX. During the ride in the car I had a chance to get to know this young man and was impressed by his gentle nature. Because of that connection, I felt a special sorrow when I found his crumpled body. We laid him on a poncho and I helped carry him as we started down the hill to the perimeter. It was hot and humid and we fell several times coming down the hill. When we got down to the valley, we were still getting occasional sniper fire. We had to drop him several times and we ended up dragging him a few meters at a time. It was hot and humid and I was extremely tired. By the time I reached our perimeter, I was dragging him and with my last ounce of strength I pushed him over the embankment and his body rolled down into the perimeter. By this time his body was covered in dried blood and mud, and his clothes were torn. I fell to the ground exhausted.

Some officer in a clean uniform, who probably had just come out to see the results of the battle, shouted at me, "That's a Marine! Treat him with respect!"

If I had the strength then, I would have stood up and slammed him for being such a pretentious prig. Some men picked up Kolbeck's body and carried him away while I knelt in the dirt seething with rage and indignation, gasping for air. But it dawned on me that he was right, I was so fixated on bringing Kolbeck home that I had forgotten about his humanity and toward the end he was just a heavy burden that I was dragging around like a sack of potatoes. Then everything came crashing down on me. I could feel the tears welling up in my eyes. I remembered that I had left two dead Marines on my field of battle last night just like the Marines I had just recovered. My young machine gunner who loved peanut butter and the 1st Platoon commander from Fox Company that I had left in the middle of a barren rice paddy. Even today, fifty years later, when I cannot sleep at night, I think of them with regret and remorse. I reached for my canteen and found that the water that I hoarded so selfishly yesterday had not been used.

****

When we made our fast retreat to the battalion command post the night of 4 March, I made it a point to account for all the men in my platoon. Unfortunately, in all the excitement and confusion, I didn't think about the radio man that had been assigned to me by Lieutenant Bonner to help me communicate with the Fox Company net. When I reached the battalion CP, I forgot to account for him and for years later I worried, not knowing if he made it back. While researching this book, I learned from Lieutenant Bonner that his name was Pfc. Glen Hensely. He had made it safely back to the battalion command post on the night of 4 March and returned to Fox Company. After 50 years, I was finally relieved to hear for certain that I had not left him behind. I would like to find him some day to thank him and apologize for not watching out for him.

Second Lieutenant Donald Richard Lumley was the son of Mr. and Mrs. Harry C. Lumley and the husband of Karolee Lumley of Sacramento, California. Donald Lumley had a promising career in minor league baseball when he enlisted in the Marine Corps in 1956. After his first enlistment he returned to playing baseball until he was forced to quit professional baseball due to an injury after the 1961 season but continued to play at the amateur level. Don Lumley was recalled to active service as a second lieutenant in June 1965 and trained with his Company before they were deployed to Vietnam.

Lance Corporal Robert Lee Smith was the son of Robert Albinas Smith and Annie Mae Smith of Newport News Virginia. He was born in Newport News July 31, 1945 and attended Ferguson High School and enlisted in the Marine Corps after graduation on June 19, 1964. He received basic training at Parris Island, S.C., and infantry training at Camp Le Jeune, N.C., before being sent to Camp Pendleton for the formation of 2nd Battalion 7th Marines where he was assigned as a machine gunner. Lance Corporal Smith was a big, husky Marine who was known as "Sonny" to his family of three adoring sisters. He was "the sunshine that made them happy when skies were grey." His youngest sister Thelma Kay learned of his death when she was called out of her high school English class. Lance Corporal Smith was the type of Marine who seemed indestructible, so it was a shock when we found he had been killed.

Lance Corporal John Jay Edwards was the son of Ralph F. Edwards Jr. and Jacqueline T. Edwards of Dillsburg, Pennsylvania. He enlisted in the US Marine Corps on August 31, 1964 in Philadelphia, Pennsylvania. Lance Corporal Edwards was a Marine rifleman, age 20, born February 25, 1946, from Lock Haven, Pennsylvania. Lance Corporal Edwards had just joined our platoon after Double Eagle II, so I did not know him as well as the men that I had trained and served with since the formation of 2/7 in 1964. I wrote a letter to his family explaining the circumstances of his death and expressing my condolences. I received a letter back from his father expressing how proud he was of his son. At that time, I was a young man. I was married but did not yet have children. I kept that letter and as I reread it so many years later, after having raised a son of my own. I can better appreciate how devastated a parent must feel over the loss of a son at such a young age. I learned later from his younger brother Ralph Edwards, that through respect for his father's decorated service in World War II, John had been assigned to Marine honor guard duty in Florida and was not scheduled to go to Vietnam. John was upset by that since he had signed up for the Marines to be in the fight. He finally got his assignment in January, 1966, just months before Operation Utah. When I heard that background I understood how hard it must have been for his father to write that letter to me.

Lance Corporal Kabeller was awarded a Silver Star for his alert action on Operation Utah. This solidified his reputation for "smelling" out the enemy as he successfully guided his fireteam on other missions where he was able to anticipate the enemy and deliver the first blow. *Pacific Stars and Stripes* wrote an article about him in May 22, 1966, (page 62) "Marine Strategy: Thinks Like VC, Shoots 'em."

Julio Schnars was the Marine who was burned by the WP grenade. In March 2020, he visited Gary Rood from Fox Company and appeared to be doing well. At the time I assumed that it was a corpsman that was assisting Julio, but I found out later that it was Lance Corporal William F. Costello who was an information services representative traveling with Fox Company who created the mudpack that saved Lance Corporal Schnars. Lance Corporal Costello was awarded a Silver Star for his actions.

Chapter 5
Golf Company Holds the Center

The following was contributed primarily by Captain Bill Seymour the commanding officer of Golf Company and the 2/7 Battalion After Action Report.

Golf Company was alerted at around 1800 on the evening of March 3, 1966, that they were to mount out for an operation the next morning. Golf Company Commander, Captain William Seymour, hastily called in his staff and notified them that they needed to call in their troops from their night positions, load up with ammo and rations, and march them over night to the Chu Lai airstrip where they would be helicoptered to an area northwest of Quang Ngai in the morning. They scrambled all night and arrived at Chu Lai Air Base where it was "hurry up and wait" as they awaited the arrival of the rest of the battalion.

After Golf Company arrived, they reorganized the helicopter teams as the size of the teams depended on the weather conditions. The helicopters that were used during that period were the UH-34s with the large piston engine which required an elaborate cooling system that determined its lift capacity. The hotter and more humid it became; the less troops and equipment could be carried. The distribution of team leaders and weapons was a key consideration since the company would be most vulnerable during the landing phase,

Fox Company was in the first wave and began departure around 1040. When the choppers from that wave returned, Golf Company could see that some of the choppers were shot up, and wounded Marines were being unloaded. It looked like they were going into a hot landing zone. Captain Seymour took the precaution to frontload a couple of extra machine gun teams, which he got from H&S company, into the first couple of choppers to provide extra firepower, when securing the landing zone. There was some additional trouble with the number of helicopters and the sizing of the chopper loads that delayed Golf Company's departure.

Transport to the landing zone in the operations area was uneventful and upon landing Golf Company secured the landing zone with each of Golf Company's platoons taking 1/3 of the landing zone perimeter. The last elements of Golf Company were on the ground by 1210. Since Captain Seymour was in one of the first helicopters in that wave to land, the battalion commander, Lieutenant Colonel Utter told Captain Seymour to get in touch with the ARVN Army advisor, Red Hat One, after landing, and see if there was anything the Marines could do to assist him as the ARVN battalion was reporting heavy NVA engagement.

Captain Seymour quickly found the Red Hat One, who turned out to be Captain Pete Dawkins of Army West Point football fame. He offered assistance, but Dawkins was on the radio speaking Vietnamese as his battalion was fully engaged and he was dealing with more important matters.

Shortly after talking with Captain Dawkins, Captain Seymour looked to the east and saw a group of NVA—about five or six—running from the left to right across their front. He noticed that one of them was much larger than the typical Vietnamese. They were about 150 yards away. His immediate thought was that the larger man was probably an advisor. In a previous engagement, Golf Company had been in a small fire fight where they captured a wounded man in combat gear who was about six-feet tall and muscular. It was obvious that he was not Vietnamese and was probably an advisor. They had loaded him into a chopper and sent him to HQ for interrogation. There were several occasions where the Marines had come across suspected foreign advisors.

H&S company and Lieutenant Colonel Utter landed with the tail end of Golf Company, followed by Hotel Company. The landing of 2/7 had taken about three hours. While the original orders were for 2/7 and the ARVN battalion to sweep south of the landing zone, with 2/7 on the right and the ARVN on the left, the ARVN battalion was heavily engaged to the northwest of the landing zone and was asking for help. The operations commander ordered Lieutenant Colonel Utter to coordinate with the ARVN advisor to render assistance and to also provide security for two downed helicopters.

61

Lieutenant Colonel Utter issued a frag order which essentially pivoted the direction of 2/7 to the north in line with the ARVN battalion on the left flank, to start a sweep to the northwest. In this formation, the ARVN battalion was on the left flank, Fox Company was in the middle and Golf Company was on the right flank. Hotel Company was in battalion reserve. At the same time, Lieutenant Colonel Utter directed Golf Company to detach a platoon to provide security for one of the downed choppers. Joe Lloyd's 3rd Platoon was assigned this mission and was detached to battalion control. Golf Company was now down to two platoons, about 65 men.

Almost as soon as Golf Company crossed the line of departure, they engaged a number of NVA in a short firefight where they killed four and wounded an unknown number. They came across an area where the enemy force had dropped their unessential equipment including about thirty backpacks with civilian clothes. They also found about 100 rounds of 12.5mm (.50 cal) ammo. The 12.5mm was used for anti-air as well as anti-personnel targets. The 12.5mm guns had already downed several helicopters that morning. Golf Company was receiving light small arms fire from their front. However, most of the heavy fighting was taking place to their left where the ARVN and Fox Company were located.

That changed suddenly when Golf Company was crossing some open rice paddies. Devastating fire erupted from a hedgerow that concealed two fortified machine gun bunkers and a trench line from which the NVA were firing automatic weapons. Two Marines, Lance Corporal Herberto Armenta and Lance Corporal Isiah Baker, III were killed trying to take out the machine guns, and a squad leader was wounded. Observing that his squad leader had been wounded, Lance Corporal George Norwood immediately assumed command of the squad and continued the assault on the enemy positions. Even though two Marines had already been killed in the assault, Lance Corporal Norwood assaulted the bunker twice, firing his automatic weapon and throwing grenades. He was forced to withdraw each time due to the withering fire from the trench line and nearby concealed automatic weapons. On his third attempt, he was able to hurl a grenade that neutralized the fire and enabled his squad to move forward and destroy the bunker. His actions inspired the rest of the members of his unit on the frontlines to keep going and not stop in the open rice paddy. Without his leadership and encouragement,

Golf Company would have taken a lot more casualties. Although he was painfully wounded in the arm and face by enemy grenade fragments, he refused evacuation and proceeded to position his men and direct fire which minimized the enemy counterattack which followed. Lance Corporal Norwood's quick action enabled Golf company to seize and retain that position until the end of the day, when they were called back to consolidate with the battalion command post. Lance Corporal Norwood's actions exemplified the courage and initiative of the Marines who were fighting there on Operation Utah. Lance Corporal Norwood was awarded a Navy Cross for his actions,

Captain Seymour received a call on the radio that stated that Fox Company was fully engaged and the battalion commander wanted Golf Company to see if they could shift some small arms fire from their left flank to assist them. Captain Seymour could not raise Fox Company on the radio, he decided to take the personal risk of leaving his command post and moved to the left flank of his position to see if he could locate Fox Company. He had a clear view of 50 yards of open rice paddy but could not see any of the Fox Company troops. He reported this back to battalion HQ and told them he couldn't have his troops shoot in that direction for fear of hitting unseen friendly troops.

While he was there on the left flank, Captain Seymour saw a Marine moving toward his position from the battalion command post location. It was Captain Alex Lee who had been directed to locate Fox Company and replace Captain Jerry Lindauer, the commanding officer of Fox Company, who had been badly wounded. Alex moved through over 100-yards of heavy fire to reach Captain Seymour's position. Captain Seymour told Captain Lee that he had lost contact with Fox Company but gave him a general location of where he thought they were. Alex was a good friend and he departed with Seymour warning "Keep your […] head down. There are a lot of bad guys out there" or some similar comment.

The incoming fire was increasing. The NVA were targeting radiomen by their radio antennas, with the knowledge that the radios were usually near the unit commanders. Captain Seymour had a hard time making it back to his company position. He and his radio man had become a target and had to crawl most of the way back. They were lucky not to be hit by small arms fire.

During the afternoon, Captain Seymour tried several times to call in artillery support but was told that artillery was already supporting a "priority" mission and that his request would have to wait. At the time, artillery fire was focused in the area just forward of the ARVN and Fox Company which was oblique to Golf Company's position. Golf Company had also lost their battalion mortar section forward observer and his radio man who were killed in action.

A medevac chopper showed up unexpectedly right behind where Golf Company's lines were located. Several of the seriously wounded got on the chopper while numerous puffs of smoke and paint came off the fuselage when enemy small arms fire hit the craft. But the pilot stayed there until all the wounded were loaded aboard before taking off. It was surprising how that chopper could fly after being hit so many times. Even more surprising was the calm heroics of the chopper pilot who took the hits until the wounded were loaded.

The situation grew worse when Golf Company began to receive small arms fire from Hill 37 to the right. Unknown to Captain Seymour, the 81mm Forward Observer and his radioman had been killed and without artillery or any other support, Golf Company had no way to neutralize the enemy fire. Since one platoon had already been dispatched to provide security for a helicopter that was downed near Hill 85, Golf Company only had two platoons that were already fully engaged and insufficient reserves to take on the hill. The hill to the right was critical terrain and should have been occupied if we had the forces to occupy it. The hill had a commanding position with a clear view of the whole battle area.

The situation was reported to Lieutenant Colonel Utter and he deployed the battalion reserve, Jimmy Lau's Hotel Company, to take the hill which he did briefly but he started taking heavy casualties. Unfortunately, the enemy held the position before Hotel Company could get there. It was a tough mission for Hotel Company to attempt to take the hill when there was no cover and concealment, Hotel Company was also down to two platoons Since their 1st Platoon had already been committed to helping Fox company, 2nd Platoon was overrun and consolidated with the remaining 3rd Platoon. It was getting late in the afternoon and Colonel Utter decided that the battalion needed to consolidate for the evening. His units were running low on ammunition and he didn't want to keep the battalion strung out for the night, so the companies were called back from their positions and Golf Company established a perimeter around the battalion command post. Golf Company continued to receive small arms and mortar fire into the evening. One mortar round landed very close to Golf Company's command post, killing one of the Marines who was standing between the company gunnery sergeant and Captain Seymour. Neither the gunny, Gunnery Sergeant Bill Purdy, or Captain Seymour was injured. Joe Lloyd's 3rd Platoon was released from the chopper security mission later in the afternoon and rejoined the company by nightfall.

Golf Company lost four KIA in Operation Utah, the youngest was Lance Corporal Heriberto Armenta, age 19, who was born in Mexico. His parents came to California when he was a small boy. He was a rifleman and was killed by small arms fire when he assaulted the NVA machine gun emplacement. He had only been in the Marine Corps for two years but his outstanding performance had already earned him the rank of Lance Corporal. Private Gary Charles Allen, age 20, was another rifleman who was killed by mortar fragments. Both Lance Corporal Armenta and Private Allan were from California and went through boot camp in San Diego together just before joining 2/7 in Camp Pendleton.

The other two Marines that were killed were Lance Corporal Lester Robert Atherden and Lance Corporal Isiah Baker III. Both Marines had joined three years earlier and were experienced riflemen who had served together in Okinawa with 3rd Battalion 9th Marines before joining 2/7 in 1964. Lance Corporal Atherden was a machine gunner, age 21, from Milford, Connecticut who died of small arms fire. Lance Corporal Atherden came from a proud military family. His grandfather served in WWI and his father served in WWII. His brothers also served in the Marine Corps. His platoon mate, Akhee Elsworth Boss remembers him as a hardworking, quiet, dependable guy and a good Marine who would share his rations with the kids from the nearby village who came around sometimes asking for food.

Lance Corporal Isiah Baker III, aged 23, was a rifleman from New Orleans. Lance Corporal Baker was one of the Black Marines who served with distinction in 2/7 and was awarded a Bronze Star for heroism. Lance Corporal Baker was one of the Marines that was killed assaulting an NVA machine gun emplacement that was raking through the ranks of Golf Company. The Vietnam War saw the highest proportion of African Americans ever to serve in an American war. During WWII, soldiers of color—African Americans and Japanese Americans, like my uncle Hiroshi Shikuma—served in segregated units. It was only in 1953 that the secretary of defense abolished segregated units in the armed forces.

During the Vietnam War, African Americans faced a much greater chance of being on the frontline and consequently a much higher casualty rate. In 1965 alone, African Americans represented almost 25 percent of those killed in action. During this time in the United

States the civil rights movement was reaching a peak with race riots in many large cities like the Los Angeles Watts Riot of 1965. In Okinawa, Black soldiers would congregate in towns like Koza during their off hours and there was a lot of friction among the Black and white soldiers stationed in Okinawa. When he was in Okinawa, Lance Corporal Baker had to be careful where he went on liberty. MP's warned him to stay out of some "white" sections of towns around the base. All his close friends were in 2/7 and most of them were white. Unlike the garrison units that were stationed in Okinawa, the men in combat units like 2/7 were dependent on each other and their bonds were closer than race or religion. While there was discrimination at different levels, Marines would still risk their lives for each other. Lance Corporal Baker is buried in the plot of his guardian, Mrs. Elizabeth Brown in New Orleans. There is no grave marker.

The next day, March 5, Golf Company reorganized, cleaned up the battlefield, and remained in place as a blocking force until heading back to their home base in Chu Lai on March 6. As they were in their blocking position, a lone NVA approached their lines. They beckoned him to come in as it appeared that he was surrendering. However, a shot rang out and the NVA went down. Fortunately, when they recovered him, the bullet had hit his magazine that NVA carried on their chests, and did not kill him. He said that he was a cook and was taken into custody. When questioned, the NVA stated his unit had been infiltrating into South Vietnam since August 1965. They arrived in this area in November and he had been here for a month.

1st Lieutenant Hank Barnett, Golf Company executive officer, had been seriously wounded, shot in the chest, and evacuated to the sanctuary hospital ship, USS Repose. Executive officers were prime targets for the enemy, since they coordinated the supporting arms and were usually surrounded by forward observers with their many radio antennas which are difficult to conceal. Captain Seymour felt guilty about assigning Barnett to that position as most of his executive officer's had a habit of getting wounded.

Lieutenant Barnett was leading the reserve command post back to the battalion command post when he was shot. He was shot in the lower left chest. Luckily the bullet entered between two ribs and exited through the back. If the bullet had hit a rib, the bone would have shattered and caused extensive damage, like an internal exploding grenade. Lieutenant Barnet said the force of the bullet shocked him but he did not feel any pain. He remembers praying shortly after he was hit: "I promised to do something of value with my life." He feels he was given that opportunity in 1993 when he donated a kidney to his younger brother. "I was thankful to be able to do that... I felt like I had paid a debt."

The artillery forward observer Lieutenant Dick Thatcher came to Lieutenant Barnett's aid and got him to the battalion command post. Medevac helicopters were delayed due to incoming mortar and .50 cal fire. Lieutenant Barnett remembers a corpsman coming by to triage the wounded, to see who might be saved if they could be evacuated. He was finally medevac'd late in the afternoon. He also remembers being on a table in a field hospital having his clothes cut off, then waking up in a clean bed on the USS Repose with tubes coming out of his nose and chest. The doctor made him sit up and start a routine of coughing and at some point, he was able to stand up and walk around. The ship eventually took him to the Philippines, then to the naval Hospital in Guam. After he recovered, he returned to Division HQ in Okinawa to finish out his 13-month tour and eventually flew back to the United States The efficiency of the medical care was superb.

Lieutenant Barnett and his wife, Pat, were newlyweds like my wife, Laura, and I when we joined 2/7 in 1964 in Camp Pendleton. We became good friends and did things together during the year before we shipped out to Vietnam. He and I both left the Marine Corps after we came back to the United States and joined IBM. Hank went on to have a very successful career in IBM and retired as one of their top sales executives. I doubt if anyone in the corporate world ever knew what he did that day in 1966. Over the years he sends me a Christmas card with a photo of his family, so I have seen pictures of his children after they were born, as they grew up, married, and had children of their own. Every time I see those pictures I am thankful that he was able to survive and have such a wonderful, productive, life. I am also mindful of all those whose young lives ended on that day. I can only imagine what their lives could have been.

Chapter 6
H&S company: The Command Center

This section is based on the recollections of Captain Nick Grosz, who was the H&S company commanding officer and Private Raymond Potter.

C aptain Nicholas "Nick" H. Grosz, was Company Commander of H&S company 2/7 during Operation Utah. Nick was born in Brooklyn, New York, and played football and baseball during his high school and college years at the University of Rhode Island. Nick was one of the more experienced company grade Officers, having been commissioned in 1962 and served with the Fleet Marine Force in Okinawa. He also trained Vietnamese Marines prior to his assignment to 2/7. Nick was well respected by the men in the battalion for his leadership and decisive action under fire. He had been awarded a Navy Cross for his actions less than three months prior to Utah, during Operation Harvest Moon when 2/7 was ambushed and he was able to rally his men while saving several wounded Marines.

H&S stands for "headquarters and service," and is made up of the battalion headquarters, which includes the battalion command section, the executive staff and headquarters support personnel. H&S company is a multifaceted organization. The support personnel include an intelligence section, communications, weapons, supply, and medical. When at home base H&S supports a field kitchen, sanitation, water purification, supply, transportation, armory and aid station. During field operations, H&S company is responsible for the coordinated use of supporting arms like artillery and air strikes, battalion mortars, resupply of ammunition and the care and evacuation of casualties. The largest sections are the communications and 81mm mortars. Most of the men in H&S company would remain with the battalion command post during deployment. However, forward observer (FO) teams, which consist of a spotter and a radioman as well as the teams of corpsmen would be assigned out to the rifle companies. A forward air controller was assigned from the air wing, and was a pilot who could talk to the supporting air elements. An artillery officer was also assigned to call in artillery support. While not considered a maneuver unit like a rifle company, H&S company's coordination of all these activities during combat are key to the success of the rifle companies. H&S company is the brains of the battalion and is therefore a prime target for enemy mortars and heavy machine guns, and suffers their share of casualties. Nine men in H&S company were killed on the first day of Operation Utah and many more were wounded, including Captain Grosz, and the battalion commander, Lieutenant Colonel Utter.

There were several Navy officers assigned to the battalion. They include medical doctors and a chaplain. 2/7 was fortunate in that the battalion had a chaplain, Navy Lieutenant Walter A. Hiskett (Lutheran) who had been a Marine infantry squad leader in 2/7 during the Korean War. After that war, Hiskett decided that he wanted to dedicate his life to the ministry, and joined the Navy Chaplain Corps. He asked to be assigned to his old unit, 2nd Battalion 7th Marines and joined them when they shipped out from San Diego in May 1965. At first, Lieutenant Hiskett would go on search and destroy missions with the battalion and shared the life of a grunt with all its perils. He participated in Harvest Moon, where he survived a Viet Cong ambush, and also participated in Double Eagle II just prior to Operation Utah.

The role of the combat chaplain was being redefined in Vietnam as were many other roles. Because of the tactical deployment of the troops and the fact that they were on the move most of the time it was impossible to conduct religious services except to visit as many individuals as possible during field operations. Lieutenant Colonel Utter decided that on subsequent operations, Chaplain Hiskett should station himself at the medical unit to which the wounded would be primarily evacuated. The reasoning behind this was that most operations were lasting only a few days, and due to the tactical deployment of troops the chaplain would be in contact with a relatively small number of troops in the command group. Almost all casualties are evacuated by helicopter from the area in which their individual unit was operating; therefore, the chaplain would have little opportunity to minister to the wounded and dying. It would be better for him to be at the battalion aid station which was the collection and clearing station for the casualties before they were evacuated to the appropriate medical facility. This was where Lieutenant Hiskett made his greatest contributions during Operation Utah, giving comfort and assurance to men who were suffering and facing death. Captain Walter Hiskett later served as the Marine Corps Chaplain from 1985 to 1989.

Captain Nick Grosz took command of H&S company in May of 1965 when 2/7 was being formed up in Camp Pendleton. He had just finished four weeks of cold weather training in the High Sierras learning how to fight on cross country skis which he found more challenging than his subsequent assignments. He spent the month of May as the new H&S commanding officer meeting with each of the sections and platoons to learn and get his arms around this multifaceted organization. Commanding an H&S company is one of the most challenging assignments in the Corps due to the number of combat and administrative services it supports. Captain Grosz found it very interesting but exhausting since there was so much to learn. Fortunately, he had a solid staff of very competent officers and staff NCOs. They in turn were delighted to have a commanding officer who was so keenly interested in what they were doing and was interested in their men. They took the time to teach him and worked with him to form the new leadership team. This was a good thing since they were not far off from deployment to Vietnam where they had to get this company to work well together. Organic to the company were a lot of different cats and dogs. They ranged from the battalion HQ staff officers to 106RR (106mm recoilless rifles) and Flame sections, to administrative clerks. The largest unit was the communications platoon followed by the 81mm mortar platoon. But there was also motor transport, supply, the battalion aid station, etc. When they went to Vietnam, Captain Grosz administratively joined bits and pieces like a water purification and shower unit, mess hall, small arms repair unit and others. The H&S rolls swelled to over 230 Marines for which Captain Grosz had NJP (non-judicial punishment) authority and lots of fitness reports with which to keep up.

A Marine Corps infantry battalion is an assault force with 15-day supply. It is not designed for protracted land warfare, at least not at the beginning of the Vietnam War. In World War II, Marine battalions would assault an island like Guadalcanal, then pull back to a staging area like Australia to refit for the next assault. In the early days of Vietnam, Marine battalions were landed in areas where there was nothing but open country without shelter, water, food, or other supplies except for what they carried in with them. For the first six months in Vietnam, most Marines in the battalion slept on the ground and lived on two meals of C-rations a day. They bathed in streams and rivers and drank water from the same streams or local wells lacing them with Iodine tablets and Kool-Aid sent from home. Within the first few months their jungle utilities and shoes were rotting away especially during the monsoon season from September through December. Their bodies were also worn down with blood draining leeches, immersion foot, diarrhea, heat exhaustion, and other ailments that come from unsanitary field conditions. Logistics was a major headache and it was all H&S company could do to provide combat support, ammunition and rations, maintain our communications equipment and provide medical services and supplies. This situation existed until the end of 1965 when the Marine enclaves at Chu Lai, Danang, and Phu Bai were finally built up.

Conditions were even worse for 2/7 who landed in Qui Nhon and was detached from the 7th Marine Regiment. They were assigned to

72

the Army in II Corps to provide security for the Army supply depot at Qui Nhon. According to Marine historians, the MACV (joint-service command of the United States Department of Defense) commander offered to provide rations, ammunition and other common items of supply. However, when Marine General Victor Krulak was notified of this offer, he disapproved, declaring that the Marines would be self-sufficient. As a result, 2/7 was left stranded in II Corps, 200 miles from the Marine bases in I Corps, living like homeless people while protecting the abundant Army supply depot in Qui Nhon. There was no reason for this type of hardship, except for the pride of an egotistical general. The Marines in 2/7 accepted these conditions since they didn't know any better.

Based on his experiences in previous combat situations like Harvest Moon, where H&S company bore the brunt of a Viet Cong ambush, Captain Grosz had made some adjustments to the H&S company organization which proved to be crucial for Operation Utah. While H&S companies had flamethrowers and 106 recoilless rifles in their table of organization, Captain Grosz got Lieutenant Colonel Utter's approval to turn them in and convert those two sections into a mini rifle platoon for mobile command post security on combat operations. It was impractical to lug all that heavy equipment, ammo, and fuel around, especially when assaulting by helicopter. In Vietnam, the lack of roads and the rugged terrain meant that everything had to be carried in by the troops.

The following is based on Captain Grosz's recollections of Operation Utah which he recently shared with me.

H&S company followed Golf Company from Chu Lai into LZ Alpha. Captain Grosz remembered being pretty up tight because word was going around that 2 helicopters were shot down by 12.7mm (.50 cal) machine guns going into LZ Alpha. His flight took some minor fire but made it in OK to the southwest area of the landing zone. Captain Grosz quickly established the battalion command post with the mini platoon and 81mm mortars. It wasn't the full platoon of mortars but they had a section or two and moved into a tree line a little further southwest. On his left, facing northwest, was the really big hill (Hill 50) where the ARVN paratroopers were positioned. Straight ahead across the landing zone in front of H&S, was Fox Company on the left and Golf Company on the right and a ridge line about 1/3 the size of the Hill 50 which ran from about Golf Company's right flank, pretty much all the way back to about 100 yards adjacent to the battalion command post. This was Hill 37 which was to become a key battle ground later in the day for Hotel Company.

Hotel Company came in next and was originally going to be the battalion reserve located near the ridge line but behind the 2/7 command post. The battalion reserve plan didn't last long. Hotel Company's 1st platoon was sent to help Fox Company recover one of their platoons that had been cut off and the rest of Hotel Company with only two platoons, moved onto the ridge line to protect Golf Company's right flank. 2/7 had committed their reserve and had no one behind the command post. The mini-platoon was all that was left to protect the command post.

The battalion command post was established in the hamlet of Chao Nhai (4). Command posts were usually set up in villages or hamlet areas since there was cover in terms of ditches, and built up areas with hedgerows and tree lines. There were also water wells and covered areas for the wounded. More importantly the VC were less likely to mortar these villages since this was their home area where many of their relatives lived. These villages would be inhabited so, the inhabitants would be rounded up and placed in a secure area where they would be safely out of the way. Getting the inhabitants out of their huts was difficult since many of the huts had underground holes where the inhabitants would hide. Even after an interpreter issued a warning, people would be reluctant to come out. The consequence would be to toss in a frag grenade to insure that no VC was still hiding in the hole. In September of 1965, during Operation Stomp, Lieutenant Colonel Utter decided to use tear gas to flush the inhabitants out of these family bunkers to avoid the injuries inflicted by a frag grenade. H&S was able to get a supply of gas masks and tear gas grenades and successfully used tear gas to flush out 20 armed VC and separate them from captive civilians without the need for a firefight. Unfortunately, an AP reporter who was identified to us as Peter Arnett, publicized this as the use of chemical agents. The world press soon latched on to this story and North Vietnam was accusing the US of using toxic agents to kill Vietnamese civilians. The use of tear gas was prohibited and the publicity nearly had Lieutenant Colonel Utter relieved of his command. This left the Marines with no alternative but to use frag grenades or risk the life of a Marine to go down into the bunkers and root them out one by one. No frag grenades were used to root the villagers out of their huts at Chau Nhai (4).

The ARVN Airborne had been in a fierce firefight with the NVA near Chau Nhai (5) and Hill 50 before 2/7 had arrived. At about 1330, the ARVN Commander requested help from the Marines and Lieutenant Colonel Utter changed the direction of his battalion's attack to support the ARVN with Fox Company on the left, Golf Company on the right and Hotel Company in an echelon formation to the right of Golf Company. The ARVN were supposed to tie in with Fox Company's left flank, but they failed to move. At first the Marines thought this was temporary and moved forward a few hundred meters when they came under heavy enemy fire. The ARVN had previously reported through their US Senior advisor, Red Hat One, that they had taken Hill 50 and the area was secure. But the information was wrong and Fox Company was caught in a killing zone with plunging fire from heavy caliber machine guns on Hill 50.

As the fighting increased Lieutenant Colonel Utter requested the ARVN to attack forward to support Fox Company's left flank. Utter was very upset when the ARVN ignored his request. He even requested to speak eyeball to eyeball with Red Hat One who showed up at the 2/7 Command Post. Surprise, Red Hat One was Pete Dawkins, Heisman Trophy winner for the West Point Army football team. Dawkins's responsibility was to coordinate the activity of the ARVN with the Marines and provide communications. Dawkins indicated there was no way the ARVN Commander was going to move off the hill until perhaps the next day. End of story. Not only did Red Hat One have no control over the command of the ARVN, the information he passed on was often incorrect which led to disastrous results for the Marines. He would report that the ARVN had control of an area and when the Marines moved into that area, they would be ambushed. 2/7 was now being attacked on three sides with no support from our allies who we had changed our plans to support. Fox Company had lost one platoon when it was cut off on the left flank and Hotel Company was being overrun on the right flank and the NVA were so close that supporting arms could not be used.

The fighting for Fox and Golf Companies continued for what seemed to be a very long time. It wasn't going well for Fox Company who was exposed on their left flank. Their commanding officer, Captain Jerry Lindauer was severely wounded and they lost contact with 2nd Lieutenant Lumley's 1st platoon. The 2nd Platoon Commander and acting executive officer, 1st Lieutenant Roland Johnson was also severely wounded with a chest wound. The only remaining officer was 1st Lieutenant Ed Bonham. Lieutenant Colonel Utter sent his Battalion Assistant S3 Officer, Captain Alex Lee to assume command of the Company. Pete Amish, who was a FAC (Forward Air Controller) assigned to Fox Company was also badly wounded. Both officers, Captain Lindauer and 1st Lieutenant Amish were brought back to the battalion command post area. The intensity of the incoming fire prevented the copters from coming in to bring ammo and evacuate the wounded. Everyone was running low on ammo. During the battle, Captain Marty O'Conner, the Battalion S4, made multiple trips across the open fire swept area with volunteers from the H&S mortar platoon and the mini platoon to bring ammo to Fox Company and bring back their wounded troops where they had a better chance for medevacs. Later that night, Captain O'Conner was seen in the dark landing zone with a flashlight to guide in the first helicopters who came in under blackout conditions. He was incredible and inspired everyone in the command post with his bravery and leadership.

Private Raymond Potter was a supply clerk who was assigned to the mini platoon. He went out on operations with the rest of the battalion and received a Purple Heart on Operation Harvest Moon which occurred in December of 1965. Private Potter came in on the same helicopter as Lieutenant Colonel Utter. Shortly after he landed, he was hit in the helmet by a sniper round. He was knocked to the ground, but the bullet circled his helmet liner and exited without injuring him. He was carrying extra mortar rounds for the 81mm mortars and set up in a depression near the mortars. He was near Captain Grosz and the rear command group. Being in the rear did not mean that he was any safer than the rest of the battalion. Rounds were coming in from all directions, over fire from the Fox and Golf Company firefights on the left and center and fire from the right where Hotel Company was engaged on Hill 37. During the day, he volunteered to make 4 or 5 trips across fire swept rice paddies to the

Fox Company command post, bringing them ammo and grenades and evacuating the dead and wounded on his way back. A rifle he was carrying was hit by what must have been a .50 cal round since it was shattered. Normally he would not have the opportunity to fire at the enemy since the rifle companies would be between him and the enemy, but on this occasion he could see the NVA on Hill 37 above Hotel Company and could support them with fire from where he was in the command post. He was down to three rounds by nightfall. Later he found that his canteen had a hole in it and an entrenching tool on his backpack was dented. Although he had a few nicks, Private Potter felt lucky to have survived considering all the mayhem around him.

Late in the day the NVA were observed moving up the ridge line on the right flank of Golf Company and began pushing Hotel Company's 2nd and 3rd platoons back along the ridge line. It was all very visible to Captain Grosz since the ridge line was not far away. There wasn't any call for fire support from Hotel Company as they were too busy trying to hang on. Captain Grosz directed Gunnery Sergeant Bascolupo to engage the NVA with the battalion's 81mm mortars. Gunnery Sergeant Bascolupo got his troops to fire a few rounds to get the range first and then began firing for effect. It was exciting to watch. The NVA were now taking some serious casualties and running back off the ridge line with Hotel Company in hot pursuit, inflicting small arms casualties on the NVA as well.

It seemed to get dark not too long after that. As dusk began to settle, Lieutenant Colonel Utter received word that the cut off Fox Company Platoon had been recovered. Lieutenant Colonel Utter decided to consolidate his units around Chau Nhai (4) and call in air and artillery. Fox Company was able to bring the rest of their wounded back to the Battalion perimeter with the help of the Hotel Company platoon that rescued their 1st platoon. Golf Company and the remainder of Hotel Company were also able to break contact and consolidate with the rest of the Battalion at Chau Nhai (4).

Several attempts were made by helicopters to land and evacuate the wounded, but were driven off by the volume of tracers directed at them. The best they could do was a low flyby where they could drop boxes of ammo. At mid-evening, the battalion landing zone was still too hot for evacuation of the wounded. Every time the helicopters approached, the enemy mortars and .50 cal machine gun fire would erupt to drive them away. A nearly full moon had risen early and silhouetted the helicopters in the NVA's cross hairs.

Hotel Company was the last to arrive at the command post and was assigned a portion of the perimeter on the right flank. While moving into their defensive perimeter, Hotel Company was ambushed in an open field near a drainage ditch. One man was killed and Hotel Company's 1st and 3rd platoons pulled back to consolidate before they could take the perimeter. They could hear the Vietnamese calling to each other. When they began their assault to retake the drainage ditch, they found the NVA had left and they were able to occupy the drainage ditch. That also seemed to eliminate the volume of mortar fire that had been harassing the medevac helicopters. These NVA may have been the forward observers for their mortars which seemed to have been so deadly accurate on our helicopters. H&S company hunkered in place and fired H&I (harassment and interdiction) fire and artillery illumination flares all night.

At 2130, MAG-36 once more renewed flights. Sometime late after dark they were able to get Medevac helicopters in a landing zone close behind the command post to fly out our casualties and the KIA Marines that had been recovered so far. Captain Grosz remembers helping put Captain Jerry Lindauer and 1st Lieutenant Pete Amish on helicopters. It was during that time that the NVA lobbed some 82mm mortar rounds into our landing zone.

> I didn't hear the rounds exploding initially over the helicopter's prop noise. But I realized we were getting bombarded when fragments started hitting the helicopter and the Marine I was loading. I ran for my foxhole but didn't make it all the way before a round exploded behind me. I caught some fragments in both elbows which I could pull out and some in my flak jacket which protected my lungs and kidneys. I caught one fragment about 1/4 inch square just below the right buttocks which went deep into my thigh. It's still there. It was decided to leave it be because they would cause more damage by trying to extract it. Although sore, I was able to function so I decided to stay with my company and walked out to the red line on the 7 March with everyone else.

During the next seven hours the copter pilots, under blackout conditions, brought in much needed supplies and evacuated seventy casualties, despite enemy fire. The medevac was completed by 22:10. The enemy was pounded by every supporting arm at the disposal of 2/7. At 2200, a flare ship, C-47, known as *Basketball*, arrived on station and dropped flares. Marine jets continued to strike at suspected enemy positions with bombs, rockets, and napalm, while A4s from MAG-12 made high altitude, radar-controlled bombing strikes on enemy trail networks leading into the battalion area.

Artillery kept pace with the air effort during the night and early morning hours of 4-5 March. Both 155mm howitzer batteries at Binh Son, Batteries Kilo and Mike 4/11, fired in support of the Marines and the ARVN airborne battalion further north. The batteries expended so many rounds that two ammunition resupply truck convoys from Chu Lai were required in the overnight hours to replenish the stock.

H&S company had 9 killed in action: Lance Corporal William Wesley Brown who was an FO attached to Hotel Company; Corporal Johnny Ray Holloway from 81mm mortars; Pfc. Michael Anthony Gilson, who was a radio operator; Pfc. Joseph Samuel Herron who was an anti-tank assault man; Pfc. Thomas Wardrop, III was a radio operator for Lieutenant Amish, the forward air observer assigned to Fox Company; Pfc. Frank Lopez, Jr. who was another radio operator that was assigned to Fox Company. Their KIA's included three Corpsmen who were killed when Hotel Company was overrun on Hill 37: Hospitalman Third Class Daniel Patrick Birch, Hospitalman Lawrence Everett Johnson, and Hospitalman Samuel Gizzi Orlando.

Personal account from Rudolph Barrios, H&S 2/7:

> During the first night of Operation Utah, I remember that night Joseph Samuel Herron and I were arguing about who's going to get the fox hole for the night. The next day he was killed, I still have that in my head, what a nightmare.

One last recollection from Captain Nick Grosz:

The day after our return to Chu Lai, Lieutenant Colonel Utter and the involved company commanders were standing around talking at our battalion command post helo landing zone waiting for a helo to take us out to the hospital ship where we sent a number of our wounded from Operation Utah. All of a sudden there was what sounded like a pop from an AK 47. In a flash all of us were on the ground looking at each other with that "what the hell was that?" look in our eyes. Then we heard the young Marine radio operator—who had just popped smoke for the helo to hone in on—laughing. It took a second and we were all laughing.

While that might have been amusing to see our senior battalion officers hitting the dirt, many of us experienced the same thing even years after we had returned and heard an unexpected sound like a gunshot. When I first moved to my current home in the countryside in Morgan Hill, California, I had a neighbor who was a deputy sheriff and a gun enthusiast. He had a firing range up in the hills behind his ranch and when he fired his rifles, I would get a chill that ran up my spine whenever I heard it.

****

Lieutenant Colonel Leon Newby Utter, was respected by all who served with him. Captain Alex Lee wrote a book, *Utter's Battalion* in which he chronicles the 2/7 Vietnam experience under Lieutenant Colonel Utter.

> Lieutenant Colonel Utter led us with bravery, with honor, with dignity, and with a deep sense of concern for every man who went forward to the sound of guns. He never, ever at any time, ceased teaching us the basic truths of soldiering under fire.

After Operation Utah, 1st Lieutenant Jack Archer, the platoon commander of the 81mm Mortars, ran into Lieutenant Colonel Utter as he was coming out of the battalion aid station. Lieutenant Colonel Utter had been hit by a fragment from a mortar shell which he had not reported since he did not want to be medevac'd from his command. When Lieutenant Colonel Utter returned from Vietnam, he was assigned as a speech writer for the Commandant of the Marine Corps. He did not get to command a regiment and his forthrightness may have prevented him from reaching the rank of general officer. In the early 1960s, Colonel Utter was a Marine officer instructor in the Navy ROTC unit at Yale University, as he was walking to class one morning, in uniform, he was accosted by a rather unkempt young man who declared that he was a pacifist. Then Major Utter replied, with a smile, "So am I. But I work at it."

Captain Nick Grosz went on to have a storied Marine Corp career, serving three combat tours in Vietnam where he was awarded two Bronze Stars with Combat V and the Vietnamese Cross of Gallantry in addition to his Navy Cross. He was promoted to Colonel and his career culminated with command of the 27th Regiment and he was awarded the Legion of Merit on his retirement in 1990. After his Marine Corps retirement, he continued to serve in executive positions with the Naval Mutual Aid Association. He resides in Fairfax Virginia, and like so many veterans of the Vietnam War is suffering the effects of Agent Orange.

Pfc. Raymond Potter went on 8 operations with H&S company, served two tours in Vietnam and was a drill instructor after his second tour. He had many interesting assignments including a tour at the White House with the president's Marine helicopter crew. He retired as a master gunnery sergeant, the highest enlisted grade in the Marine Corps. When I commented on his success, he replied:

> But I was and still am that private from H&S company from the 2nd Battalion, 7th Marines that served under Captain Nicholas Grosz and Colonel Leon Utter; The finest Marines that I ever served with.

Chapter 7
Dueling Mortars

This section is based on contributions from 1st Lieutenant John Archer, who was the 81mm mortar platoon leader during Operation Utah.

A mortarman in the Marine Corps operates a weapon system called a mortar. A mortar is a smooth bore, muzzle-loading, high-angle-of-fire weapon used for close-in support of ground troops. Although mortars can be as big as 160mm, at the battalion level, mortarmen are responsible for the tactical employment of the 60mm light mortar and the 81mm medium mortar. They provide indirect fire in support of the rifle squads, platoons, and companies, as well as the battalion. Mortars provide an extra dimension to the battlefield. They fire at a high angle and come down almost vertically, which is an advantage when the enemy are in trenches or spider holes. The high angle enables them to reach targets that are behind hills and other barriers. It also enables them to hit targets situated on higher elevations. Other projectiles like artillery and rockets do not do well when firing uphill. Mortars can fire white phosphorus as well as high explosive rounds to inflict casualties and can be used to create a smoke screen or mark targets for close air support or medevacs. Illumination rounds can be fired to expose enemy troops at night without giving away the location of the mortar if they are hidden behind a barrier. They are the battalions "artillery" for quick, close in support, and are highly mobile, on the backs of your sturdier Marines. In addition to having the strength and stamina to carry an extra 100 lbs. of gear, Mortar men also need to have the skills to be able to read topology maps and chart the trajectories for the rounds.

During the period of Operation Utah, the Marine Corps started to replace 3.5-inch rocket launchers, more commonly known as the bazooka from WWII and Korea, with 60mm lightweight mortars, at the company level. While the 3.5-inch rockets were effective against armored vehicles and tanks, these types of targets were not common in Vietnam and mortars were more effective for firing into defilade without relying on direct line of sight between the gun and its target and had a larger kill radius. At the same time some of the rocket teams were replacing the 3.5-inch bazookas with the M72 LAW (Light Anti-Armor Weapon) 66mm rocket, a small, armor-piercing explosive rocket contained in a disposable firing tube. It was first developed to destroy tanks and was very effective against bunkers. Each rocket man carried four M72 LAWs.

During Operation Utah we still had a. mixture of 3.5-inch rockets, M72 LAWs, and mortars. A rocket crew consisting of a gunner and a loader and were officially known as anti-tank assault men and carried the bazooka or the LAWs and were usually assigned out to a rifle platoon during field operations. The 60mm mortar team would remain at the company weapons platoon and the 81mm mortars were kept at the battalion level due to the need to coordinate the targeting and supply of the mortars.

The two mortars used by the Marine Corps are the MM224A1 (60mm) and the M252 (81mm). There is a big difference in size, weight, and effectiveness of the two mortars in use by the Marine Corps: The M224 60mm lightweight mortar was used at the company level. Depending upon the configuration, the M224 will weigh between 18-45 lbs. Each of the 60mm rounds weighs 4 lbs. The M252 81mm medium weight mortar was used at the battalion level. The M252 weighs 90 lbs. and each round weighs 15 lbs. There were basically four types of rounds. High explosive rounds with a quick or delayed fuse setting, Smoke for marking targets or providing a smoke screen, White Phosphorus for marking targets or creating fires, and Illumination rounds for visibility at night.

60mm mortarmen form a squad located in the weapons platoon of the rifle companies and the 81mm Mortars were organized as a platoon in the H&S company of the battalion. The 60mm mortarmen were kept with the company command center and were usually not deployed with the rifle platoons. They were organized in squads and kept in the company command post under the direction of the company gunnery sergeant. A 60mm mortar squad was a nine-man squad that had two tubes. The squad was composed of a squad leader, two gunners, two assistant gunners and four ammunition carriers. NCOs were assigned as mortar gunners, forward observers, fire direction plotters, and squad and section leaders. Mortar men were expected to be carrying heavier weights than the rest of the platoon/squad and were tasked with a variety of responsibilities within the mortar platoon. Many men preferred the mortar squad, since they were kept with the command post at night and were not required to go on night patrols.

1st Lieutenant Jack Archer was the mortar platoon commander on Operation Utah. Jack was from Elmhurst, near Chicago, and was a three-sport athlete in high school. He graduated from the University of Miami, where he played baseball and had offers to play professionally for the Cincinnati Reds and the Milwaukee Braves. Since he had met and married his wife Vicki on graduation, he decided to join the Marine Corps and apply for OCS (officer's candidate school), instead. Jack was a classmate of the other platoon commanders in 2/7 and was the weapons platoon commander for Hotel Company when we first formed up at Camp Pendleton. However, since the machine gun and rocket teams would usually be assigned out to the rifle platoons during operations in the field, Jack was looking for more direct involvement in operations with the battalion mortar platoon. When Jack took over the mortar platoon, he inherited a group with many discipline problems. When they were in Okinawa, some of the platoon had even been involved in the murder of a taxi driver. His first challenge was to instill pride and discipline in a group that felt over-burdened, neglected, and unappreciated. By the time of Operation Utah, Jack had revitalized the mortar platoon and the men were operating at a high level.

The 81mm Mortar platoon had four sections made up of 8 men each with 2 guns per section. One section to support each rifle company in the battalion, if you were to break it down to that level.

The table of organization calls for a sergeant E-5 as the section leader. There is a corporal gunner, lance corporal assistant gunner, and 2 or 3 PFC ammo humpers, if we had the manpower available. There is a radio operator and a forward observer as well with each section. Other riflemen in H&S company or the rifle companies were often assigned to carry extra mortar rounds as the value of the mortars was important.

Mortars required more training to set the right charge for distance, the right azimuth for direction, and the timing of the fuse. The gunner and assistant gunner carried the tube and base plate with several rounds of mortars and were armed with a .45 automatic pistol. The ammunition men would carry 4 to 6 rounds of mortars in addition to their M14 rifles and a hundred rounds of M14 ammo. Each Marine was expected to carry about 100 Lbs. of additional weight. Jack appreciated the extra physical demands of the Mortars and was always looking at ways to make life better for the men. When Jack went to cold weather training in the Sierras, he noticed that the pack boards that were used to handle the bulky cold weather gear were very good at distributing load. Applying what he learned in cold weather training, he ordered these pack boards for his troops' use in Vietnam which made it easier for them to carry their loads.

After landing at LZ Alpha, the mortar platoon was deployed in a tree line to the south, behind the battalion command post. Jack assigned a forward observer and a radio man to each of the three rifle companies. Their job was to spot targets for the rifle companies and communicate the targets to the fire direction center at the battalion command post. Unfortunately the forward observer and radio man for both Fox Company and Golf Company were killed early on in the engagement

Mortars played a key role in turning back the NVA when they threatened to overrun Fox Company on the left flank and Hotel Company on the right flank. With the attacks happening so quickly there was no time to call in artillery or airstrikes. The positioning of the artillery northeast at Binh Son also made it difficult to call in artillery on the NVA who were attacking from that direction since the over-splash from that direction would fall on 2/7's position. Mortars were the ideal weapon to use when being attacked from that direction and when the enemy were within several hundred meters.

The NVA's attack on Hotel Company's position on Hill 37 was clearly visible to the battalion command post. Late in the afternoon, the command center could see Hotel Company was under heavy attack, being pushed off the high ground and hanging on by sheer will power. There was no request from Hotel Company for a fire mission since it was obvious that they were heavily engaged. Gunnery Sergeant Bascolupo was able to initiate a fire mission on behalf of Hotel Company from the command post. The NVA were easy to spot with branches tiered around their backs and moving across the ridge line where all the natural vegetation had been blown away. From their position they were able to bracket the NVA and fire for effect inflicting heavy casualties on the NVA. This pushed them off the ridge with Hotel Company in hot pursuit. The characteristics of the mortars, being able to be quickly deployed at close range and fire at targets uphill, turned the course of battle.

The 2/7 and NVA mortarmen were in a duel all afternoon and into the night. Whenever the mortarmen marked landing sites with WP smoke rounds for the helicopters to drop supplies and evacuate the wounded, the NVA mortars would hone in on them. The Marines would mark where the rounds came from and fire back. There were so many fire missions, the mortars had to be resupplied three times. In between resupplies, the mortarmen risked their lives carrying regular ammo across the open rice paddies to the rifle companies that were heavily engaged with the NVA. The rice paddies were swept with NVA mortars and 12.7mm (.50 cal) machine gun fire. A 12.7mm machine gun had an effective range of up to a mile and would blow huge holes in whatever it hit. The 12.7mm is like a mini cannon. The rice paddy dikes would explode when a 12.7mm round hit it. The 12.7mm was powerful enough to bring down an F4 Phantom on a napalm run at the beginning of Operation Utah. Imagine what it did to human flesh and bone.

****

Jack Archer was decorated for his service in Vietnam and he left the Marine Corps after he returned from Vietnam. He raised a family and had a successful career as a financial planner and has retired on a small ranch in the foothills of Southern California. Like many of the veterans of Vietnam, he is on disability from the effects of Agent Orange, but he is proud of his service and the men with whom he served and feels lucky to have survived.

Mortars played a key role in determining the outcome of Operation Utah. If the mortars had not turned back the NVA on Hill 37, they could have overrun Hotel Company and split Golf and Fox Companies from the battalion command post at Chau Nhai (4). The battalion could have been destroyed before they could consolidate for their night defenses. The mortarmen had their share of casualties and many more risked their lives volunteering to carry much needed ammunition to the rifle companies across open fields of fire. They also saved many lives as they helped to evacuate the wounded across those same exposed areas. While this is a description of what the 2/7 mortarmen did, the same type of stories could be told of the mortarmen in the other three battalions. Those of us who survived Operation Utah owe our deepest gratitude to these mortarmen.

Chapter 8
Hotel Company Takes the High Ground

In Sun Tzu's *The Art of War*, he advises military leaders to take the high ground and force the enemy to attack from a lower position. Fighting from an elevated position is said to be easier for a number of tactical reasons. Holding the high ground offers an elevated vantage point with a wider field of view, enabling surveillance of the surrounding landscape. Additionally, soldiers fighting uphill tire more quickly, have less visibility of the enemy positions, and move more slowly when compared to soldiers fighting downhill who do not have to struggle against the forces of gravity while struggling over natural obstacles in the terrain. In modern warfare, fighting uphill means that straight trajectory weapons like rifles and artillery are less effective and weapons have to be held higher—from the shoulder or the hip to get the right angle—which exposes more of the shooter's profile to enemy fire. Soldiers who have the high ground can fire from a prone position which presents a minimal target, and use plunging fire to cover more of the target area. The ideal position on a hill is the military crest which is an area on the forward or reverse slope of a hill or ridge just below the topographical crest from which maximum observation and direct fire covering the slope down to the base of the hill or ridge can be obtained. The military crest is used in maneuvering along the side of a hill or ridge to provide the maneuvering force maximum visibility of the terrain below and minimize their own visibility by not being silhouetted against the sky, as it would be at the actual or topographical crest of the hill. Controlling the high ground is a major tactical advantage .

This section was largely based on the memoirs of Frank Picon who was the platoon sergeant for 3rd Platoon, Hotel Company, 1st Lieutenant Harry Ketchum who was the platoon commander of 3rd Platoon, Herman Busse, 1st squad leader of 2nd Platoon, and Gary

Watkins the only corpsman who survived while supporting Hotel Company on Hill 37.

Frank Picon was born in Trona, California. His parents were immigrants, his mother was from Sonora and his father was from Chihuahua, Mexico. He was a star football player and team leader in high school and played quarterback for Coalinga Junior College until an injury ended his career. One day, he decided to learn a trade by joining the Air Force. It turned out that the Air Force recruiter was away on vacation so Frank decided to join the Marine Corps. He did well in boot camp where he was given a meritorious promotion to PFC and was selected for sea duty as an orderly to Admiral William Gentner aboard the USS Lexington. He later joined 3rd Battalion 9th Marine in Okinawa, before joining 2nd Battalion 7th Marines as platoon sergeant for 3rd platoon, Hotel Company. Frank was an exceptional platoon sergeant who knew what was required of his men in combat and cared for them. He tried to know each man's strengths and weaknesses in order to make them better Marines and better human beings.

While Frank was the picture of a squared away Marine, his platoon Commander, 1st Lieutenant Harry Ketchum was more casual. Harry Ketchum was a maverick, a man of few words. He was an outdoorsman from the Dalles in Oregon where his family had homesteaded a large ranch. He had an independent streak and didn't always follow the rules. He was no nonsense, but fair to his men, respected for his tactical decisions, with an outdoorsman's instincts for navigating through the jungle and avoiding dangerous situations. He carried a non-regulation .44 magnum revolver and a large 11-inch bowie knife. He didn't like the standard issue .45 semi-automatic since it took two hands to chamber a round and the regulation, 7-inch KA-Bar, felt like a toothpick.

Frank and Harry were a great combination and their leadership and coolness under fire saved 3rd Platoon and 2nd Platoon when they were about to be overrun on Hill 37.

When Frank boarded the helicopter at Chu Lai, he asked the crew chief if they were going into a hot landing zone. In response, the crew chief pointed to a hole in the floor. There had already been some damage to other helicopters and there were reports that an F4 Phantom jet on a napalm run had also been downed. Frank always sat by the door so that he would be the first one out to organize his

Marines when they landed. Just as they were coming in, the helicopter banked sharply to the side and an A4 Skyhawk came screaming in just below the helicopter with an ear-splitting shriek and dropped some napalm. The heat and the roar of the flames were intense. It was like looking into the depth of hell. It was like nothing Frank had ever experienced.

When they were a few feet above the ground, Frank and his men started jumping out and quickly took cover. They linked up with the rest of the 3rd Platoon and set a perimeter. There were no incoming rounds. Some of the men noticed some movement in the grass ahead, and Frank took two men to investigate what was there. They discovered an NVA in an officer's uniform who was badly burned from the napalm. He had a map case which they took and they called up Watkins the Corpsman to see what they could do for the NVA. The Corpsman said that there was nothing they could do since his flesh was dripping from his bones. The decision was made not to call in a medevac, and one of the men, Pfc. Odem shot the NVA to put him out of his misery on the advice of the corpsman.

The other two companies of 2/7 had already landed. Fox Company was in the first wave, followed by Golf Company and the command group with H&S company. It was past noon by the time Hotel Company had landed. Then the battalion sat there in a holding pattern with Fox Company on their left flank and Golf Company to their right with H&S behind them and Hotel Company behind them as a reserve. They sat there for about an hour before the orders came to move out. Since one of the helicopters was having engine trouble, 1st Lieutenant Yoshida's 1st Platoon, Hotel Company, was told to stay behind as security until the helicopter could be repaired and retrieved. The rest of Hotel Company moved out as the battalion reserve behind Fox and Golf Companies and behind H&S company.

Fox Company became engaged in a fire fight on the left flank and Golf Company was called up to protect Fox Company's right flank where they were also quickly engaged in a firefight. Golf Company reported heavy contact from machine guns in the hedgerows and trench line in front of them. Then they reported seeing NVA moving around to the ridge line on their right flank and getting in position to outflank the battalion. That's when Lieutenant Colonel Utter committed his reserve. Hotel Company was called up to take the high ground on Hill 37 to the right of Golf Company to protect the battalion's right flank. Hill 37 was a ridge line that ran north and south. It was mostly bare hard ground with a high peak on the east side. They began to move out with Ketchum's 3rd Platoon on the left flank and 2nd Platoon led by Staff Sergeant McDermitt on the right flank. They had no reserve since the 1st Platoon had been providing security for a downed helicopter and was later sent to support Fox Company. Hotel Company was able to reach the military crest of the ridge in short order with 2nd Platoon taking the higher peak on the right side. Between 3rd Platoon and 2nd Platoon the angle of the slope did not allow for physical contact or visibility. The radio chatter from Hotel was increasing, but it was hard to tell what was happening since the noise of the battle was so intense that it was hard to hear and understand what was being said. The sounds of F4 jets screaming overhead, napalm bombs exploding and the increasing fire of machine guns and mortars was deafening. The 3rd Platoon radio man, Herbert McInville, was kneeling next to the radio

91

cupping his hands to his ear, but he couldn't make out what was being said.

Ketchum's 3rd Platoon was deployed along the lower crest of Hill 37, but the 2nd Platoon was in a bad situation. Unable to hear what was being reported to assess the situation, Ketchum and Picon physically went to the right flank to see what was happening to 2nd Platoon. They saw them in a pitched battle. 2nd Platoon was caught on a slope with hard ground where they could not dig in and had no cover. They were totally exposed.

Sergeant Herman Busse remembers 2nd Platoon moving up Hill 37. Sergeant Busse's 1st Squad was on the right, 3rd Squad was to his left and Corporal Hooper's 2nd Squad was on the far left. At first the progress was relatively easy as they reached the top of the ridgeline. Then the mortars hit them. Sergeant Busse had taken over an M79 grenade launcher and asked his machine gunner Lance Corporal Taylor to fire some tracers to mark where he thought the mortars were coming from. He raised himself up on his knees to locate the target just as a mortar landed in front of him and severed an artery in his right arm. He could see the blood spurting out over several feet with each heartbeat. Behind a pile of rocks, he found a corpsman who applied a tourniquet and gave him a shot of morphine. Sergeant Busse was feeling the effects of the morphine and decided to make his way to the battalion aid station. He left his grenade launcher, M14 and seven magazines of M14 ammo with his squad.

While 2nd Platoon was concentrating on the action in front of them, they were being outflanked on the right by a large group of NVA wearing branches for camouflage. Busse looked back and could see a swarm of camouflage NVA attacking 2nd Platoon. He felt hopeless as he watched his squad being overwhelmed by the swarm of NVA. That is an image which haunts him to this day. He had lost so much blood he could not possibly make it back up the hill to help his squad, but in his mind he feels he could have done something.

2nd Platoon Commander Staff Sergeant McDermitt was a veteran from the Korean War and was well respected as an experienced combat leader. While leading his men uphill, he was wounded in the leg and could not walk. When Lieutenant Ketchum saw the sea of NVA coming over the hill, he called out to the 2nd Platoon to fall back through the 3rd Platoon perimeter. McDermitt was trying to rally his men and refused to be evacuated. One of the 3rd Platoon Marines went over and forcefully moved McDermitt to the rear. As 2nd Platoon joined 3rd Platoon, a Marine from 2nd Platoon suddenly came running out from the middle of the pack of NVA, yelling "Don't shoot, don't shoot!" This surprised everyone and both sides stopped shooting as the fleeing Marine made it safely to the 3rd Platoon perimeter. There were several 2nd Platoon Marines intermixed with the NVA when they were overrun. Several of the Marines appeared to be wounded by booby traps, which indicated that the NVA had been there before.

Ketchum sent a fire team to the left flank to hook up with Golf Company, but instead of Golf Company they were met with automatic fire from an NVA machine gun and the three Marines in the fireteam were killed. Rupert Carven, Lewis Kimmel Jr, and Franz Kolbeck were killed immediately. There appeared to be two interlocking machine guns covering the area. Corpsman Lawrence Everett Johnson, attempted to go to their aid and was killed by the same machine guns. Other Marines including their squad leader, Sergeant Ruiz, tried to go to their aid but were driven back. The three men and Corpsman Johnson had to be left where they fell and 3rd Platoon was cut off from Golf Company. Ketchum could not contact Golf Company on the radio.

Sergeant Picon was with Sergeant Maynard who had taken over an M79 grenade launcher. They spotted the two machine guns that had hit Sergeant Ruiz's squad and attempted to take out the machine guns. Sergeant Picon acted as his spotter while Sergeant Maynard fired a grenade then ducked down as the machine guns zeroed in on their position. Sergeant Maynard fired back and was laughing as he seemed to be enjoying the duel. Sergeant Picon told him to stop messing around and Sergeant Maynard finally took out one of the machine guns before they were called to consolidate with the rest of the platoon to repulse the next assault.

The NVA now had the high ground and appeared to be massing for an attack from the high ground on the right ridgeline. A Marine shouted that hundreds of them were coming over the crest of the hill. One of the men jumped up and began to run to the rear, but was quickly shot down. A spotter plane later described the valley behind the Hill 37 ridgeline as a moving sea of camouflaged NVA. While there was initial panic, the Marines returned fire to repulse the attack. Harry Ketchum later described it like mowing down hay. The NVA with branches tied around them for camouflage were being cut down as they charged. The attack was repulsed with the help of 81mm Mortar fire from H&S company who had a clear view of the ridgeline where all this was happening. Initially the Marines thought it was NVA mortars until they saw the barrage bracketing the NVA positions. Although the 2/7 mortars were on lower ground behind the battalion command post their high trajectory made it possible to fire uphill while passing over 2nd and 3rd Platoons. Another spotter plane that flew over the scene later described seeing at least a hundred bodies strewn across the crest of Hill 37.

The attack was repulsed but they had lost contact with Golf Company as well as their own company command post and there was confusion as to whether they should stay or pull back. Radio communications were useless due to the noise of the battle and the poor quality of the PRC 10 radios. The 3rd Platoon and 2nd Platoon formed a perimeter and during a lull in the fighting, Lieutenant Ketchum left Sergeant Picon in charge while he went to find 1st Lieutenant Lau to find out what was happening. After a while he came back without much more information. Harry had picked up an M14 that he found along the way for additional fire power.

Accompanying 2nd and 3rd Platoons was a Marine war correspondent, Corporal Lester Arthur Wesighan, and his photographer Corporal Ken Henderson from 3rd Marine Division HQ. Corporal Wesighan had dropped out of preflight school to be a correspondent and had hoped to work for his hometown paper when his tour was done. Corporal Wesighan left his cover to crawl through the grass to recover Lance Corporal William Brown who had been wounded. As AK-47 rounds cut through the grass, he signaled for a corpsman but instead fell to a sniper round. There were no corpsmen available because three had already been killed and the remaining corpsman had been commandeered by Fox Company. His photographer, Ken Henderson, then crawled through the grass to recover Corporal Wesighan. After Corporal Henderson determined Lance Corporal Brown and Corporal Wesighan were no longer alive, Ken himself became pinned down by small arms fire. Realizing that they were being overrun, he dug a depression into the ground to avoid enemy rounds and hoped to avoid detection. After several harrowing hours surrounded by the enemy, Corporal Henderson was able to crawl back to Marine lines after dark.

Corporal Wesighan was the first Marine correspondent to die in combat during the Vietnam War. His fiancée, Patricia Kessler, wrote:

> Lester was optimistic and had a very cheerful disposition. He had so many hopes and aspirations for his future. His plan was to work at his hometown newspaper and eventually land a position at the *Washington Post* or *New York Times*.
>
> Lester volunteered to go to Vietnam and died fighting for a cause in which he believed. Although I really did not want him to go, I was proud of him...I attended his funeral in Franklin, New Jersey, with his mother and afterwards we drove to Arlington National Cemetery for his military burial service. I cannot describe the profound sadness we felt. I loved him and have often fondly thought of him over the years.

There was a lull in the battle and by this time it was getting dark and they were low on ammunition. Although Lieutenant Colonel Utter had already sent out the word to consolidate at the battalion command post for the night defense, Ketchum had not gotten the word due to poor radio connections. Ketchum decided to withdraw to the Battalion area on his own, taking the remnants of 2nd Platoon with him. They organized a retrograde maneuver, where one squad covered the withdrawal of the other squad as they leapfrogged down the hill. Once they reached the bottom of the hill, Sergeant Maynard's squad went back along a tree line while the rest of 3rd and 2nd Platoon opted to take the shorter route across the open rice fields. It was impossible to get a clear headcount as the men were scattered. Five men were missing. By this time, all the corpsmen were dead, so the men tended to their own wounds and helped each other traverse down the hill. They gathered up the wounded and left the dead and missing behind. As soon as they got into the open field, the NVA opened fire at them. The 3rd Platoon machine gunner dropped down and was setting up to fire back but Sergeant Picon made him withdraw since he did not want anyone pinned down in the open field, especially his machine gunner.

As they made their way back, they had to cross an open area that was covered by an NVA machine gun. They took turns, timing their crossing between machine gun bursts. When the radio man McInville ran across, he dropped his radio. Rather than try to retrieve it, Lieutenant Ketchum blew it up with a grenade. Sergeant Picon was the last to cross over. Everyone was able to make it across safely.

As they straggled back to the battalion command post it was getting dark and when they were challenged, Harry announced it was 2nd and 3rd Platoons. Lieutenant Geoff Hartman, who had been a classmate with Lieutenant Ketchum from Quantico, called out to Ketchum and expressed surprise saying that they had written them off a while ago. Due to lack of radio communications, the battalion had assumed that Hotel Company had been overrun and wiped out. Ketchum was then told to deploy his men on the battalion perimeter where there was a gap and no one knew if anyone was there. Sergeant Picon remembered being annoyed that no one in the command post had checked it out while his platoon was busy on the hill. As they were moving to that area, Picon heard a grenade being armed and shouted for everyone to hit the ground. The grenade went off and the NVA opened fire. Two men were killed as they took cover and returned fire. They could hear the NVA talking and calling out to each other. Soon it was quiet and the NVA appeared to have left. The 3rd Platoon was joined by the 1st Platoon and they were able to occupy the position which was in a drainage ditch. After that there were a few harassing shots, but the NVA appeared to have left the area and 2/7 was able to get helicopters in to resupply ammo and water and evacuate their wounded. This encounter might have been a forward observer post for the NVA mortars, since the incoming mortars that were targeting the helicopter landing zone, seemed to trail off. The accuracy of their mortars also indicated that they had to have eyes on the landing zone. It was past 2130 and the full moon that had been silhouetting the helicopters as it rose in the east was now setting down behind the Annamite Mountains to the west, much to the relief of the helicopter pilots.

While Sergeant Busse was waiting to be evacuated, he could see what was happening to his platoon on Hill 37 and decided to go back up the hill despite his wound. Then he saw one of his squad members Lance Corporal William Hrinko who had been shot several times in the chest and was brought to the aid station. It was about 1430 when the first medevac helicopter attempted to land. Sergeant Busse put his arm under Lance Corporal Hrinko's arm and was helping him get to the helicopter when four mortar rounds landed in the landing zone. Lance Corporal Hrinko was killed by the mortars just minutes before he was to be evacuated. The mortar also blew off Sergeant Busse's right thumb, which meant he could not hold a rifle to go back into the fight. He managed to find his thumb and take it back with him when he was evacuated later the next morning. The medevac helicopter took off immediately and medevacs were cancelled until 2130 that evening. Sergeant Busse was not evacuated until 0230 or 0300 the next morning. The doctors were able to reattach his thumb.

Sergeant Busse also remembers Captain Marty O'Conner standing in the dark landing zone with a flashlight, guiding the first helicopters in under blackout conditions, to drop supplies and evacuate the wounded. This was typical of Captain O'Conner, not to ask others to do the high risk jobs. Captain O'Conner was the company commander of Hotel Company prior to Operation Utah and was the battalion S4 officer in charge of logistics during Utah. His leadership was sorely missed that day by Hotel Company. As the S4 officer, he personally led many heroic efforts to distribute ammunition and supplies and evacuate the wounded.

On one of Sergeant Picon's trips to get ammo at the helo site, Frank passed by a group of wounded Marines and Staff Sergeant McDermitt called out to him to ask what happened to the 2nd Platoon. Frank told him it wasn't good and McDermitt just buried his face in his hands.

When Frank got back to the 3rd Platoon position, he decided to spell McInville who had been on the radio all day. Frank took over the radio, but must have fallen asleep since he was awakened by the Hotel 6 radio man (Hotel 6 was the call sign for the Hotel Company commander) saying that they were trying to reach them. The adrenalin was wearing out and a lot of the men were starting to crash from exhaustion. There were only about 8 Marines in the 3rd Platoon and 6 in the 2nd Platoon, who had not been killed or wounded, out of nearly 70 Marines who landed that morning. 1st Platoon was fortunate in that they had only two killed in action and two wounded in action when they were assigned to rescue the Fox Company Platoon and were spared the battle on Hill 37.

The next day, it appeared that the NVA had left Hill 37 during the night. The 1st Platoon was sent up the hill to check it out. The smell of blood and gore and decaying flesh hung heavy in the morning air. The hill was pockmarked with bomb craters and shattered trees. The ground was littered with shell casings, discarded gear, and battle dressings. The NVA had removed their dead and collected all the weapons, which must have been a considerable effort, given the quantity of the men that were killed the day before. The NVA had removed an estimated hundred bodies or had hidden them during the night while we were strafing and bombing Hill 37. In the light of day, the area seemed so much smaller. The 1st Platoon was later joined by the 3rd Platoon as they moved back up on the ridge to retrieve the Hotel Company dead and look for the missing. They found all the missing, dead.

They found Orlando, the corpsman who was awarded the Navy Cross for his heroic actions the day before. His wallet, watch, and ring had been taken. Frank remembers the ring that Orlando had bought in Oceanside, the town outside Camp Pendleton, before they left. He remembers the ring since Orlando had bought it on payments and the 1st Sergeant had called him in for not making the payments. It was difficult to get money orders to make payments when we were out in the field. Somewhere in Vietnam, that ring is a trophy in someone's collection.

They found the five men who had been missing from the day before. They were together as though they were making a last stand. All were dead. They had traumatic wounds and the ants were already crawling through their mouth and eyes. Sergeant Frank Picon helped the corpsman, Doc Watkins identify and tag each of his own. Some of them he had known and trained with for three years in the old 3/9 before the formation of 2/7. There was Lance Corporal Rupert Carven III, who had been extended on lock down when his enlistment ended in February. He was lying near Pfc. Kolbeck, who had given Sergeant Picon a roll of Life Savers from his stash of goodies when they were waiting for the helicopters only 24 hours before. It was especially sad for Sergeant Picon to find Pfc. Henry Odem, who appeared to have died from a massive wound to this leg.

Odem was a good Marine who was always ready to take on the tough jobs. Although he was in 3rd Platoon, he disobeyed orders from Lieutenant Ketchum and stayed behind to help his friends in 2nd Platoon. Odem was very resourceful and Frank had been hoping that somehow Odem would find some way to survive. Odem was the Marine who killed the badly burned NVA officer when they first landed at the landing zone.

There were some reports that the bodies of our Marines had been stripped and mutilated with ring fingers cut off. I personally did not see that, nor did Frank. Some of the wounds were traumatic due to the large .50 cal machine guns. Bodies were torn apart by horrific wounds and personal items like watches, rings, and wallets had been taken, but the bodies had not been purposely mutilated. Unlike the VC, the NVA appeared to be more disciplined.

While they were on the ridgeline collecting the dead, they saw a number of NVA moving around a village on the other side of the ridge. 1st Lieutenant Ketchum got on the radio and called in artillery which scattered the NVA. They could hear the battle being waged on the other side of Hill 50 where the ARVN and 3rd Battalion, 1st Marines were engaged with the NVA.

When they finally brought the bodies back to the battalion area, the local villages were gathering around. One old lady was jabbering and nagging at the Marines, until one of the Marines slammed her with a rifle butt and dropped her to the ground. Normally this would have been a serious offense, but after all the death and carnage, no one batted an eye and the Marines just carried on, stepping over her body, carrying their dead to the helicopter pad.

****

Several Descriptions of Operation Utah had 2nd and 3rd Platoon on Hill 85. This is wrong since Hill 85 was behind 2/7 and Utter's After Action Report shows the map coordinates to be a small hill which I identify as Hill 37. Hill 37 is not mentioned in any other literature on Operation Utah.

Several other reports have Hotel Company attacking an NVA mortar position at night and killing 20 NVA. No survivor of Hotel can support that claim. This was most likely the interaction that 1st and 3rd Platoon had when they tried to secure the perimeter and were ambushed, The NVA left after the ambush and were probably a forward observer post for NVA mortars, since the mortars stopped after that encounter. The location of the NVA forward observation post would have explained the deadly accuracy they had on our battalion landing zone.

Contrary to other reports, the successful 81mm barrage that turned the tide on the NVA counter attack was not initiated by Hotel 2/7, but by Captain Nick Grosz and Gunnery Sergeant Bascalupo from H&S company who could see the action on Hill 37.

The squad leaders—Sergeant Maynard and Sergeant Ruiz—were key to the survival of Hotel Company. Their experience and leadership helped to inflict many casualties while organizing an orderly withdrawal. Both survived the war and returned home.

Sergeant Maynard left the Marine Corps and went home to Kentucky to work with his father in the coal mines. Many remember Sergeant Maynard as a wild man, laughing as he traded shots with the NVA. Years later Sergeant Picon invited Maynard to visit the Vietnam Memorial Wall, but he declined, saying that he would not be able to handle it.

Sergeant Danny Ruiz joined the Marine Corps during the Korean War. After surviving Operation Utah on his first Vietnam tour, he joined the 4th Marines in Hawaii just before they shipped out to Hue where he participated in the street-to-street fighting during Tet. In his third tour, he joined the 27th Marines who were engaged in Operation Allen Brook. Sergeant Ruiz probably survived more combat than most Marines who served as an infantryman. He retired from the Marine Corps, went to trade school and had a second career repairing large engines. At the age of 88, he was residing peacefully in Phoenix Arizona.

Frank Picon returned to the United States and trained new Marines at the Infantry Training Regiment at Camp Lejeune, trying to teach the hard earned lessons he had learned in Vietnam. Unfortunately, the curriculum had not been updated, and the senior staff NCOs in charge did not have Vietnam combat experience. When they finally offered him a promotion to staff sergeant, a job which he had been doing for a year as a platoon sergeant in Vietnam, he decided to leave the Marine Corps after nine years and joined a technology company and worked for them until he retired. After he left the Marines Corps he suffered debilitating headaches for many years which were finally diagnosed by a VA doctor who had been in Desert Storm, to be due to Post-Traumatic Stress Disorder.

Sergeant Herman Busse recovered from his wounds and left the Marine Corps. He was upset by the lack of intelligence and support that Hotel Company received prior to and during Operation Utah which caused so many casualties among his friends, many of whom he knew from boot camp. How could a regiment of NVA, thousands of people, be building fortifications within 10 miles of Chu Lai and the Marine Corps and ARVN not provide that information to the troops and provide them with enough manpower to do the job. Busse had a flying service for a while then had an adventurous, international, career with Bechtel Engineering as a power system mechanic in many global hotspots.

First Lieutenant Harry Ketchum left the Marine Corps after Vietnam and returned to his ranch in the Dalles in Oregon and expanded his ranching activities. Several of the men from 2nd and 3rd Platoon have stopped by to visit him at his ranch and several reunions have been held there. Harry is on disability, suffering from Parkinson's disease which was diagnosed as resulting from exposure to Agent Orange. Harry and Frank have stayed in contact on a regular basis.

Chapter 9
Above and Beyond

During the research for this short history of Operation Utah, I have come across so many amazing stories that were told to me so matter-of-factly, as if it was no big deal. What amazes me is how these young Marines did what they did in the confusion and uncertainty of battle, despite the pain and fear and disorientation caused by traumatic injuries, how they continued to fight and support each other with no thought for themselves. While these Marines received Purple Hearts, none of them received any medals for valor for what they did, even though I would consider it above and beyond what would have been expected of ordinary men.

Shot in the Head

Jim Nor was raised on a dairy farm in Hebron Township, Illinois. He graduated from Alden-Hebron High School where he made All Conference in football. After graduation, Jim joined the Marine

Corps, thinking there had to be something out there besides farming. He felt that he had to get away for a while and left for Boot Camp in January of 1964. He went to boot camp in San Diego, California, and completed Infantry Training at Camp Pendleton, just in time to join 2/7 in July 1964. By July 1965, a year later, he was running patrols and ambushes in Vietnam.

Utah started for Jim when he was airlifted with the rest of Hotel Company into a hot landing zone that had been established at the base of a small hill near Quang Ngai. When the UH-34 landed, he disembarked, but at that time there was not much going on. His platoon was told to start advancing up the small hill which was to their east. There were a lot of downed trees & rubble from previous bombings. They had just come off a large-scale search and destroy mission called Double Eagle II and this started off feeling like so many other operations that the company had been on. Then they started to receive heavy incoming fire. The men were wondering about getting some artillery support, but were told that they were "out of range." It would have been more accurate to say that the NVA were too close, within a few yards, to employ any weapons like artillery. The incoming fire was increasing and the NVA were impossible to see, as they were heavily fortified and dug in.

Jim was with Sergeant Maynard, the 3rd Platoon squad leader who had picked up an M-79 grenade launcher. Jim was trying to spot targets for Sergeant Maynard, and they were down under a large tree that had been blown down. The sun was setting and he tilted his helmet to reduce the glare, and that was all he remembered until he woke up a few minutes later.

A 7.62 sniper round that had been aimed to hit him between the eyes, hit the exact rim of his helmet and fragments from the bullet lodged in his forehead. When he regained consciousness Doc Orlando, a corpsman, was trying to stop the bleeding with a battle dressing. The front of his uniform was drenched in blood and he could barely hear anything. Although his head was ringing, he was aware of what was happening around him. When he looked up the hill, he could see the NVA advancing down the hill. Jim looked around and found an M14 and was shooting at the attackers when he noticed that others around him were starting to back down the hill. Jim couldn't hear if any orders were given, but he realized that they were not going to make it if they stayed where they were and managed to get himself down the hill to the command post.

The sun was setting and he found a stretcher and laid down on it. There were quite a few dead and wounded laying around him. An hour later, Sergeant Maynard came through and announced that some of the helicopters had been shot down and he needed every man who was able to walk, to grab a weapon and go back up the hill to take out the opposing forces so the Marines could get some choppers in to evacuate the wounded.

Jim thought to himself, he could walk and get back up there. So, he got up off the stretcher and started to look for a rifle, when an officer came up to him and asked where he was going. Jim tried to tell him he had orders to go back up the hill but the officer told him to go back to the stretcher, that he was done for the day. Jim was still trying to go although he could barely walk. A corpsman came up to him and gave him a shot in a vein in his arm.

That is all he remembered until he woke up on the USS Repose hospital ship, six days later. The doctors had done a craniotomy on Jim to relieve the pressure, and stop any more hemorrhaging. Jim lost 60% of hearing in his left ear and 30% in his right ear, ending up in a disability termination from active duty, and retired from the Corps.

Jim returned to Hebron and picked up some factory work for a while before joining his father on the farm. Eventually he took over the farm and expanded its operation until he retired and turned the family farm over to his sons. Jim suffers from prostate cancer due to Agent Orange and is on disability for both the cancer and hearing loss.

He considers himself to be very lucky to have survived. He credits Doc Orlando for saving his life. He was unconscious and bleeding to death when Orlando found him and stopped the bleeding. Orlando was killed shortly after he attended to Jim and was awarded the Navy Cross. Jim made it a point to visit Orlando's grave at Arlington to pay his respects. Jim showed a tremendous amount of strength and courage to be able to continue fighting and make his way back to the command post after suffering such a horrendous wound and losing so much blood.

Jim also credits his survival to the strength & stamina he developed growing up on a dairy farm, and all the training he did at Camp Pendleton before shipping out to Vietnam: "The Marines knew where we were headed and the physical training helped us."

The Death of a Fire Team

| Rupert Sadler Carven, III | Lewis Kimmel | Franz Joseph Kolbeck |

The fireteam is the basic combat unit in the Marine Corps. At full strength it consists of four Marines, a fireteam leader, automatic rifleman, assistant automatic rifleman, and a rifleman. At the time of Operation Utah most fireteams were down to three men. Lance Corporal Rupert Carven was a fireteam leader, Lewis Kimmel was his automatic rifleman and Franz Kolbeck was his assistant automatic rifleman. This fire team was caught in the crossfire from two machine guns when they were sent to establish contact with Golf Company. Carven was hit first and his fire team tried to come to his aid. As Kimmel and Kolbeck tried to retrieve Carven's body they were killed, as well. Their squad leader, Sergeant Ruiz, and a corpsman, Doc Johnson, tried to go to their aid. Doc Johnson was killed and Sergeant Ruiz had to pull back due to the intense fire. The NVA knew that Marines would try to help each other when they were down, so they trained their guns on the area of the downed Marines.

The worst of this tragedy was that none of these three men should have been there on Operation Utah. The fireteam leader, Carven, had finished his enlistment in February, but was extended for 6 months when 2/7 went into lockdown. His close friend and teammate, Lewis Kimmel, was still recovering from malaria and should have been in the rear recovering. Kolbeck, the youngest member of the team, was an only child of a widowed mother and could have been exempt from combat duty. Looking back, it appeared that they all had a premonition of what was to happen to them.

Rupert Sadler Carven, III, came from a wealthy family in Massachusetts. He was well-educated and had attended a university before he was drafted. At 24 years of age he was four or five years older than most of the enlisted men in the company. Some say that he went to Harvard or MIT. He did not talk about his background but his maturity and demeanor set him apart from the others. His squad leader Sergeant Ruiz, said he was intelligent and was always respectful. He was an experienced Marine having trained with the 9th Marines in Okinawa before joining 2/7. He was upset with the Marine Corps for extending his enlistment that should have ended in February, a month before Utah, but he did not let that interfere with his duties. While waiting for the helicopters that were to take him into Operation Utah on the morning of March 4, 1966, Carven made a comment to Watkins, a corpsman, that he did not think he would make it.

Lewis Albert Kimmel Jr. had served with Carven in the 9th Marines in Okinawa and they were good friends. When they were training in Camp Pendleton, Carven would spend weekends with Kimmel at his home in Camarillo which was 120 miles north of the base. Shortly before Utah, Kimmel came down with a severe case of malaria and was sent to a hospital in Danang. Marine Corps General Victor Krulak, came to the hospital and ordered everyone in sickbay to go back to their units or be transferred to another billet. Kimmel opted to return to 3rd Platoon. His platoon sergeant, Sergeant Picon could see that he was not fully recovered and tried to keep him on light duty. But when the call came to mount up for Utah, Kimmel said he was ready to go. Kimmel's father, Technical Sergeant Lewis Kimmel Sr. was stationed at Tan Son Nhut Air Force Base in Saigon, when he was notified of his son's death. Technical Sergeant Kimmel Sr. had the sad duty of escorting his son's body back to Camarillo.

Franz Joseph Kolbeck was a sweet, mild-mannered, boy in a big man's body. He was big, barrel-chested and well over 200 lbs. Jim Nor knew Kolbeck since they were both from the Chicago area and played football on opposing teams. Jim remembers Kolbeck making All-State in1963. Kolbeck failed his last inspection before leaving for Vietnam because he did not have a second pair of boots. His feet were too large for any of the boots in supply. I happened to be the duty officer on our last day in Camp Pendleton, when his squad leader told me of his failed inspection. I drove him in my private car to all the PXs in Camp Pendleton until we found a pair that fit so he could pass that inspection. (I sometimes wonder what would have happened if I left him to fail the inspection. Would that have kept him from shipping out to Vietnam? I'm sure it didn't make a bit of difference.) But it did give me a chance to get to know Kolbeck, as we searched for his boots. Although he wasn't in my platoon, I felt a special loss when I found his body on Hill 37.

Kolbeck was the only child of a widowed mother and could have been exempt from combat duty. His platoon sergeant, Sergeant Picon offered to transfer him to a non-combat billet since he was an only child but he refused to be transferred. His obituary quoted his mother as saying, "We didn't even know he was in combat."

He loved to eat and his mother would send him weekly care packages filled with all sorts of treats. Normally, he would not share his treats. However, when the platoon was waiting for the helicopters to fly them into Utah, Kolbeck was seen passing out his treats and emptying his backpack. He gave Sergeant Picon a roll of Life Savers.

The Unwanted Child

The fourth member of 3nd Platoon that was killed on Operation Utah was Henry Duane Odom. He was from a small town in Texas. He was only 19 when he was killed by small arms fire.

Odom told Sergeant Picon that he was abandoned when he was a child in grammar school. One day he came home from school and found that his parents had taken everything and left without a word. An aunt took him in. He finished one year of high school and joined the Marine Corps as soon as he was 17.

Odom was a good Marine, he knew his job and was always available to volunteer for the next assignment. During the battle when 2nd Platoon was being overrun, Lieutenant Ketchum remembers Odom wanting to go back up the hill to help his friends in 2nd Platoon. Lieutenant Ketchum told Odom to stay with his squad, but Odom was missing in action when the platoon consolidated that evening in the battalion command post.

The next day when 2/7 went back up the hill to search the battle field, they found Odom's body in the area where 2nd Platoon was overrun. He had a large leg wound and probably bled to death. When Odom's body was sent back to his home town in Texas, there was no one to claim his body. Later his mother wrote to Lieutenant Ketchum to claim his $10,000 death benefit. Years later his squad leader, Sergeant Maynard, found his grave in Eldorado Cemetery in Jackson County, across the Texas border in Oklahoma.

Losing an Arm Didn't Stop Him

This Marine has not been positively identified. This action was reported by Doc Watkins. Since Doc had only been with 2nd Platoon for a few months he was not familiar with all the personnel and did not know this Marine's name.

Doc Watkins had been tending to the wounded in the Hotel Company battle area with 2nd Platoon when he treated this young Marine who had been injured by a mortar explosion. His left arm had been blown off below the elbow and he was suffering from a sucking chest wound. Doc Watkins applied a tourniquet above the elbow and covered the chest wound so that air could not be sucked in, but air from inside could be expelled. The Marine appeared to be mobile and started to move downhill toward the landing zone for evacuation on his own power.

Doc went on to treat other casualties until he came to Corpsman Birch, who was badly injured and needed help getting down to the landing zone. Doc Watkins was able to get Birch down to the landing zone with the help of a Marine named Maples. Just as they got to the landing zone, a machine gun opened up on the evacuation helicopter causing it to abort its landing. The landing zone was littered with the dead and wounded from Fox Company including the Fox Company Commander, Captain Lindauer, who had a badly shattered arm and other injuries. There were 18 bodies that were covered with ponchos and abandoned gear and bandages were scattered around the landing zone.

A sergeant from Fox Company decided that this landing zone was too hot for medevac helicopters and that the wounded needed to be taken to the battalion command post for evacuation. He ordered Doc Watkins to triage the wounded and move them to the battalion command post. Doc Watkins protested that he needed to be back on the hill with 3rd Platoon, but was given a direct order.

Doc Watkins gathered up the walking wounded and got them to help move the more critical casualties. He and three of the walking wounded used a poncho to carry Captain Lindauer. One of the walking wounded who helped carry Captain Lindauer was the young Marine with the one arm and a sucking chest wound! They managed to make it to the evacuation area near the Battalion command post, but just as they were loading the medevac helicopter, the NVA mortars began to zero in on the landing zone. The medevac was able to take off with many of the wounded, but the young Marine with the one arm and a sucking chest wound was hit in the head by a mortar fragment and killed before he could be evacuated. From records of men who died from fragmentation wounds, I believe that Marine was Lance Corporal Klaus Jurgen Herms, the son of Walter B. Herms

109

and Hildegard M. Herms of Covina, California. Lance Corporal Jurgen was born in Poland but gave his all for his adopted country.

These Marines were representative of the men that fought in Utah and throughout the Vietnam War. They did not hesitate to step up and go beyond to help one another.

Part 3
Operation Utah
Phase Two

Chapter 10
Mike Company 3/1: A Tiger by the Tail

E
ven as the first wave of ARVN troops began to land on D-
Day, March 4, 1966, the damage to the incoming helicopters
and the downing of an F4 Phantom jet made it clear to the
commanders that this was not going to be the typical search and
destroy operation where the VC would melt away to avoid
confronting our fire power. After leading his gunships in the pre-H-
hour, Lieutenant Colonel Robert J. Zitnik, the commanding officer
of VMO-6, reported something to the effect that we had "a tiger by
the tail." Agreeing with the VMO commander that the heavy anti-
aircraft fire indicated the presence of a sizable enemy force, Colonel
Peatross returned to Chu to Lai to give General Platt a first-hand
report and alert additional Marine forces. At this point—
approximately 1130—General Platt decided to reactivate Task Force
Delta which had been in place for Operation Double Eagle. Colonel
Peatross was assigned as Chief of Staff and personnel from the 7th
Marines and 4th Marines headquarters made up the rest of the staff.

General Platt had already begun to take measures to reinforce 2/7.
His main concern was that the North Vietnamese might evade the
allied forces as they had done during Operation Double Eagle. He
had ordered the deployment of another 155mm battery to Binh Son
and Lieutenant Colonel James R. Young's 3rd Battalion, 1st Marines
to establish blocking positions north of Utter's battalion. Young's
Kilo Company was assigned to provide route security for the Task
Force Delta command center which would be located outside of
Quang Ngai, located on Hill 101 (known as Buddha Mountain)l
overlooking the southern area of the battlefield about seven miles
southeast of the Utah area. This meant that another rifle company—
Kilo 3/1—would not be involved directly in Operation Utah.

Because of the heavy resistance encountered by Utter 's battalion
and the desire to encircle the NVA, General Platt alerted yet another
battalion, Lieutenant Colonel Paul X. Kelley's 2nd Battalion, 4th

Marines still at Chu Lai, for helicopter movement the following morning to a landing zone 2,500 meters South of Utter's night perimeter. This would have the Marines pressing from the north and the south. At the same time, the South Vietnamese called up extra units to block any escape to the east and the west.

March 4 was a busy day for MAG 36. After making two hotly contested air assaults with an ARVN battalion and Utter's Marine Battalion 2/7, in the morning, MAG 36 was called upon to make yet another air assault. At 13:10 on March 4, a verbal frag order, which was not preplanned, was given to MAG 36 to provide 28 helicopters for the transportation of two rifle companies from 3/1 in Chu Lai to an area north of Utter's Battalion and 5000 meters west-southwest of Binh Son. Lift off was scheduled for 1500 based on the availability of the helicopters. Initially the frag order was for two rifle companies, reinforced by 81mm mortars, but Lieutenant Colonel Young, the Commanding Officer of 3/1, requested and received authorization for a third rifle company, India Company, as a reserve. By 1800, the command group, companies Lima, Mike and two platoons of India were landed and in position on the high ground south of the Tra Bong River and north of Chau Nhai (4) where 2/7 had consolidated for the night. They were within 1000 meters of Hill 50 where the main battles would be fought the next day. Companies Lima and Mike moved to assigned blocking positions and held those positions throughout the night while India Company provided security for the landing zone. One platoon from India Company was delayed until it landed in the morning of March 5. While moving into position, Mike Company engaged in a brief firefight with two NVA and used their 81mm mortars to silence a 12.7mm machine gun nest. During the night, they could see the air strikes and artillery hitting Hill 50 and the two villages Chau Nhai (3) to the southeast and Khanh My to the southwest. There was no further enemy contact during the night in this area.

During the night of 4-5 March, the enemy continued to harass Utter's battalion in Chau Nhai (4). The NVA became especially active when helicopters tried to fly in for medevacs. Because of the intensity of the enemy fire, Lieutenant Colonel Utter had called off helicopter missions during the day and early evening. There was nearly a full moon that had risen during the afternoon which silhouetted the helicopters until it set around 2100 behind the

Annamite Mountains to the west. Around 2130, MAG-36 once more renewed flights. During the next seven hours, much-needed supplies were brought to the Marines and 70 casualties were evacuated by those brave helicopter pilots who flew through a hail of bullets each time they arrived at the battalion's perimeter.

During that night, Marine supporting arms played a large role. An Air Force AC-47 arrived on station and dropped flares. Marine jets continued to strike at suspected enemy positions with bombs, rockets, and napalm, while A4s from MAG-12 made high altitude, radar-controlled bombing strikes on enemy trail networks leading into the battle area. Colonel Leslie E. Brown, the MAG-12 commander, recalled:

> We were just in a long stream of bombing and coming back and rearming and going back as fast as we could. You were not necessarily flying with the same squadron that you left with. You came back and joined up and the next two to four airplanes off became a flight. The level of proficiency was so high that it didn't matter who was leading.

Artillery kept pace with the air effort during the night and early morning hours of 4-5 March. Both 155mm howitzer batteries at Binh Son, Batteries K and M, 4th Battalion, 11th Marines, fired in support of the Marines and the ARVN airborne battalion further north. The Marine artillerymen expended so many rounds that two ammunition resupply truck convoys from Chu Lai were required to replenish the ammunition. Just as the second convoy arrived at Binh Son shortly after 0500, the North Vietnamese launched a major attack against the 1st ARVN Airborne Battalion's defensive position near Hill 50. Major Elmer N. Snyder, at that time Task Force Delta operations officer, asked the artillery liaison officer to call for "maximum fires on the four grid squares that comprised the battlefield." In the largest single fire mission yet conducted in the Chu Lai area, the two Binh Son batteries, reinforced by a 155mm gun battery at Chu Lai, fired 1,900 rounds in two hours.

While this was all going on in the early hours of 5 March, Staff Sergeant Leonard Hultquist, the Platoon Sergeant for 2nd Platoon, Lima Company 3/1, was on radio watch and was using the light of the flares to write a letter to his wife Nancy and their three daughters. Staff Sergeant Hultquist used every opportunity he had to write to his wife. Leonard Hultquist was born in Omaha, Nebraska and was sent to Boys Town, Nebraska and completed grades 7 to 12 before he enlisted in the Marine Corp in 1954. In 1958, he left the Marine Corps and worked in a Bakery where he met and married Nancy Blomenkamp of Keystone, Nebraska. He reentered the Marine Corps in 1960 and was stationed at Kaneohe, Hawaii before he joined Lima Company, 3/1 when it was formed at Camp Pendleton. He wrote to his wife about the awesome display of the air and artillery strikes that he saw that night. It seemed that nothing could survive that pounding.

 At 0630 on March 5, the remaining platoon from India company arrived and shortly afterward, Battalion 3/1 was ordered to leave their blocking positions and move southward to relieve pressure on the 1st ARVN Airborne Battalion's northern flank on Hill 50. Captain Pete Dawkins, the US ARVN advisor reported that they had half the hill and the NVA had the rest. During the night, their front lines were only about 10 meters apart. By morning, they were still heavily engaged with the NVA. Mike Company led out with Lima Company on their right and India Company in reserve.

 Pfc. Danny Hernandez, a machine gunner in Mike Company, remembers how they deployed for battle:

> By 0700H, 3/1 was ordered to move down the hill. It took us about 40 min to get down, and once we reached the flat land at the bottom, our company was ordered to form a line from west to east, shoulder to shoulder. We were on the left, or west flank of Lima Company, while India was kept in reserve. At 0900H, we stood there ready to march shoulder-to-shoulder into the battle. I looked to my right, then to my left, and saw Marines as far as the eye could see.
>
> As I looked up and down this line of courageous men, I couldn't help but feel a sense of invincibility and power. Standing shoulder to shoulder with Gunnery Sergeant Downing, Staff Sergeant Thompson, Staff Sergeant Crutchfield, Staff Sergeant Maloon, Staff Sergeant Jellas, Sergeant Anderson and the other sergeants and corporals gave me a sense of solidarity in fighting ability, no matter

the rank. Today we would all go into battle as warrior equals.

The battalion's mission was to attack the NVA's regimental headquarter which was reported to be located in a bunker complex on Hill 50. The plan was for Mike Company to attack Hill 50 from the rice paddies on the east and Lima Company to attack Hill 50 from the north and link up with the 1st ARVN Airborne Battalion who supposedly occupied the southern portion of Hill 50. At about 1000 hours Mike Company had gotten halfway across the rice paddies when 1st Platoon became engaged with a small group of NVA in Khanh May on the right flank. The rest of Mike Company pressed forward. Suddenly, as they drew abreast of Chau Nhai (3) on their left, which was supposed to be secured by the ARVN, all hell broke loose. Enemy fire exploded all around them. The NVA held the high ground in the village in Chau Nhai (3) protected by hedgerows and a network of bunkers and spider holes. They were heavily armed with 60mm mortars, .50 cal machine guns, 57mm recoilless rifles, grenades and a large number of automatic weapons.

Mike Company was caught in a horseshoe killing zone. With incoming fire coming from the village of Khanh My on their right, incoming fire from the village of Chau Nhai (3) on their left and Hill 50 to their front. The NCOs tried to keep the unit together and pivot the assault toward Chau Nhai (3) but the formation had been broken. Men dived for cover in the rice paddies, seeking cover behind the rice paddy dikes. This is where their training kicked in. Individual squads and fire teams began to press forward to Chau Nhai (3). The battle was now a number of little battles where individual fire teams fought their way across the rice paddies, focusing on groups of NVA hot spots. They were crawling through the mud and firing from behind the paddy dikes, while bullets and mortars rained down around them. Some fire teams focused on taking out enemy gun positions, while others were trying to recover their wounded that were caught in a killing zone. Mike Company was heavily engaged by a large NVA force that was entrenched in-depth in well-prepared positions with excellent fields of fire. They fought from an extensive tunnel system which connected bunkers and spider holes protected by minefields, booby traps and punji stake pits. They held the high ground in the village and were masked by hedgerows and bamboo fences. The only way to target them was through their muzzle flashes and the sounds of their weapons. Mike Company was in a major battle.

The sequence of events that follow was recorded by Danny Hernandez in his book, *Silver Star: An American Story* and is repeated here to illustrate how Marines work together in combat.

Danny Hernandez and his assistant gunner, Severson, were a machine gun team that was assigned to a platoon that was led by Lieutenant Lupori of Mike Company. When the firing broke out they dove for cover and in the confusion were separated from their squad. Without hesitation they began to maneuver toward the edge of the village. Although they could see men being hit around them, they knew they had to reach the cover of the village and set up their machine gun. It never occurred to them to hide behind a paddy dike and wait it out. With bullets flying all around them, they crawled over the paddy dikes until they reached a small plateau that gave them some protection, about 25 yards into the village. They didn't know who was in charge, as they assessed the situation.

On the left there was an NVA machine gun position about 20 yards away battling a group of Marines led by Gunnery Sergeant Downing and on the right there was another Machine gun nest about 30 yards away that was engaged by another group of Marines. Although there was no voice or radio communication between the groups of Marines, Danny's training told him that Gunnery Sergeant Downing along with Corporal Sanchez of H&S company were

117

preparing to storm the machine gun bunker from the back side. Understanding their intent, Danny began to unload all the ammo he had on the bunker to give Gunnery Sergeant Downing's men a chance to reach the bunker. Finally, he saw a Marine throw a grenade into the gun position which silenced the machine gun.

Gunnery Sergeant Talmadge R. Downing was a combat veteran from the Korean War and was the weapons platoon sergeant with Mike Company. Gunnery Sergeant Downing had trained these troops in Okinawa and was instantly recognizable and his presence on the field of battle helped to focus the efforts of the men around him. One of the machine gun squads and a rifle squad were pinned down by intense automatic weapons fire and hand grenades from concealed, fortified positions. In the confusion of battle, fire from maneuvering friendly forces threatened to endanger another group of Marines who were wounded. Gunnery Sergeant Downing immediately exposed himself in order to correct the friendly fire and was wounded in the shoulder by an enemy grenade. Despite his wound, he helped the wounded men to relative safety. He then organized an assault unit which attacked and destroyed an enemy position which was manned by a numerically superior enemy force. He single-handedly destroyed another enemy position with his pistol and a hand grenade. Running low on ammunition, he calmly picked up an automatic weapon from a destroyed enemy position and directed the final assault on an NVA machine gun bunker. With the help of covering fire from Danny Hernandez's machine gun, Gunnery Sergeant Downing was able to get close enough to hurl the grenade which completely silenced the enemy gun position.

When Danny turned his attention to the other machine gun bunker he saw that they were focused on something in the kill zone of that enemy machine gun. Since he had expended all his ammo on the other bunker he was not able to support this group of Marines with fire power. He realized that a Marine was badly wounded and was caught in the kill zone and the Marines were preparing to assault the machine gun to rescue him. The rescue from their position would result in more casualties since there was no cover for them in the kill zone. Danny felt that he had a better chance to reach the wounded Marine since there was enough cover to get him within a few yards before he would be exposed to enemy fire. Danny made eye contact with the Marines and using hand signals and body language he got them to understand that he was going to make the attempt. As Danny prepared to make his attempt, he realized that the wounded Marine was Joel Rodriguez, who he had just met the night before when they shared a forward gun position.

Joel and Danny discovered that they both shared a birthday on March 11. Joel made an impression on Danny. Although they were both Mexican American, Danny was from the mean streets of East LA while Joel was from a farming community in Texas where the type of family foundation was completely different. Joel was very respectful and had a strong sense of optimism which made an impression on Danny. Danny vowed that if he made it back to East LA, he would do everything possible to make a difference not only for himself and his family but also for his community.

Every Marine carries a battle dressing on their cartridge belt and one of the basic rules is that you never use your battle dressing on another Marine. You use the other Marine's battle dressing so that you have your own in case you need it. However, Danny could see that Joel was bleeding badly and he wouldn't have time to unpack Joel's battle dressing while they were in the kill zone, so he took out his battle dressing and got it ready before he made his run. He made eye contact again with the other Marines and they instinctively understood what to do next. They opened fire on the enemy bunker and Danny made a mad dash to Joel's side where he quickly applied the battle dressing while he was shielding Joel from enemy fire. Within seconds the fire around them increased and Danny felt a blow like a sledgehammer hit his back. At first he had no feeling in his body. After a few seconds his feeling came back and the firing paused. Danny quickly moved around in front of Joel and began dragging him backwards toward the Marines who again began firing at the bunker to pin them down. This coordinated effort enabled Danny to get close enough to where the other Marines could pull them in. A corpsman applied a battle dressing to Danny's back and he and Joel were moved to the medevac area. Unfortunately, Joel died later from his wounds but his brief connection with Danny left a lasting impression.

The medevac area was behind a hill, north of Chau Nhai (3). When Danny reached the medevac area, his heart fell as he saw many of the dearest and most respected Marines in Mike Company lying dead or severely wounded. Lying there, motionless, were

Sergeant Anderson and Sergeant Crutchfield, who had lined up with him shoulder to shoulder as they began the attack earlier in the morning. Both of these sergeants were loved and respected by the troops. When Sergeant Anderson found out that Danny did not have enough money to go home on leave before they shipped out to Okinawa, he insisted on loaning him $200. This was the type of loan that Danny has been paying forward ever since.

The medevac area was guarded by a sergeant and several Marines. The NVA were popping up all over from their underground positions. The medevac guards noticed enemy movement to the north of them and moved in that direction to cut them off. Danny's A-gunner, Seversen, had managed to scrounge up some ammo for their machine gun and came over to see Danny. Suddenly, enemy fire began to come from the east into the medevac area. There appeared to be a tunnel nearby and NVA were emerging to fire on the wounded Marines in the medevac area. Although his back wound hampered his movement, Danny grabbed the machine gun and put himself between the NVA threat and the wounded Marines. He charged the NVA which attracted their fire to him and away from the wounded Marines. Firing from the hip he exchanged a maelstrom of fire killing several of them before they ran back into the tunnel. The tunnel collapsed before Danny could pursue them any further. Although several NVA had fired automatic weapons at him he miraculously was not hit, but several of the wounded that he had saved were hit in the exchange of fire. Among the wounded was Lance Corporal Johnny Enriquez, who was wounded by the enemy machine gun fire from the bunker that Danny helped to silence earlier. Lance Corporal Enriquez was sure that Danny's quick action saved him a second time as he repulsed the attack on the medevac area. Realizing that there were other NVA tunnels all around them, Danny refused to be evacuated and joined another squad and continued to support the battle with his machine gun until another bullet hit him in the head later in the evening. At first, the Marines around him thought he was dead, but he surprised everyone when he asked someone to retrieve his dented helmet so he could keep it as a souvenir. He was finally evacuated to a hospital in Guam. Pfc. Danny Hernandez was recommended for the Silver Star Medal but the paperwork was lost. He was finally recognized with a Silver Star Medal for his actions in 2009.

Pfc. Danny Hernandez

Mike Company battled an estimated NVA battalion for nearly 3 hours until they finally penetrated the NVA position around Chau Nhai (3). There were 59 confirmed NVA KIA and possibly another 50 that the NVA carried away. There were also a number of civilians, old people and children who were killed in the crossfire. Mike Company casualties were 15 KIA and 46 WIA.

The disposition of 3/1 Rifle Companies by the afternoon of 5 March 1966 is shown on the following map. Mike company had taken the brunt of the battle in Chau Nhai (3) where they had engaged an estimated battalion of NVA forces who were dug into a series of tunnels and fortified positions. Lima Company had bypassed Chau Nhai (3) and was positioned to join the 1st ARVN Airborne Battalion that had supposedly taken Hill 50. India Company was initially in reserve, then passed through Mike Company when Mike Company had taken Chau Nhai (3) and was positioned to advance on Hill 50.

Disposition of 3/1 Forces On 5 March 1966

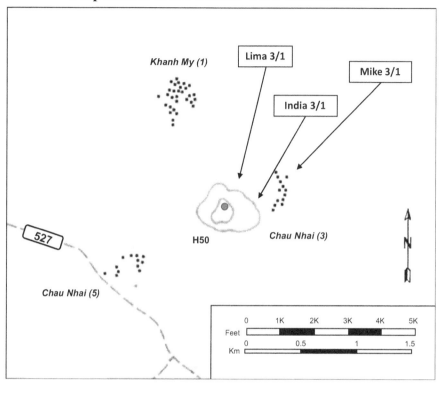

****

Lieutenant Colonel James Young retired after 30 years in the Marine Corps as a Colonel. He was awarded a Silver Star and Legion of Merit with V device for Valor for his performance during several battalion combat operations as Battalion Commander of 3/1. His career culminated as Chief of Staff Marine Corps Schools.

Gunnery Sergeant Talmadge Downing was awarded the Navy Cross for his inspiring leadership and fighting spirit which contributed in large measure to the success of Operation Utah.

Pfc. Danny Hernandez returned to his East Los Angeles "barrio neighborhood" after Vietnam. He remembered the vow that he made there to make a difference to his family and his community. Inspired by his experiences there and the people that influenced his life like

Joel Rodriguez and Sergeant Anderson he became active in community causes. He earned a BA Degree from Cal State Los Angeles and joined the Hollenbeck Youth Center in 1981 where he worked with inner city youth and is currently their President and CEO. While at Hollenbeck he helped to spawn the Inner City Games Foundation which is currently in 14 cities nationwide. He was awarded a Silver Star for his actions on Operation Utah in 2009 and has written a book about his Marine Corps experience in *Silver Star: An American Story.*

Chapter 11
India Company 3/1 In the Killing Zone

At 1330, India Company, led by Captain Lecky passed through Mike Company to increase pressure on the NVA. India Company lined up in assault formation, shoulder to shoulder as they prepared to assault Hill 50. India Company was aligned north to south, facing Hill 50. Suddenly there was a burst of automatic fire and mortars which tore through the formation. Most of India's casualties occurred in the first fifteen minutes of this firefight. India Company continued the assault and remained in heavy contact from 1330 to 1630. The NVA were well entrenched and heavily armed. The hostile fire was so intense that the Marines' movement was limited to fire and maneuver by individual fire teams a few yards at a time.

Michael W. Hastriter, who was a corpsman in India Company wrote this memory which describes some of the action that occurred with India Company:

The fiercest battle we fought was on 5 March (my dad's birthday). We were serving as a reinforcement reactionary company just outside of Chu Lai. We rarely knew what was going on. We just went where we were told. Helicopters picked us up and we soon knew it was a multiple battalion operation called Operation Utah. As we gained altitude in our bird, I counted over 40 other UH-34 helicopters in the air. We climbed higher and higher while circling until all were airborne. As we peeled off away from the airstrip at Chu Lai, I could see black puffs of smoke exploding 50 to 100 yards off our chopper: They were anti-aircraft weapons firing at us. After a few minutes we were out of there and dropped in elevation to tree top level. It is more difficult for ground fire to hit you when you pass over the trees so fast. If you are higher, the enemy can see you longer and let a rocket off at you, so we stayed low and fast. As we were zipping along over the treetops, I remember sitting on a five-gallon water can in the tail of the chopper. You always wonder if a round will come ripping through the floor and up through you. As I sat there on the water can looking down at the floor, I was thinking of just that, when *pu du du du du*! A string of rounds came ripping right up the middle of the chopper floor. I literally saw a bullet rip through the floor 6 inches from my right foot and shrapnel hit my leg. I thought I was shot for sure and one man did receive minor flesh wounds. His name was Steven Anthony Church, and I took care of him and we all thought it was very exciting to get some real action. This would have been Steve's second Purple Heart—which we all thought was pretty cool at that moment.

We landed on the top of a mountain, got out quickly, and cleared the landing zone for other choppers to touch down and dump their payloads of US Marines. After forming up, our company was told we had a hard core Viet Cong force in the valley below and we were to replace Mike Company who had taken a beating the night before and needed relief. It was later described as the elite 21st Viet Cong Regiment, hardcore NVA. We observed our F4 Phantom jets bombing and strafing the valley below. How could anything survive that we thought?

As India Company worked its way down the mountain to the smoke-filled valley below, we contemplated what we were getting into. As we arrived at the valley floor, we approached Chau Nhai (3) where Mike Company was heavily engaged. We were to pass through Mike Company's lines and apply pressure to the NVA. Gunny Greer came down the line checking each man and offering encouragement.

This was our first hardcore challenge. It was going to be hard combat and we all knew there would be casualties and some of us would not make it. I was packing a machine gun tripod, light backpack, my Unit-1 (medical bag), a .45 pistol, and was wearing a flak jacket.

Our line was ready to advance in a broad sweep of the village. The signal was given to advance. There were hedges of trees, bamboo and other vegetation growing in the bottom. There were also dykes, rice paddies, potatoes, and cane fields. We lined up on a broad line about 3-5 meters apart to begin a sweep of the area. I remember the word coming down the line to shift to our left and approach 90 degrees from how we were lined up (this would prove to be a fatal mistake as the NVA were now entrenched at our front).

As the weapons platoon corpsman, I wanted to be right alongside the Marines in my unit. Sergeant Eaglin said, "Doc, you just set here [by a well] and wait till we call you." He probably saved my life! It wasn't long until all hell broke loose with an explosion of all kinds of automatic weapons and mortar fire. The quiet air was suddenly shattered by fire like I'd never heard before. Men began screaming, "corpsman! corpsman!" Vegetation was falling from bushes and trees from flying bullets. Grenades were exploding here and there, and mortar rounds were coming in on us. We were pinned down by VC who were within 50 yards of us. I ran to the front (about 50 yards) to find a number of marines hit and everyone in a prone position and pinned down by heavy enemy fire. Sergeant Eaglin was shot several times. His head was severely damaged and his left arm was shot in the elbow. As I took off his helmet, the back left side of his head was gone. His brains were showing and his teeth were broken from gritting them. I couldn't get his mouth open to check his airway, but he was breathing through his nose, gritted teeth, and locked jaw. I couldn't help but think how helpless I was to help him. There was little I could do except to pull him behind a tree, cover the open head wound with a dressing, apply a dressing to his arm and keep him comfortable. He was in severe shock, conscious, but not in pain. Sergeant Goodwin came with a pack board, and he and I put Sergeant Eaglin on the pack board and together dragged him to a rear area where he was evacuated on a medevac chopper. I was told later that he was flown to the hospital ship USS Repose, where he received the very best of medical care. He lived until 11 April 1966. While we were training in Okinawa, he was so faithful and he proudly bragged of his wife and young daughter.

After Sergeant Eaglin was evacuated, I returned to the same site where Sergeant Eaglin was shot and took care of several more wounded marines along the line. We were all lying on the ground facing the fortified VC positions. We had only a sparse hedge of vegetation between the VC and us. Within a couple minutes Staff Sergeant Wiener received a thigh wound while lying on the ground. Hospital corpsman Lazarius moved to bandage him and was also shot in his thigh. Laz treated Staff Sergeant Wiener and himself and they assisted each other to the rear for evacuation. It is amazing how instant shock can cover the pain and men respond to their own needs. 2nd Lieutenant Mulcahy also received a bullet through his calf. I picked up a rifle that was laying on the ground and crawled up to a tree with a fork about a foot up, placed the rifle between it and began to shoot at NVA that were entrenched about 50 meters to our front. I could see the heads and shoulders of numerous VC firing at us from a trench. They had us pinned down.

Steve Church crawled up beside me as I was shooting and he fired his rifle about a foot from my right ear. It was so very loud that I turned and screamed at him and he crawled up right beside me and began to shoot. He was so excited as he was obviously taking a toll on the enemy. Suddenly, incoming rounds split down his rifle stock and entered his chest. I shall remember as long as I live: He flipped onto his back and said, "My God, I'm hit."

I reached over and ripped open his flak jacket and shirt. I could see three holes in the center of his chest. I didn't know what to do except put my hand over the holes, as if to somehow stop the sucking, bleeding chest wound and restore his life. It was only seconds before he was dead. I knew there was nothing more that I could do. I felt so helpless. It was only seconds before he was dead. He was killed almost instantly. Something left him as I watched and witnessed him die. I knew the body that lay next to me was simply that:--a body, Steve's spirit (soul) had departed and was elsewhere. I could see his spirit leave his bullet-ravaged body as his eyes lost the luster of life. He didn't even know what hit him; it was so quick.

Steve was a good Marine and always did his part. He often humped the company radio for the command group. It is a testimony to me that when a man dies, his spirit does, in fact, leave his mortal body. You can feel it and see the absence of it at the moment of death. It is ironic that he would have been 21 years old the next day and as they lifted us out on the 7th of March it was also my 21st birthday. I never got to know Steven Anthony Church very well, but know that he was an outstanding Marine and gave his life for a just and noble cause in abating communistic dominance of the South Vietnamese people. Never let an American tell you differently. He will always be remembered for good by those who knew him and his family can be proud of his courage in the face of mortal danger. Know that he died for a worthy cause; We all have to believe that.

I picked up his damaged rifle, placed it in the crotch of the tree, and begin to pick off the entrenched enemy. It was a strange feeling. It wasn't like killing another human being, but a feeling of both self-defense, and revenge for Jim Keeler, Sergeant Eaglin, Steve Church and the others. I was always a good shot... Maybe it saved someone's life or maybe even my own.

I soon ran out of VC to shoot at and worked my way to the left side of the pinned-down platoon where I learned that Pfc. Charles Sherlee Satcher from Vallejo, California had been hit in the leg and was laying in an opened sweet potato field between two rows. At the same time, we were receiving machine gun fire from a grass hut on a slightly elevated hillside up behind the trench line. One of the Marines had a disposable LAW, much like a bazooka. The guys called me *Dinger* when we were in the states, because I could shoot, or *ding*, 55-gallon drums with the 3.5 rocket launcher at 250-300 yards, so I was the designated shooter. Pfc. Royce Glenn Scoggins was on the M60 machine gun and covered me while I kneeled and fired the LAW which silenced the gun in the thatched hut!

Then we turned our attention on getting Satcher out of the open field. Our platoon commander, 1st Lieutenant Simms ordered Pfc. Mai to go out and get him. Mai ran across the field twice with plenty of semi- and automatic weapon fire directed at him. Mai was smaller than I was and unable to move Satcher, but Pfc. Lamprich, being larger in stature, tried also without success. Seeing the needless danger of sending men out in the open without a plan, I suggested to 1st Lieutenant Simms that we gather everyone's rifle slings, tie them

128

together to make a rope and drag him back to the safety of the large clump of bamboo that a half dozen of us were using as cover from the VC fortified trench. Lieutenant Simms said, "Good idea, Doc!"

I figured he was going to get somebody else killed, so I made the suggestion and volunteered to go after Satcher. He said, "Ya! Get ready Doc!" Now there was no turning back. Little did I know that this very action would save my own life.

Once we got the slings rigged, I crawled behind a dike and jumped over into the potato field. Pfc. Scoggins again provided covering fire with the M60 machine gun. Fortunately, the rows paralleled the VC trench, which allowed me to roll over each row out of sight into the next one. It became kind of a game, as I would work my way up or down the row quickly rolling over to the next getting closer to Satcher. Each time that I would roll over a row, automatic weapons would fire at me. There were about 6 to 8 rows. After what seemed like an eternity, I got to Satcher. Because of the pain caused by the tourniquet, Satcher had removed the tourniquet and bled to death. I tied the slings around his legs, but they could not pull him out of the row in which he lay. Working myself under him and lifting, Tom Peters and Peterson were able to drag him over a half dozen-or-so rows to the field behind the dike.

Once Satcher's body was secure, I made a beeline for the large clump of bamboo. To my great dismay, Corporal Leland Francis Dixon of Whistler, Alabama lay dead in the exact spot that I had been sitting. The guys told me that as soon as I moved to get Satcher, Dixon moved right to the spot where I had been previously sitting for 30 minutes, lit up a cigarette, and received a .50 cal through his chest. Corporal Dixon was a very large man, probably 240 pounds. When hit, he had fallen over on a very young and small marine and bled all over him. The marine went crazy and was evacuated even before I returned from getting Satcher. Pfc. Royce Glenn Scoggins, our M-60 machine gunner of McKinney, Texas was also shot in the head and killed while I was getting to Satcher. Royce probably saved my life with the fire he laid down to cover me.

Between the entrenched VC and us was a dike footpath about 5-6 feet wide. About 250 yards up the path, a Vietnamese woman was approaching us with a baby on her back, two small children in hand, and a yolk on her shoulder with probably all her worldly belongings. We yelled at her to go back, but she continued on without shots being fired until she got in the middle of both enemies. Somebody fired and both sides opened up. They were all shot down. Everyone was sick inside... Just can't describe it. We got all our dead and wounded out that was possible over the next couple of hours. The sun set quickly and we pulled our dead and wounded back to the command post and set up a hasty perimeter for the night. Pfc. Fred Howard Horton, Denver, Colorado received a severe abdominal wound and suffered a lot of blood loss. HM2 Herzog and HM1 Keigley set-up an IV on him and tried to get medevac choppers to pick him up. There was a delay in medevac, but he was finally picked up. He died before the day was out as indicated on the Vietnam Memorial records (5 Mar 66). Several Marines, Sean (I think his last name was Higgins) and Stanley Quail were missing. The VC followed us to the command post and fired at us at very close range. You could see their muzzle flashes in the dark.

For unknown reasons, they pulled back and we were not probed again that night except for two Marines...Ya! Sean and Stanley. Sean had found Stanley in a sugar cane field with a head wound. A bullet had entered his helmet and ringed his helmet on and off his skull. He was a mess, but no internal brain injury. It left him stunned and unaware of where he was. Sean caught a VC about to kill Stanley and he reportedly killed him with his knife. He was out of ammo, but had depleted a Chinese communist AK-47 confiscated from a dead VC. We were glad to see those two Marines crawl back through our lines.

The next morning, everything was quiet. My nerves were shot. We were told we had to go back into the VC strong hold again and complete the mission. I couldn't understand why we just couldn't bomb the area and not risk more losses. We already had sixteen dead and many more wounded. That was the closest I have ever been to a total emotional breakdown. When we went back into the same area we found a mass grave in which the VC had tried to bury their dead. It was supposed to be a victory, but what a price to pay. There were no feelings of victory, but the dreaded agony of the dead and wounded from both sides. The forked tree that I had been behind the day before had more than thirty bullet holes in it. The Vietnamese woman and kids were lying where they were shot. Their bodies crumpled randomly on the ground. The baby still bound to its mother's back had the top of its head shot off and the chickens had completely pecked the brain clean. An entire family gone... Was there a loving father/husband to grieve the tragedy, or was he also among the VC casualties? We also saw the bodies of an entire squad of Marines from Mike Company, 3rd Battalion, 1st Marines lying where they fell within a 20-yard radius.

A few hours before we relieved them, the VC had dressed up like ARVN troops (Army of the Republic of Viet Nam...friendly forces) and yelled to the squad of Marines to come up and join them. Totally unaware, the Marines fell into the trap. When they got close enough, the VC opened up on them. We also found four of our Marines lying within 10 feet of each other. A burst of machine gun bullets had caught all four in the head. They were Corporal Roy Gonzales, Jr., San Antonio, Texas, Lance Corporal Robert Lani Nueku, Nanakuli, Hawaii, and I think the last one was Corporal Albert Cabanayan, Kahului, HI. The fourth man was not identified.

Nueku and Cabanayan had a close bond since they were both from Hawaii. Nueku was from the big island and Cabanayan was from Maui. Although they were in separate platoons, Nueku was from 3rd Platoon, and Cabanayan was from 2nd Platoon, they would spend their spare time together and share their letters and packages from home. Normally platoons would be operating in different areas and men from different platoons would not be killed together. But on 5 March, Nueku and Cabanayan were found close together in death. Perhaps one tried to go to the aid of the other when he saw his buddy in trouble; Ohana mau loa.

We spent the day doing body counts and exploring tunnels. Tunnels are explored by stripping to t-shirts and pants and entering with a flashlight in one hand and .45 pistol in the other. The air strike had done a lot of damage. Bodies were scattered here and there. One was blown 20 feet up and was hanging from two crisscrossing bamboo limbs. It was during this bombing mission that I saw one of our F4 Phantom jets shot down. We saw the pilot eject and float down in the distance. After spending one more night (6 March), we were lifted out of the area and returned to Chu Lai on 7 March 1966. It was a very nice birthday present! I was written up for a Silver Star which was downgraded at battalion to a Bronze Star with V device. I've always been proud of the Star, but often wonder about the lives I might have saved if I had not been so scared. So many others performed so heroically and I know they were as scared as I was. At one point while concealed behind the tree previously discussed, I nearly jumped up and ran towards the upper end of the entrenched VC. In retrospect, such an action would have put me in position to easily direct fire the length of the trench (instead of perpendicular to it). I wanted to but was just too scared. What makes some men react without regard for their own lives? That is a question no one can answer unless they have done it and their answer would likely be, "I was just too scared to do anything else!" Because of our heavy casualties during Operation Utah, we were thereafter assigned to guard the airstrip at Chu Lai.

Another Marine, Pfc. Robert A. Biskey, noticed that one of the fire teams had become separated from the platoon and all members had been wounded, Pfc. Biskey immediately went to their aid, advancing across seventy-five meters of fire-swept terrain. Despite the savage incoming fire, he administered first aid to the wounded men. Realizing that the men were unable to move on their own, he remained in the exposed position for most of the afternoon while his company was evacuating other casualties and reconsolidating forces for a flanking attack on the enemy. While protecting his stricken comrades, he killed a VC officer and possibly killed two other guerillas. As the battle around him grew more intense it became increasingly more apparent that the casualties needed to be evacuated. Pfc. Biskey picked up one of the wounded men and ran with him through a hail of enemy automatic weapons and mortar fire to a safe position. Pfc. Biskey was awarded a Silver Star for his actions which undoubtedly saved at least one man's life, and was an inspiration to all who observed him. One of the men in the fire team that did not survive was Pfc. Mario Ybarra.

Mario G. Ybarra was born on May 1, 1943 to Felipe and Fidela G. Ybarra in the Southern border town of Weslaco, Texas. The Ybarra family was a close-knit family and Mario was the first born of eleven children. Mario was a giving and compassionate person who started working in the fields gathering seasonal crops at a very early age and helped with the care of his younger brothers and sisters. He did well in school and played clarinet in the Weslaco High School band. When Mario was not busy taking care of his siblings, attending school or working he was occupied with boxing, which was one of his favorite pastimes. In the ring, he was called *El Indio* ("The Indian"). This was a nickname that was given to him by his neighborhood friends because he was a fierce fighter and always wore a red bandana on his forehead when he fought.

Upon graduation from Weslaco High School in 1961, Mario enlisted in the United States Marine Corps. Although this was a decision that his parents did not agree with, Mario knew that he needed to do it for his country. Because his country needed him! While on leave, Mario dressed in the Marine uniform, something he wore proudly. It was during one of his scheduled leaves that he returned to the Rio Grande Valley and married his sweetheart, Manaen Hernandez. On March 13, 1965, his son, Mario G. Ybarra, Jr. was born. In the summer of 1965, while with the 3rd Battalion, 1st Marines, Mario Sr. was given orders to go fight in Vietnam and was assigned to India Company. During Operation Utah, Pfc. Ybarra was observed going to the aid of a few of his fellow Marines who were wounded in an ambush when he was killed by enemy fire.

Pfc. Ybarra was one of the first of many young men from rural Hidalgo County, Texas, to be killed in Vietnam. Hidalgo County lost 71 of their finest young men to the Vietnam War, the vast majority of which were of Latino heritage. Pfc. Ybarra's flag-draped coffin arrived in Weslaco, just three days after his son's first birthday. Mario Ybarra Jr. attended his father's funeral at Highland Memorial Cemetery. Although his son was a baby when his father was killed, he was inspired by his father's life and worked to keep his memory alive as an author, artist, and veteran's advocate. In 2010, the Pfc. Mario Ybarra elementary school was named in his honor as an inspiration to the young children of Hidalgo County.

The results of India Company's engagement were 9 NVA KIA with possible four more. India company casualties were 20 KIA and 34 WIA. At 1630 hours, The NVA mounted a counter attack which drove India Company back down the hill. India was directed to remain in place while the ARVN Battalion was to link up. At 1900 hours the ARVN Battalion Advisor informed 3/1 that physical contact with ARVN would not be established. Contact had reduced to sporadic small arms fire.

****

Michael W. Hastriter left the Navy and served in the Army where he retired as a Lieutenant Colonel He went to Brigham Young University where he became an Entomologist, specializing in fleas and bat parasites and is currently the Museum Curator, Monte L. Bean Life Science Museum. He has discovered more than 80 new species and several new genera of fleas. "I am a Vietnam combat veteran," says Hastriter, "and I named a number of the species after my friends who died on the battlefield."

Chapter 12
Lima Company 3/1 Takes Hill 50

While the ARVN Advisor, Pete Dawkins, could not direct the actions of the commander of the ARVN battalion, he did have the responsibility to deliver accurate information to his Marine counterparts. 1st Lieutenant Gregory who was the company commander of Lima Company had been told by Dawkins, known as Red Hat One, that two companies of ARVN rangers had moved forward and cleared the ridge (Hill 50) of NVA and Lima Company was to join up with them and secure the northern flank of the ARVN Companies and assume a blocking position.

Lima Company skirted the Mike Company fight in Chau Nhai (3) and one of its platoons was ordered to "join the ARVN" on Hill 50. As the 3rd Platoon moved to carry out these orders, it soon became clear that the NVA, not the ARVN, held Hill 50. 1st Lieutenant Gregory's Lima Company continued to advance to link up with the ARVN forces and began to receive opposition on their right flank. By 1100, 3rd Battalion 1st Marines was fully engaged, with Mike and India Companies fighting an estimated NVA Battalion. Mike and India Companies were on the east or left flank, and Lima Company in conjunction with the 1st ARVN Airborne Battalion was fighting what was later estimated to be a company-sized force on the north or right flank on Hill 50. The enemy confronting the 3rd Battalion Companies had the advantage of prepared positions and terrain; they held the high ground. Bamboo fences and hedgerows masked the enemy position from the Marines. The NVA were fighting from an extensive tunnel network which connected bunkers and tunnels, the enemy lay in wait in elaborate entrenchments protected by minefields and booby traps. The heavy air and artillery bombardment of Hill 50, the night before, seemed to have had no impact on the fortifications.

As Lima Company approached the ARVN on Hill 50, they could see what appeared to be ARVN soldiers standing on the crest of Hill

50 waving them on as though everything was clear as reported by Pete Dawkins their US advisor This turned out not to be the case. The NVA were concealed in spider holes immediately forward of what was assumed to be the ARVN positions. Lima Company did not see them due to the heavy underbrush and the ARVN did not alert Lima Company of the danger. The NVA withheld the main volume of their fire until Lima Company was within fifty meters of the crest, then they opened their ambush.

Fortunately, 1st Lieutenant Gregory had deployed his platoons in a V-formation with Lieutenant Dan Walsh's 2nd Platoon and Lieutenant Eugene Cleavers 3rd Platoon up front and Lieutenant Steve Crowley's 1st Platoon in reserve. When the ambush was triggered, the platoons up front were able to respond with a volume of fire and the platoon leaders were in position to direct their response. The NVA had chosen their targets and some of the first to go down were the machine gunners, Lance Corporal Phillip Fitch and Sergeant David Shields. Both lead platoon commanders were also hit. 1st Lieutenant Walsh was hit in the shin, thigh and hip with machine gun fire, but continued to direct his troops. 1st Lieutenant Cleaver was shot twice in the chest and was barely kept alive by Pfc. Gary Harlan and Lance Corporal Gary Hester from 3rd Platoon. They found him in the underbrush, administered CPR, and brought him to Doc Reyerson who applied a patch to his sucking chest wound, which extended his chances of being evacuated. Cleaver and Doc Reyerson were able to meet at a company reunion in 2014. The Platoon Sergeant for 2nd Platoon, Staff Sergeant Hultquist was also seriously wounded and later died of his wounds. Despite the loss of key leaders, Lima Company pressed on through the ambush and eventually took Hill 50.

Pfc. Gary Harlan had just completed six months of active duty with the Marine Corps reserves in Springfield, Missouri when he read about Operation Starlight, which occurred in August 1965 and was the first major Marine Corps battle in Vietnam. He went to his Marine Corps recruiter and requested active duty on the condition that he be assigned to the infantry and receive orders for Vietnam. He was afraid that the war would end before he got there. Less than five months later, he was landing in Vietnam on Operation Double Eagle.

On March 5, 1966, Pfc. Harlan was approaching Hill 50 with Lima Company. 2nd and 3rd Platoons were in the lead and his Platoon, 1st Platoon was in reserve. When the ambush occurred, 1st Platoon moved up to join the assault. Harlan's rifle jammed and he picked up another rifle from a dead Marine. Several meters from him Sergeant David Shields, a machine gunner who was born in Scotland, was firing his M-60 from the hip. Suddenly the thumping sound of a 12.7mm machine gun joined the battle and a 12.7mm round hit Shields in the head and exited the back of his helmet releasing a fountain of blood. Shield stood motionless for a moment before falling backwards.

Gary describes his feelings during combat. An awareness of time seemed to vanish and sounds became muted. When someone asked him how long the fighting lasted, he had no idea. He doesn't remember being afraid. He just kept moving, mostly helping the wounded and providing covering fire. After the action the men gathered in small groups, most were in shock, not caring what happened next.

When Lima Company was taken under heavy fire, and prevented from further movement. Pfc. Rickey D. Garner, a runner in 2nd Platoon and four others advanced into the NVA positions where two of the three leading men were severely wounded, one of them fatally. Garner fiercely attacked the enemy in their dugouts. Observing a group of five NVA soldiers in a trench about twenty yards from where he stood, he charged the trench, firing his weapon on automatic as he ran. As a result, he succeeded in destroying the enemy positions, but sustained mortal wounds. Pfc. Ricky Garner was posthumously awarded a Silver Star.

Corporal Jimmy P. Sanchez, a fireteam leader from the 3rd platoon, saw another fire team from his platoon receive two casualties, and become pinned down by heavy automatic rifle fire and hand grenades. Corporal Sanchez maneuvered his fire team forward to aid the trapped fire team. After positioning his fireteam out of immediate danger, he moved forward to observe the situation. In order to observe the enemy positions, he stood and exposed himself to enemy fire until he spotted them. He then took cover and informed the trapped men that he intended to throw a smoke grenade to cover their maneuvers, then directed his fireteam to cover him by fire. He again rose to his feet and threw the smoke grenade and was immediately shot and killed by the NVA, but not before he had accomplished his intended purpose. Corporal Sanchez was posthumously awarded a Silver Star.

Lima's Company Commander, 1st Lieutenant Gregory moved among his platoons, controlling their movements and encouraging his men to pursue the attack. Although continuously exposed to heavy hostile automatic weapons fire, he directed the fierce hand to hand fighting for the positions on the crest of the hill over the next three hours. He coordinated the attack through its final phases and successfully linked his unit with the Vietnamese battalion, while ensuring that the casualties were evacuated to protected areas. Lima Company cleared the objective of all NVA resistance through a systematic search and destroy of the area. This required engaging and rooting out individual NVA from prepared positions.

Later 1st Lieutenant Gregory had choice words with Pete Dawkins, the ARVN Advisor, who he thought had misled the Marines about the ARVN situation which led to their ambush.

During the battle Lieutenant Gregory captured an NVA soldier after jumping into a shell crater with him. They were both surprised, but Lieutenant Gregory had the advantage as he later discovered that the NVA was wounded.

It was a very definitive moment as I first believed that I would have to kill him, but since I had him by the front of his shirt with my left hand, I was unable to pull my pistol and cock it. This meant that all I had left was my combat knife. Although I drew the knife, I could see in his eyes that he had surrendered. I carried him down the hill to the improvised aid station the corpsmen had set up for treating the wounded. Unfortunately, he died later that day. The NVA soldiers we engaged that day fought to the last man.

Despite being ambushed, the aggressive efforts of Lima 3/1 produced 33 NVA KIA with a possible additional 55 KIA. Friendly casualties were 10 KIA and 20 WIA. Both Pfc. Rickey Garner and Corporal Jimmy Sanchez would be posthumously awarded the Silver Star for their actions. 1st Lieutenant Gregory was also awarded a Silver Star for his leadership during the ambush. After clearing the objective, Lima Company turned the objective over to the ARVN battalion and moved to consolidate with the rest of 3/1.

Years later 1st Lieutenant Gregory wrote to a Corpsman, Bob Ingraham, who was assigned to Lima Company and was wounded on Hill 50 explaining that he had spent a lot of time over the years second-guessing his actions at the very beginning of Lima Company's engagement with the NVA on Hill 50.

"After the initial bursts of fire that morning, it was all that I could do to maintain a cohesive presence on the battlefield. The wounded were in need of attention, the dead had to be removed, the enemy had to be dealt with as I determined that there was no way to disengage without taking more casualties. The urge to flee affected some of us initially I am sure, but it soon became obvious that we all knew the course of action required and stood our ground. I had one deserter that day, which was a difficult situation to deal with, on top of everything else.

My own mental state had put me past the fear stage quite early on and I essentially was comfortable with the fact that I could die at any moment. A calmness came over me that allowed me to function with effectiveness. Some have described it as an 'out of body experience.' Needless to say the emotions, sights, sounds and smells of that battle still remain with me and rarely a day goes by that I don't recall the experience.

I still wish I could do Utah over again. Maybe you would not have been wounded along with the eighteen others, maybe the ten dead would be alive. If only I had done things differently. Should I have questioned the info received from the ARVN unit? Sent scouts out in advance of our moving to the hill? Waited with two platoons on line and effected reconnaissance by fire? Withdrawn a few hundred yards and asked for more mortars, artillery, naval gunfire, close air support? Tried a flanking movement? Unfortunately I had about sixty seconds to process all of the choices and in fact had no time at all. As Caesar said when he crossed the Rubicon, '*Alea jacta est*,' The die has been cast. Also, flight crossed my mind as well, but my makeup eliminated it as an option. We were just little teeth on the gears that had been turning since the 1850's when the French dropped anchor in Danang harbor."

One of the Lima Company Marines who was killed in the ambush was Staff Sergeant Hultquist, the platoon sergeant of 2nd Platoon. Staff Sergeant Hultquist was leading his men in an assault against an entrenched position when he was shot in the chest. A corpsman, Robert Ingraham, rushed to his aid to treat his pumping chest wound. Staff Sergeant Hultquist was still alert as he was able to warn Ingraham of an incoming grenade in time for him to take cover and avoid the blast. Staff Sergeant Hultquist was evacuated by helicopter to an aid station but died there from his wound.

He was loved and respected by his men and many of them wrote letters to his widow Nancy and their daughters, expressing their sorrow and respect. When his effects were gathered, they found the last letter that he wrote on 5 March under the light of the flares over Hill 50, and it was sent to Nancy. Unfortunately, the notification of his death was mishandled and the news of his death was announced in the newspaper before Nancy was officially notified by a telegram from the Marine Corps Headquarters which came nearly a week after his death. No officers were sent to notify her in person and no apology was given. Staff Sergeant Hultquist and his family deserved better. While the Marine Corps Brass may have failed one of our own, his fellow Marines responded with heartfelt letters of condolences.

The Commanding Officer of 3/1, Lieutenant Colonel Young requested permission to maintain positions and call in massive air and artillery preparation to be followed by a continued assault by 3/1. This request was approved for the next morning. On March 6, at 1030, massive air and artillery preparation commenced and at 1245, 3/1 began their assault. There was no enemy contact during the assault. They did discover a vast interconnected, well-developed cave complex that required 5000 pounds of C4 explosives to destroy, 300 meters of entrenchments, and two overhead bunkers that were suitable as command post bunkers for a large headquarters. The search of the cave complex continued through March 6.

On March 7, the search and destruction of the cave complex continued. No further enemy action was encountered. By 1830 the last elements of 3/1 were helicoptered back to Chu Lai.

Total friendly losses for 3/1 numbered 41 KIA and 102 WIA.

Gary Harlan was a Pfc. in Lima Company on Operation Utah and served two tours in Vietnam. You can see how he aged after a several months in combat. These pictures show Gary as a 19-year-old in Vietnam. The picture on the left shows Gary when he was promoted to Lance Corporal after Operation Utah, less than two months after landing in Vietnam. The picture on the right shows him after he returned from a patrol after six months in Vietnam. When he left the Marine Corps he pursued an academic career in philosophy then left that path to lead the establishment of the Ozarks Vets Center in Springfield, Missouri. When he enlisted he was anxious to fight, but after two tours he became an anti-war activist.

Gary Harlan has written a book where he interviewed many of the individuals in Lima Company who are mentioned in this book. The most heartbreaking story is that of Staff Sergeant Leonard Hultquist and his wife, Nancy, who shared many of their letters during his time in Vietnam. Gary Harlan's book is *Always Faithful: Returning to Vietnam*, published in 2020. It is well worth reading for his views on the war and the views of the Marines, corpsman, and Vietnamese, who he interviewed so many years after the "American War."

Simon Gregory left the Marine Corps after his commitment was up and was successful with a career in corporate management including ownership of Vanguard Electronics. He is an avid art collector and photographer and active member of several museums, conservation societies, South East Asian coalition, Indochina Arts Partnership, and youth centers. He has generously contributed articles and interviews in support of authors like Gary Harlan, mentioned above, and Bob Ingraham, published at EphemeralTreasures.net.

Part 4
Operation Utah
Phase Three

Chapter 13
2/4 Ambushed in the LZ

The task of forming the southern part of the encirclement was assigned to Lieutenant Colonel P. X. Kelley's 2/4. Just the day before, 2/4 had relieved 2/7 on the Chu Lai defensive perimeter when 2/7 was called out to initiate the assault on Operation Utah. That meant that 2/4 had to leave a part of the battalion behind in Chu Lai to maintain the defensive positions. Lieutenant Colonel P. X. Kelley had to hastily form a combat unit out of an assortment of different elements. Although it was basically the 2/4 battalion command group with Golf Company and Hotel Company from 2/4, it also included some additional units. Since 2/4 had been in-country since May of 1965 and had suffered some major casualties in previous operations like Operation Starlight (August 18-24, 1965), the battalion was severely understaffed. In fact, Golf Company was previously India Company 3/7 and had joined 2/4 after Operation Starlight to bring them back up to strength. Golf Company went into Operation Utah with 104 men and Hotel company was not much better with 138 men (a rifle company would normally be over 200 men). 2nd Platoon Fox Company 2/4 with 43 men was added to the mix, attached to Golf Company, as well as a raider platoon of 24 men.

The raider platoon was unique to 2/4 and was started by Lieutenant Colonel Bull Fisher who was the previous Battalion Commander before Lieutenant Colonel P. X. Kelly. The raider platoon reported directly to the battalion commander and was made up of all enlisted volunteers. It was about 24 men including the S2 scouts and snipers. They had their choice of weapons and many of the NCOs carried sub machine guns or grease guns. This was similar to the 2/7 H&S company's mini rifle platoon, except the Raider Platoon was permanently assigned and had their own tactical area of responsibility. H&S company with the command group, comm and mortars was about 71 men. The biggest addition to this force was

143 men from Bravo Company 1/7 which had been designated as a Sparrow Hawk, or Quick Reaction Force for situations such as these. In total 2/4 fielded 498 men compared to about 600 men in 2/7 and nearly 800 men in 3/1.

On March 5, the 2nd Battalion, 4th Marines began landing shortly after 0830 on a clear grassy area near An Tuyet (1), 3,000 meters north of the Tra Khuc River. Despite air preparation of the landing zone, enemy gunners were well entrenched and contested the helicopter landing of the Marine battalion. First to land was the 2/4 Raider Platoon led by Sergeant C. R. Peterson. The Raider Platoon met some resistance when they landed from the high ground to their southwest and from the nearby village west of the landing zone. They were followed by Hotel Company 2/4, then the 2/4 command group, Golf Company 2/4, then Bravo Company 1/7. Each wave of helicopters received fire from that hillside which caused confusion in the drop off and each heli-team had to be sorted out after they landed. The landing zone was situated about 400 meters to the east in the shadow of a multi-peaked north-south ridgeline where the enemy had dug well concealed trenches and tunnels with clear fields of fire on the landing area. This was probably the worst place for a landing zone: an open clearing with entrenched enemy firing down on them from the surrounding high ground. Here again, for whatever reason, the commanders of the task force, handicapped the battalion by sending in only three, understaffed rifle companies into a hot landing zone. They compounded this by replacing one of their rifle companies with a company from another battalion and another regiment, Bravo Company 1st Battalion 7th Marines. The mixing of battalions and regiments meant that radio communications, command relationships and delivery of supplies and supporting arms were severely hampered. The lack of logistic support almost cost the loss of Bravo Company 1/7.

The landing zone was under heavy small arms fire resulting in several Marine KIAs and WIAs during the landing. Most of the helicopters were hit and two were forced to land in the landing zone. The helos were setting down wherever they could, causing units to be separated and intermingled. The door gunners in the helicopters added to the chaos by spraying the area without regard for the friendly troops that had already landed. It took a few hours for Hotel and Golf Companies of 2/4 and B Company 1/7 to consolidate under the withering incoming fire. In his After Action Report, Lieutenant Colonel Kelly recommended that after the first troops land that the door gunners do not fire unless they have a clear enemy target or are instructed by the senior ground commander.

The following is a recollection of Hospital Corpsman Carl Dunaway who was on his last mission. Dunaway says of that mission:

We were carried into this engagement on a UH-34, a helicopter capable of carrying twelve to sixteen men but limited by heat and humidity to seven to eight combat loaded Marines. Upon reaching the LZ (landing zone) the UH-34's came under heavy small arms fire. We were all lifted in with these UH-34's (ugly-looking helicopters). He (HC Tommy Miller) was on another chopper but on the same third wave. I remember waiting for the choppers to come back for us and it seemed like forever. When they did, most of them all had many, many bullet holes in them. The chopper I boarded had a hole in its side bigger than a watermelon. I could stick my head through it if I wanted to. When we landed, a firefight was already going on. I thought we were surrounded. We basically got ambushed as my diary described it. I think I was kneeling, trying to figure out which way to go when I heard someone behind me get hit. I heard my name called out which surprised me. Before I knew it and could turn around, he (Tommy) was thrown down on me. I kept looking at his face wondering who this man was. I knew it couldn't have been the same Tommy Miller I knew. But it was.

Then I saw another corpsman by the name of Lockhart get hit when he ran across a dike. The same two Marines that pulled me away from Tommy went for Lockhart and were killed. This all started about 9:00 in the morning and was still going on at 11:00 at night when we had an emergency ammo drop.

Dunaway went on to say that:

Tommy never—and I mean this with my whole being—never felt a thing. He did not die like so many hundreds that I saw where they laid in pain and agony." "We had so many Marines that were wounded that day that after we were able to get them to the landing zone they bled to death because we couldn't get choppers in to pick them up. If Tommy would have only been wounded, he may still have died because there was no way of getting him out until the next day." On March 8, 1966, his parents received a telegram informing them that he had been killed in action. His body was returned to the Bender Funeral Home in North Manchester, and he was buried in Pleasant Hill Cemetery just west of North Manchester, Wabash County, Indiana. [Taken from ingenweb.org]

Pfc. Bob Hodges was one of the first men to land in the landing zone with Golf Company 2/4. When they approached the landing zone, the UH-34 began receiving incoming fire and the crew chief was yelling for the Marines to jump off the chopper even though they were still four to five feet off the ground. Bob jumped off the chopper and saw the tops of the tall grass around him being chopped off. At first he thought it was the blades of the helicopter but immediately heard the sound of machine guns and realized it was incoming fire that was chopping everything down. His immediate thought was to get off the landing zone and find some cover. Bob was the point man for his squad and his squad leader was yelling at him to find a way out of the killing zone that they were in. Although

147

they were getting incoming fire from a hill to his front which was west of the landing zone, he ran in that direction since the hill was the only place that afforded any cover.

Pfc. Gil Litton was 19 when he landed in the third wave with Golf Company 2/4. He was a scout and point man for his squad. His team had been told that the landing zone was supposed to be secure and had been instructed not to lock and load their weapons (load a magazine with live rounds in their rifles) while in the helicopter. As they approached the landing zone, he could see that the area was covered with smoke, and he could see the machine guns cutting through the grass. He jumped off the helicopter before it landed and looked for cover. There wasn't any on the landing zone, so he directed his squad to a grove of trees that was about 200 yards away. The rest of the battalion was engaged in a fire fight with a large enemy force that was firing down from the north-south ridgeline that overlooked the landing zone from the west. It felt like 2/4 had been helicopter into an ambush.

Corporal Conrad A. Sipple was a squad leader with Golf Company 2/4 when his platoon came under extremely heavy small arms and automatic weapons fire from VC/NVA forces, entrenched on the ridge line to the west of the landing zone. Numerous casualties were inflicted on his platoon and many fell in areas exposed to annihilating fire. Corporal Sipple repeatedly assisted in the evacuation of wounded Marines despite the incoming fire. He braved the fusillade of automatic weapons fire alone on two occasions to assist wounded comrades to safety. On two other occasions Corporal Sipple returned into the enemy fire to assist others in the evacuation of seriously wounded Marines who had to be carried bodily from the extremely hazardous area. On his 4th sally into the hail of enemy fire, he was mortally wounded. When Corporal Sipple was hit, Pfc. Litton picked him up and moved him to an evacuation area, but the corpsman there said the Sipple had been shot in the spine and was dying. Conrad Sipple would be posthumously awarded the Navy Cross Medal for his actions.

Litton returned to his squad as they were working their way up the hill to take out the enemy positions. They found the enemy were well entrenched in the hill with tunnels and spider holes, which must have taken weeks to build out. Some of them were also protected by booby traps.

As the squad paused for a moment, Pfc. Litton knelt on one knee and noticed that his pant leg was torn from his pocket down to his boot. He also noticed that his knee was resting on a device with three prongs. He froze and the squad leader called for engineers to defuse the booby trap. After what seemed like an eternity, the engineers arrived and defused the boobytrap. Pfc. Litton decided that he wasn't meant to die that day. But the VC were trying hard to get him. By the end of the day, Litton had been shot four times, twice through his shirt, once in his backpack and once through the heel of his boot. But none of the bullets ever broke his skin.

On the afternoon of 5 March, the disposition of forces in the southern area of Operation Utah is shown on the following map. Bravo 1/7 established a defensive perimeter around a downed helicopter in the LZ. Golf 2/4 was engaged assaulting the hill to the west of the LZ and the rest of 2/4 was sweeping toward Chau Nhai (4).

Disposition of 2/4 Forces On 5 March 1966

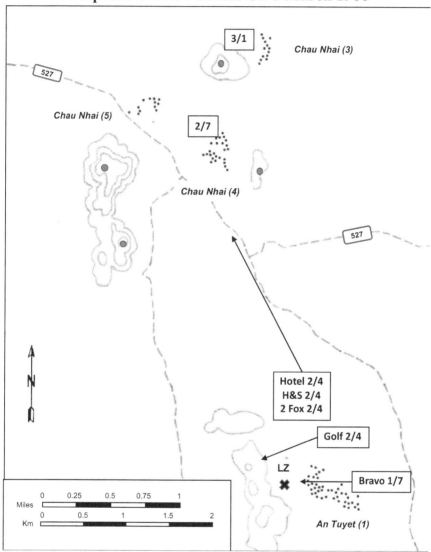

Golf Company spent the rest of the day fighting to take the hill that was west of the landing zone. They fought all day and into the night clearing holes and trenches on their way up the hill. That night, Golf Company sheltered in the trenches that they had cleared so far. At day break (6 March), Golf Company lined up and made a final assault. Their assault was witnessed by Bravo 1/7 Marines who were still at the landing site. Pfc. Dave Shelton of Bravo Company described it like witnessing a rebel charge, a line of crazy Marines yelling and firing as they charged from the backside and over the crest of the hill. The VC were routed and running away as fast as they could. This was a great relief to Bravo Company since they had been defending the landing zone from wave after wave of VC attacks over the last 24 hours and taking incoming fire from the VC on that hill.

Although the 2/4 After Action Report says that Golf Company joined Hotel Company in a sweep to the north to set up a blocking position near 2/7 at Chau Nhai (4), the survivors of Golf Company recall that they stayed in the fight for the hill near the landing zone at An Tuyet (1) and stayed there over the night of 5 March until they took the hill the next day. It was a hard-fought victory that cost them five of their own: Beauregard, Jimenez, Johnson, Sipple, and Stoudt. The next morning when they were told to vacate the hill and join the rest of 2/4, many of the men expressed their anger at having to sacrifice so much for nothing. To add insult to injury this action was not even recorded in the 2/4 After Action Report.

According to the 2/4 After Action Report, Lieutenant Colonel Kelley's battalion met stiff resistance on the west and in the villages, northwest and southwest of the landing zone. Two of Kelley's companies were engaged at close quarters until 1100 on 5 March. At that time, General Platt ordered the battalion commander to continue the original mission of closing the southern flank of the objective area. The After Action Report has Kelley disengaging the two companies, Golf and Hotel, along with the Raider platoon and the 2nd Platoon of Fox Company, from the firefight and began a sweep to the north. However, according to members of Golf Company, they stayed engaged on the hill west of the landing zone until they were able to take the hill the next morning (6 March) and occupy the fortifications that were established there by the VC/NVA. In the confusion of battle, part of Golf Company along with the platoon from Fox Company may have joined Hotel Company while the rest of Golf Company stayed engaged where they were. The battalion's Hotel Company and command group reached Lieutenant Colonel Utter's battalion without incident and established night defensive positions. In addition to the five men killed in Golf Company, H&S company also lost Lance Corporal Michael Linn Bianchini from the

Raider Platoon to a booby trap and Corpsman Tom Miller to rifle fire. The rest of 2/4 did not have any KIAs.

In the morning on 6 March at 0745, 2/4 received orders to conduct a search and destroy operation back to the landing zone to relieve Bravo 1/7 who had been under attack all night. According to the After Action Report, Golf Company led the way and established a base of fire at the bottom of the hill and Hotel Company was to follow in trace. Engineers came on site to destroy the fortifications.

Chapter 14
Bravo 1/7 in No Man's Land

Bravo Company, 1st Battalion, 7th Marines, landed with 2/4 on 5 March to provide a blocking force on the southern part of the Operation Utah area in an attempt at encircling the North Vietnamese Regiment that had engaged 2/7 the day before. The last of Bravo Company had landed in the landing zone by 1100 despite heavy small arms fire. Machine gun fire from a nearby ridge line hit and disabled two helicopters. They established a horse shoe perimeter facing the hill and were immediately in a close range firefight. Bravo Company was ordered to remain in the landing zone to provide security for the two downed helicopters and evacuate the 2/4 Marines who were wounded during the landing. Although the situation was still hot, 2/4 was ordered to disengage and move north to link up with Utter's 2/7. If the objective was to engage the NVA, the task force leaders should have left 2/4 where it was since they were already heavily engaged.

Most of the men in Bravo Company did not know that the rest of 2/4 had left the landing zone. Bravo Company was isolated in a rice field in no man's land, an under-strength infantry rifle company of 165 young Marines fighting one of the most intense battles in the Vietnam War against an estimated five hundred or more elite North Vietnamese soldiers. Bravo Company had landed in Vietnam on November 18, 1965, and had not had any major firefights prior to Utah. Their commanding officer, Captain Robert Prewitt, had just assumed command of the company in the last few months. Bravo Company was surrounded by an NVA battalion and under almost constant fire throughout the day and night of 5 March. Bravo Company was in for the fight of its life.

With the departure of 2/4, Bravo Company was on its own in a remote, isolated position with no physical contact with any friendly forces. The ridge line that was overlooking their position ran from

153

their northwest to their southeast at about 400 meters distance and provided the NVA with excellent observation of their position. A cane field grew along the base of the ridge line that gave good concealment to the enemy. It allowed them to move undetected very close to their perimeter. Bravo Company was thinly spread out in a large semicircle in the dry rice field. 1st Lieutenant Dave Brown's 1st Platoon was positioned to the north. 1st Lieutenant Ken Nisewarner, a Naval Academy graduate, had his 2nd Platoon defending to the west, and Staff Sergeant McClelland's 3rd Platoon was in the southern sector. Each platoon had a machine gun squad and a rocket launcher squad attached to it. A dozen or more walking wounded Marines from 2/4 filled in their backside facing An Tuyet (1). A forward air control team and mortar and artillery forward observer teams had fortunately been attached to the company. Including those attachments, the total strength of Bravo Company that day was only five officers and 160 enlisted Marines, well under strength.

Captain Prewitt described his situation in an online post in 2004:

> So there we were in no man's land—165 "good guys" against who knew how many "bad guys"—with the sun baking down, searing the still, hot air. The good news was that one of the downed helicopters had been repaired and was able to fly out. We were also able to evacuate 2/4's casualties. The bad news was that we were still under fire, and we were getting low on water and ammunition. We had only what we carried with us on our backs and cartridge belts. Our uniforms were soaked with sweat and clung to our bodies like Saran Wrap. Our heavy armor vests (which were mandatory to wear) made us even hotter. Each man started with two full canteens of water, but in the blistering and brain-burning heat, even disciplined and acclimatized Marines were compelled to drink water. Each time that a helicopter landed in our perimeter to evacuate casualties, the NVA opened fire on it, and each time we immediately returned fire, expending more ammo to protect the helo.

By well-directed use of supporting arms and disciplined small unit fire control, the intense enemy attacks were repulsed, one after another. The forward air controller, 1st Lieutenant Bob McCormick directed twenty one air strikes of rockets, bombs, napalm, and strafing by A4 and F4 jets and gunships, the most in one day in Vietnam to that date. At night a C47 flare plane dropped beautiful flares that slowly descended around them casting eerie shadows and providing illumination throughout the night that helped them see enemy movements. Because of the intense surrounding enemy fire, medical evacuations were not possible during the night and the wounded had to wait until the next day (6 March) to be evacuated.

Dave Shelton was a 19-year-old Pfc. fire team leader when he landed with Bravo 1/7 at Operation Utah. He arrived in Vietnam in November of 1965 with Alpha Company 1/3 and the whole company was re-designated to be Bravo Company 1/7 in January 1966. Although he had been on several smaller search and destroy operations, Operation Utah was to be his first major battle. As a fire team leader, he was also the heli-team leader. Dave sat in the door of the UH-34 with his feet dangling over the edge. As he approached the landing zone in the third wave, he could hear the noise of battle and at first, he thought the landing zone was covered with fog until he realized it was the smoke of gun fire. After they landed, the landing zone was relatively quiet and his squad, which was down to eight men, made a quick sweep of the small hamlet of An Tuyet (1) before settling into the south side of the landing zone perimeter.

Pfc. Dave Shelton Getting water from a well

Dave was armed with an M14 that was set for full automatic. He had picked up six bandoleers of M14 ammo before leaving Chu Lai and had about 520 rounds of ammo. As he set up his fire team on the south side of the landing zone perimeter, he noticed a Marine machine gunner to the right of him, firing at a row of trees to his front and receiving enemy fire in return. He directed his fire team to fire into the side of the same row of trees and he began to fire his automatic as well. Although they couldn't see any specific targets, the noise indicated that they were having some effect.

Between his position and the row of trees there were two rice paddies. The first rice paddy closest to him was dry and barren while the second rice paddy was about 15 meters further away and was full of rice stalks and two green bushes. Beyond that about another 15 meters was the row of trees.

While Dave was firing another magazine at the row of trees, one of the green bushes popped up at the edge of the rice paddy less than 15 feet away, and Dave saw a round face peering out of the bush. As the NVA was reaching around for a Chicom grease gun that was slung on his back, Dave shot him. He immediately thought about the other green bush that he had seen in the rice paddy, and he saw it rising up a short distance away. He emptied the rest of his magazine

156

into the second bush. That was the first time he saw the faces of the men he killed.

Around 1600 (5 March) Bravo Company 1/7 came under heavy attack from the south by several companies of VC. Unlike the enemy forces who were engaging 2/7 and 3/1 on Hill 50, the enemy here were not wearing the NVA Green Uniforms and pith type helmets. They also had a wide assortment of weapons instead of the AK-47s that were used by the NVA. The heaviest action of the night and early morning hours of 5-6 March occurred at this relatively isolated position near An Tuyet (1). Large groups of VC were seen on the ridge to their west during the afternoon. 3rd Platoon was sent to take out a position which was pouring heavy fire on the landing zone. But 200 meters into the attack, they became pinned down.

The heaviest fighting was on the southern portion of the company perimeter where four of the six Bravo Company Marines were killed. Three of them were in the same eight man squad as Dave Shelton. They were Sergeant Charles Frederick Setzenfand, the squad leader, Pfc. John Henry Bell, and Corporal Roy John Higgins. The fourth Marine was to the right of this squad. He was the machine gunner, Corporal Mario Clayton Kitts who was firing into the tree line that Dave Shelton described.

When Corporal Mario Kitts was wounded by a mortar round, several of the Marines were able to reach him and carry him back to the medical aid area. They rolled him onto a poncho and tried to carry him without bumping him against the furrows and paddy dykes, knowing that each bump would cause him excruciating pain. One of the Marines called for the others to carry him higher to avoid causing him pain, but Mario told them to stay low so they wouldn't get shot. By the time they reached the aid station, it was dark and the medics worked on the wounded holding red flashlights. No medevacs were able to get in due to the heavy enemy fire that erupted whenever the helicopters made an appearance. Corporal Mario Kitts bled to death sometime during the night.

Pfc. John Henry Bell heard the call for more machine gun ammo. He gathered up whatever ammo could be spared and attempted to run it over to the machine gun team. His helmet fell off when he ran by Pfc. Dave Shelton. Pfc. Bell was able to deliver the ammo and when he was returning, he bent over to pick up his helmet. When he bent over, a round split his skull and he fell over onto Dave Shelton.

157

He landed laying across Dave's lap and his eyes met Dave's. Dave described it as a 1000-yard stare. He didn't know if John recognized him, but he could feel the tension in his body so he knew he was alive. Dave placed his hand on John's head and his brains oozed onto his hands. Dave felt John's body go limp and knew he was gone. Of all the deaths that Dave witnessed during his tour in Vietnam, Pfc. John Henry Bell's death was the one that he remembers most vividly. Later he noticed that the wooden grip on his M14 was sticky with John Henry Bell's brain matter.

I have asked Dave if experiences like this have caused any symptoms of PTSD. Dave has told me that he does not suffer from PTSD, because he is able to compartmentalize his experiences. He felt honored to have been able to share John Henry Bell's last moments.

The whole company was running low on ammo. Dave Shelton was firing full automatic, a full 20-round magazine at a time. At one time the front stock of his M14 ignited from the heat. He had to throw it in a rice paddy to put out the flames. By evening he had fired over 500 rounds and was down to his last seven bullets. There were multiple requests for emergency supply of ammunition at 1700 and at 1830. One medevac helicopter was able to land and evacuate some wounded but no ammo came with it. All during the night Airforce C47s were able to drop flares continuously so that the surroundings were always lit up.

As night fell, Captain Prewitt decided that his men were too spread out and consolidated the night perimeter, with his men forming a smaller 360 degree perimeter around the downed helicopter that was closest to the center of the landing zone. Pfc. Dave Shelton and Pfc. Tommy Alexander were the farthest away toward the south when the order to consolidate was given. Since they both had automatic rifles they provided covering fire while the rest of the squad moved back. When everyone else had left they each loaded a full magazine into their M14s, stood up and blasted the tree line where they were being fired from. As soon as they emptied their magazines, they turned and ran toward the perimeter that was about 70 meters behind them. When they were running a machine gun opened up on them stitching divots between them. Suddenly Tommy pitched forward sprawling in the dirt. At times like this, the adrenalin takes over and men have super human strength. Shelton wasn't about to leave his buddy behind so with one hand he reached down and picked Tommy up by the back of his flak jacket and kept on running. Tommy's legs were flayling in the air as if he was in his death throes. Just then, Shelton heard Tommy yell at him: *"Put me down, Damit! I tripped!"* Dave and Tommy made it back to the perimeter without any further incident.

While one helicopter was inside their small perimeter, a second helicopter was located about 10 meters outside the perimeter and was guarded by two fire teams. During the night an alert Marine noticed a bush that was moving toward the outside helicopter and he fired an illumination grenade at it. The phosphorus ignited the bush and a camouflaged NVA jumped up and started to run back and was cut down by gun fire.

By 2300 (5 March), six hours after the first emergency request for ammo, Captain Robert C. Prewitt, the company commander, was still looking for a resupply of ammo. Captain Prewitt reported to the 2nd Battalion, 4th Marines that he was under mortar and heavy small arms attack and was running extremely low on ammo. According to the battalion commander, Lieutenant Colonel Kelley, "Prewitt advised me that he was dangerously low on ammunition." Lieutenant Colonel Kelley informed General Platt of the situation and asked for an emergency resupply for the company. The task force commander approved the mission, and two HMM-364 helicopters took off from Chu Lai to deliver the needed ammunition.

The two helicopters came in low, about 50 feet off the ground, from the northeast. As soon as they cleared the trees from An Tuyet (2) which was the village next to An Tuyet (1), the enemy opened fire on the two helicopters. There was an eruption of automatic fire which looked like a cone of fire, criss crossing around the helicopters. The helicopters were unable to land and pulled back behind the trees. The flight leader, First Lieutenant Terril J. Richardson, radioed Prewitt and regretfully announced that they would not be able to land. After Prewitt informed him of the severity of the need (less than 100 rounds of rifle ammo left in the company), the pilot (Richardson) said in effect that they would get the ammo in somehow. The result was that the two helicopters came across the zone a few feet off the ground and at about 10-20 mph while the crewmen kicked the ammo boxes out the doors. Both aircraft were hit by ground fire, but no crew member was hit and the helicopters managed to flounder back to Chu Lai.

On the ground, Prewitt's company came under increasing pressure. Supported by mortars and automatic weapons, two VC companies closed in on the Marine perimeter. About 0130, 6 March, the enemy attacked the Marine positions from three directions—north, south, and west. With the help of Marine artillery at Binh Son and an ARVN 155mm battery at Quang Ngai, the newly replenished Marines repulsed the NVA attack at ranges of less than 30 meters. Even after the attack failed, the North Vietnamese continued to subject the Marine company to heavy mortar, small arms, and automatic weapons fire until early morning. Golf Company 2/4 was also engaged in a fire fight nearby and when they called in artillery fire, one round fell within Bravo Company's perimeter. Lance Corporal Harry James Stateczny lost his leg to the short round. He could not be evacuated until the helicopters were able to land the next day. Lance Corporal Stateczny was later evacuated to Great Lakes Naval Hospital, Great Lakes, Illinois to be near his home. He was able to see his parents, but unfortunately he died of gangrene on July 3, 1966. Although he was not listed as a KIA from Operation Utah, I include him in this book as a KIA from Operation Utah.

Pfc. Gary E. Sooter, was a rifleman with Bravo Company when the unit came under repeated infantry attacks and a heavy barrage of accurate enemy mortar fire. Realizing the seriousness of the situation, Pfc. Sooter exposed himself continually to intense small arms and destructive mortar fire to cover and defend approaches to his platoon's position. Later that night, observing the enemy attempting to penetrate on his left, he again ran through a heavy volume of mortar and automatic weapons fire to block the advancing VC/NVA, until he fell mortally wounded.

Pfc. Gary E. Sooter would be posthumously awarded the Silver Star for his actions. Although Pfc. Sooter was with Bravo Company 1/7, he was recommended for the Silver Star by a Gunnery Sergeant from Golf Company 2/4 who was still with Bravo Company. Bravo Company lost six Marines in the day's fighting. Five were KIA on March 5, 1966 and a sixth, Lance Corporal Stateczny died of his wounds on July 3, 1966.

The issue of resupply of ammunition as reported by Captain Prewitt was a curious sidenote to me. After several requests for emergency resupply, it wasn't until 2300, (5 March) when Captain Prewitt finally got through to the Battalion Commander Lieutenant Colonel Kelly, that they were dangerously low on Ammo. Lieutenant Colonel Kelly then had to contact the Task Force Commander, General Platt, inform him of the situation and ask for approval for an emergency resupply before two helicopters were dispatched with the needed ammunition. Considering the heavy contact that Bravo Company was experiencing all day, why had they not had an earlier resupply of ammunition and why did it take the approval of General Platt to authorize an emergency resupply? The After Action Report of another battalion, 3/1, indicated that they received a resupply that may have been intended for Bravo Company due to a mix-up in call signs. The battalion S4 officer is responsible for resupply and should have been proactively monitoring the supply situation. In the case of Utter's battalion, 2/7, the S4 officer, Captain Marty O'Connor, kept up the resupply of ammo during the conflict on 4 March and personally led volunteers across fields of fire to resupply Fox Company when they were running out of ammo. Where was the S4 for 2/4? Since Bravo Company was from another Battalion, 1/7, their supply needs might have been overlooked when they were assigned to Kelly's Battalion 2/4. The After Action Reports of 2/4 and Bravo Company 1/7 make no mention of the supply shortage or any recommendation for correcting this in the future. If it wasn't for the foresight of the individual riflemen who grabbed extra bandoleers of ammo when they got on the helicopters, Bravo company would have been sunk.

The next day, 6 March, at 0745, General Platt ordered the 2nd Battalion, 4th Marines to return to the landing zone and relieve Bravo Company. The battalion left the blocking positions that it had established the night before, leaving the 2nd Battalion, 7th Marines in place. By midafternoon, Kelley's battalion had moved overland and seized the high ground west of the landing zone. There was only light enemy resistance to the move; The main enemy force had withdrawn, but not without heavy losses. Captain Prewitt confirmed 38 enemy dead and estimated that at least twice that figure had been carried away. Bravo Company was too busy fighting for its life to worry about sophisticated estimates of enemy KIA. Bravo Company's casualties were miraculously only five killed and twenty four wounded. Outstanding combined arms support, fearless helicopter support for medevacs and resupply, Marine training, and combat experience no doubt kept casualties to a minimum.

Captain Prewitt summed up the action of Bravo Company 1/7 on March 5 and 6, 1966.

> At that time we were not fighting for our country or the Corps ... we were fighting for each other! We knew that we were accountable for our actions and deeds to our team members and fellow Marines. They were dependent upon us, as we were upon them. We were not about to let one another down.

****

Captain Prewitt documented Bravo Company's heroic stand in an online article: "Fix Bayonet: Bravo Company on Operation Utah." Captain Prewitt was awarded the Silver Star and Bronze Star medals for his service in Vietnam. He later commanded an infantry battalion and then an infantry regiment in the 2nd Marine Division. During the Cold War, he was the senior emergency actions officer in the Military Command Center at the Pentagon in Washington, D.C. After retiring from military service as a Lieutenant Colonel in 1981, Robert Prewitt directed an outreach ministry in Dallas that taught conversational English to more than 800 South East Asian refugees and other foreign-born adults.

Dave Shelton left the Marine Corps after his enlistment was finished. He was trained in electronics and served with the Army for 10 years, followed by 20 years in the Air Force. In both tours, he worked on aviation electronics and flew to many destinations in Europe and the Middle East. He has maintained his contacts from the Marine Corps during Vietnam and was the source for much of the input for this chapter.

Part 5
Supporting Units

Chapter 15
The Indestructible UH-34 and the Men Who Flew Them

T he Vietnam Helicopter Pilot and Crewmember Monument, located in Arlington National Cemetery, commemorates the nearly 5,000 pilots who lost their lives while serving in Vietnam.

One of the iconic images of the Vietnam War is that of a helicopter carrying troops into a hot landing zone. One of the highest risk assignments in the Vietnam War was to be a pilot or crew member in a helicopter.

The helicopter that the Marines used during Operation Utah was the Sikorsky UH-34. It was accepted by the Marine Corps in 1960. It was developed as an upgrade to the Korean War H-19. It had a crew of three (two pilots and a crew chief/gunner) and was built to haul around twelve to sixteen troops, but in Vietnam it was usually restricted to seven to eight combat-loaded Marines. The engine developed less power at higher elevations and higher temps. It was the last evolution of the large piston-engine helicopters. A nine-cylinder air-cooled Wright R-1820-84 reciprocating engine powered the single rotor UH-34 and the massive engine required an elaborate blower system to keep it cool. As a result, the lift capability of the UH-34 was sensitive to the heat and humidity of Vietnam and restricted the number of men and equipment that could be carried on any trip.

The engine was located to the front of the cabin, closer to the axis of the main rotor, increasing the center-of-gravity envelope which made it a very stable platform. However, this configuration required the relocation of the cockpit to a position on top of the engine. Shafts and gearboxes were situated along the spine of the fuselage and substantial tail pylons drove the tail rotor. Helicopters were not meant to fly like fixed-wing airplanes.

It is a delicate balance of opposing forces. One rotating blade forced the air down while the next blade forced the air up and the tail rotor kept it from spinning in circles. You don't see helicopters gliding in for a landing. The fuselage was all metal. However, the metal did not protect against incoming rounds since it was principally magnesium alloy for weight savings. Operationally, in Vietnam, it was vulnerable to small arms fire if the exposed oil cooler under the engine compartment was hit, but early on the Marine Corps added armor plate shields that helped. They also found that the big 2200 HP front mounted engine could take a lot of hits and still operate ok, plus it protected the pilots from frontal small arms fire.

Pilots of UH-34s flying in Vietnam discovered that some of the design's innovative features carried penalties in the combat zone. The high cockpit made it an obvious target, and the drive shaft created a partition that made it difficult for crew chiefs to come to the aid of the cockpit crew if they became injured. The UH-34's magnesium skin resulted in very intense fires, and contributed to significant corrosion problems. The airframe was also too weak to support most of the weapon systems that would have allowed the UH-34 to become an effective ad-hoc gunship compared to the newer Huey helicopters. The only armament on a UH-34 was an M60 machine gun which was mounted at the door and operated manually by a door gunner.

Seeing a UH-34 come lumbering in for a landing makes a tempting target, especially when you could see the pilot sitting on top behind a large windshield. They looked like dinosaurs compared to the faster, turbo-powered, streamlined Huey helicopters that were used by the Army.

While there were stories of UH-34's being downed by arrows, they proved to be very reliable in a hot situation. The UH-34, proved to be a stable platform that could maneuver in very tight situations, and demonstrated an ability to sustain a substantial amount of combat damage and still return home. During Operation Utah, four of the new Huey gunships were used to escort the UH-34's. However, on the first wave, one was shot down and the other three were damaged and had to leave the assault. The UH-34s were also shot up and riddled with holes but continued to support wave after wave of troop insertions. They served two major roles in support of combat troops. First was the mobility to insert troops into tight landing zones, and the second was to deliver ammo and evacuate the wounded within minutes of an engagement.

While infantry Marines were most familiar with the UH-34 which carried them into battle, the new turbo-powered Hueys (Bell UH-1 Iroqouis) were being introduced to the Marine Air Group (MAG-36). While the HMM Squadrons used the UH-34 for troop transport, resupply and medevacs, The Huey was armed with rockets and machine guns and assigned to VMO squadrons as gunships providing close air support for infantry and recon units. During Operation Utah, helicopters from HMM-261, HMM-364 and VMO-6 supported the troop lift of the 1st ARVN Airborne and 2/7 on D-Day March 4. Fourteen were heavily damaged during the insertion by intense anti-aircraft fire from numerous 12.7mm (.50 cal) anti-aircraft machine guns. This was the first major contact with the 21st NVA Regiment and they had the firepower to take down the helicopters. On D-Day 4 March, one Huey was downed near Hill 85 and the crew was evacuated by a HU-34 crew. Another UH-34 was downed at the landing zone. The ARVN and Marines were then reinforced by HMM-363, while MAG-36 helicopters provided overnight resupply and medevacs. HMM-261 helos were again heavily damaged when inserting 2/4 the next day as a blocking force. Two UH-34s were downed in the 2/4 landing Zone. A section of UH-34s from HMM-364 provided an emergency resupply of ammunition to Bravo Company 1/7 at night on 5 March, as two helicopters came across the zone a few feet off the ground while the crewmen kicked the ammo boxes out the doors under extremely heavy fire. This was to be a common sight for the next six years. Fortunately, none of the helicopter crews on that run were killed.

Resupply was a difficult problem especially as the NVA held the high ground in Operation Utah and could fire down at the landing zones with their .50 cal Machine guns. Unlike the NVA and VC forces who had caches of ammo on-site, the Marines had to bring all their ammo with them and were dependent on helicopters to resupply them. The firefights on Utah, unlike previous operations, went on for hours and Marines were chewing up their ammunition at a fast clip. Marine riflemen were armed with the M14 rifles which fired a 7.62mm round. Normally, a Marine rifleman carried five magazines of twenty rounds each which amounted to 120 rounds with one in the rifle. A hundred rounds do not last very long in a fire fight. Most Marines on Operation Utah who had experience in previous firefights had loaded up with several extra magazines and bandoliers of ammo, carrying about 200 rounds. While every M14 could be set to automatic fire, for fire control purposes, only one member of a fire team was set to full automatic and the rest were set to semi-automatic. The NVA seemed to have a limitless supply of ammo and all of them seemed to be firing in bursts of automatic fire. In previous wars many infantry troops did not fire their weapons, but this was not the case at Operation Utah. The Marines were burning through ammo just to keep up with the NVA. The NVA were armed with AK-47's which had a 30-round magazine. The NVA usually had one magazine in the rifle and carried three extra magazines in a pouch carried on their chest for a total of 120 rounds. It was obvious that the NVA were fighting from prepared fortifications where they had a limitless cache of ammunition while the Marines only had what they brought with them. After a few hours of contact the Marines were in dire need of ammo, M14 rounds, linked ammo for the machine guns, mortar rounds, M79 grenades, and hand grenades.

Helicopter resupply and medevacs were critical to the battle. One of the resupply missions was documented in a *Stars and Stripes* article from April, 1966. This involved Bravo Company 1/7 who had been assigned to 2/4 to set up a blocking position on March 5 several kilometers south of 2/7. They landed at a landing zone near An Tuyet and met heavy resistance. Multiple copters had been shot down during the insertion and Bravo Company was assigned to provide security for the copters while the rest of 2/4, which consisted of two companies, was ordered to proceed to a blocking position near 2/7's location at Chau Nhai 4. While the bulk of the fighting was in the Northern Sector around Hill 50, Bravo Company was left alone to battle the NVA from early morning with the supplies that they had carried in on their backs. By 1700, they were out of M-79 grenade and rocket launcher ammunition, and machine gun and rifle ammunition was almost exhausted and the NVA were circling around for the kill. By 1830 they were down to only a handful of bullets per rifleman, when the emergency supply request was finally approved. The resupply copters finally arrived at 2300 hours. However, it was already dark, and the situation was near desperate. The following description of the resupply run was reported in the Stars and Stripes.

CHU LAI, Vietnam (ISO) - A Marine pilot from the state of Utah can testify to the intensity of Viet Cong fire at landing zones during Operation Utah.

"It seemed as though the whole world started firing at us," commented 1st Lieutenant Terril J. Richardson of Vernal, Utah, a pilot with Marine Medium Helicopter Squadron 364.

Richardson's helicopter received several hits from the enemy during one mission. It begins when he received word to launch on an emergency resupply mission for a ground unit (Bravo Company 1/7) 18 miles south of here.

Approaching the landing zone, he followed a small light from a Marine unit into a clearing. As the rear wheel touched down, the enemy opened up with an intensive sheet of automatic weapons fire. The Utah Marine immediately flew the aircraft out of the zone. as the 'copter climbed, crew chief Sergeant James R. Vance of Barlow, Kentucky. and crewman Lance Corporal George E. Sexton counted eight automatic weapons and two .50 cal machine guns firing at them. The two crew members were blazing away at the enemy positions with their machine guns.

Richardson radioed the ground unit to see if they would agree to a low altitude airdrop of the critically needed ammunition. The ground unit replied, "affirmative," and Richardson again began the descent.

Silhouetted by a full moon, the helicopter came in at top speed at an altitude of only 50 feet. The enemy held their fire. Getting closer to the zone, 1st Lieutenant Richardson stared intently at a small light marking the drop area. The copilot 2nd Lieutenant C. Eric Cederblom of Malvern, N.Y., kept checking the instruments and calling off speed and altitude to the pilot. Nearing the light, Richardson pulled back hard on the cyclic stick and reduced engine power, slowing the aircraft but maintaining altitude. Suddenly the enemy opened fire again. Tracers flew at the chopper from all sides. Vance was already dropping the ammunition from the aircraft. Sexton was exchanging a steady stream of machine gun fire with three enemy automatic weapons in a tree line on the left of the helicopter.

The ammunition off-loaded, the pilot lifted up and away from the zone as enemy gunners with automatic weapons and .50 cal machine guns began playing a deadly game of tag. Richardson pulled a hard left, then a right, and the enemy gunners would follow, trying to lock their fire on the chopper to shoot it down. "I even leveled off hoping they would fire over me, but they leveled off too," the pilot commented. At 1,500 feet Richardson banked the aircraft to the right again and headed for the mountains. With the mountains between his 'copter and the moon, the aircraft was no longer silhouetted and the enemy fire ceased.

Lieutenant Richardson flew his UH-34 aircraft over an hour after that with no problems, but when a warning light came on, he taxied to the flight line and shut it down. A bullet had hit a tail rotor gearbox, cracked the casing, and was about to fail. If that had happened while Richardson was airborne, he most probably would have lost control of the helicopter and crashed. Without the ammunition that he delivered, Bravo Company had little chance of survival. Inspection showed over forty bullet holes in his machine (including eight through the cockpit and fourteen through the troop compartment), but miraculously, not a single crewman was scratched.

The helicopters were also critical for evacuating the wounded. In a country that consisted of mountains, valleys, waterways, rice paddies and very few manageable roads, helicopters were the only way to evacuate the wounded even though they drew intense fire whenever they appeared and slowed down to land or hover over an landing zone. For a wounded soldier, doctors were discovering that there was approximately a six-hour window after injury or what they refer to as the "golden hours" to treat a wound before the soldier went into shock or cardiac arrest.

In Vietnam, dust-off helicopters touched down on the battlefield itself and removed the wounded to air-conditioned hospital ships or fixed-facility hospitals as sophisticated as those in the United States. Because of the speed of evacuation and the quality and proximity of these hospitals, the died-of-wounds rate in Vietnam sank to 2.5 percent, the lowest of any war. In Utah, the battle was so close that it was difficult to evacuate the wounded in a timely manner. landing zones were targeted by long-range .50 cal machine guns and 82mm Mortars. The bravery of the helicopter crews was amazing. Many of our seriously wounded would not have survived without the bravery of the pilots to fly into the hailstorm of fire and remain exposed while we loaded our wounded. For many wounded Marines, the first indication they would see their families again was the sound of helicopter blades beating against the sky. Without the valor of the helicopter pilots in Vietnam, many more names would have been added to the memorial in Washington D.C.

The decision to leave rifle company units behind to guard downed helicopters has been a subject of debate, since it diminishes the rifle company's strength to carry out their primary mission. With two helicopters down in two different locations, 2/7 had to dedicate two rifle platoons, a quarter of their remaining forces, to guard the helicopters when they were sorely needed for combat.

Years later, Colonel Peatross would explain that he decided not to destroy and leave the downed helicopters unless they were already destroyed beyond repair for two reasons: The first was to keep up the morale of the helicopter crews who knew that they and their craft would be protected. The other reason was that a downed helicopter almost invariably drew enemy action near it when it went down. Since we were constantly searching for the enemy, why leave the helicopter when we knew that they were going to come to it? In the case of Bravo Company 1/7, the downed helicopters attracted a lot of attention, and almost resulted in the loss of the company if other helicopter pilots had not delivered the ammo that they needed.

For more information about Marine Corps helicopter experiences and capabilities check out the USMC Combat Helicopter and Tiltrotor Association website (https://www.popasmoke.com).

Chapter 16
Fire For Effect

The artillery support for Operation Utah was assigned to 4th Battalion 11th Artillery Regiment. At that time 4/11 was based in Chu Lai and consisted of two Batteries, Kilo and Mike, which were each equipped with six new M109, self-propelled 155 mm howitzers. The M109 was essentially a tank with a 155 mm howitzer mounted on a turret with an inch of armor plating protecting the crew. This made it faster to set up compared to a 155 mm howitzer that was towed and had to be dug into place to stabilize the placement of the weapon and provided better protection for the gun crew. The turret enabled it to rotate 360 degrees to change direction of fire without having to reposition the emplacement saving even more time and effort. The M109 used the same firing tables as the M114 towed howitzer for calculating the gun's deflection and elevation during targeting. The 155mm howitzer had a high trajectory which enabled it to fire over hills and reach a maximum range of 9 Miles. The impact and explosion of a 155mm shell is tremendous. According to quora.com the kill radius is 50 meters with a casualty radius of 100 meters. The danger zone extends to 250 meters where a small fragment as small as a half a dime could kill a person in the open.

The disadvantage of the M109 was that it was too heavy to be transported by helicopter and was largely road-bound due to its weight. For mobile operations the Marine corps used the lighter 105mm howitzers or the M144 155mm towed howitzer that could be lifted by the Army skyhook helicopters but required 48 hours to schedule. Although they were few roads in Vietnam at that time, there was one main road that ran the length of Vietnam, connecting the coastal cities on the east coast. This was Route 1, which was known as the "Street Without Joy" from the French Indo China War.

Although the M109 could not be transported by helicopter like the towed version of the 155mm howitzer, M109s were in virtually every battle in northern and central South Vietnam, defending bases and providing counterbattery fire against North Vietnamese threats to Marine bases and large cities situated along the Coast. The M109 proved its worth during the Marine battle of Hue during the Tet Offensive of January/February 1968.

In the first few battles of the Vietnam War the Marines would attack from the sea on amphibious assault vehicles or landing crafts and push inland as they did in World War II. The artillery would be located on the coast and could support the assault by firing over the Marines into the enemy forces. However, this allowed the enemy to escape into the mountains. In Operation Utah, the plan was for the Marines to land inland by helicopter and drive toward the coast in an attempt to trap the VC against the sea. However, this presented a problem where the artillery would be firing into the advancing Marines if they remained on the coast. In order to avoid this conflict, the artillery would be moved to Binh Son which was about seven miles north and perpendicular to the direction of attack which would be from west to east. This enabled the artillery to provide supporting fire that was oblique to the direction of the advance. The planning for Operation Utah was very minimal and the commitment to the assault was over night. The self-propelled M109s were able to respond to the short lead time, moving to Binh Son, and setting up overnight to be ready for action by the morning of March 4. Two batteries, Kilo and Mike, with 12 M109s and ammunition trucks moved from Chu Lai to Binh Son. Security was provided by Easy Company from 2/7, who would remain with the artillery during Operation Utah since the enemy could attack from any direction. A 105mm battery from 3/11 was also added to the convoy. However, the range of the 105's could not support the distance needed to support the area of operations of Operation Utah, and was probably added in the event that the Binh Son location came under attack and close in 105 support was required while the 155s continued to support Operation Utah.

On D-Day March 4, the ARVN met heavy resistance from Hill 50 after they landed and the direction of attack was shifted from heading east toward the coast to heading north toward Hill 50. This new direction meant that the enemy would be between the Marines and Binh Son and the Artillery would be firing toward the advancing Marines and would be restricted in the fire missions that they could support. For the most part they would be limited to firing to the left flank of the ARVN position and Hill 50. On March 5 and 6 they were in a better position to support 3/1 in their assault on Hill 50 and 2/4 in their engagements in the southern portion of the Utah area.

There are basically three functions in an artillery battery: Forward Observer (FO) teams that identify the targets and adjust fire, Fire Direction Centers (FDC) that do the calculations and coordination of the guns, and the Firing Unit or Gun Line that loads and fires the guns based on directions from the FDC.

Since the howitzers are firing at indirect targets often miles away, the FO teams have to be positioned within direct sight on the target. Their job is to provide the coordinates of the target location, the target description and recommended munition, and other information like the proximity of friendly forces and communicate that to the FDC. After the first round is fired, they communicate the necessary adjustments, then call for *fire for effect* to have all the guns in the battery fire on the target. The FO position is a high-risk job since they are in the front lines with the infantry, carrying radios with whip antennas which tend to attract attention. Sometimes they are called to be on covert missions in enemy territory.

1st Lieutenant Dick Thatcher was an FO assigned to Golf 2/7. He joined the Marine Corps because he wanted to be with the best ever since he read Leon Uris's book *Battle Cry* as a kid. He chose Artillery since "Arty lends a bit of class to what is otherwise a brawl." Dick and his five-man team were assigned to Golf Company 2/7 where they stayed to provide support even when they were in defensive positions in Chu Lai. Dick came to know the officers in Golf Company better than the officers in the Artillery Battalion. When they got on the helicopters for Operation Utah, he split his team in two groups. His scout, who could call in targets, and a radio man were in one group while he and the other radioman flew in with Captain Seymour, Golf Company commander. They were soon engaged in a close-in fire fight, but the enemy were too close to call in artillery.

Dick was with the command group when the call came to consolidate with the battalion near Chau Nhai (4). The command group was split up and Dick joined 1st Lieutenant Hank Barnett, Golf Company executive officer, and some others going back first. They pulled back a couple of hundred meters and were laying

175

in a farmed plot with high furrows. They could see the muzzle flashes aimed at them. Hank was in a furrow about 30 feet away when Dick heard him grunt—he'd been hit. A corpsman got to him and put on a dressing; the whole time rounds were hitting around them. Dick remembers seeing .50 cal rounds blowing away the paddy dikes that men were trying to use for cover. Hank was shot in the chest and Dick was able to be with him a while before he was evacuated. He wrote a letter to Hank's wife trying to explain what happened. Fortunately, Hank survived his wound.

1st Lieutenant Thurston Roach was the Fire Direction Office (FDO) for the FDC in Kilo Battery. The FDC computes firing data, *fire direction*, for the guns. The process consists of determining the precise target location based on the observer's location if needed, then computing range and direction and propelling charge and fuse to reach the target from the guns' location. During Vietnam this data was computed manually, using special protractors and slide rules with precomputed firing tables. Corrections can be added for conditions such as a difference between target and howitzer altitudes, propellant temperature, atmospheric conditions, and even the curvature and rotation of the Earth. In most cases, some corrections are omitted, sacrificing accuracy for speed. However, a one degree error could mean hundreds of feet in deflection and range when firing over several miles. The FDC must also coordinate their fire with air support, location of friendly ground forces, and other artillery FDC's.

1st Lieutenant Thurston Roach with an M109 at Chu Lai

176

On Operation Utah, both Kilo and Mike batteries' FDCs got their targets from the 4/11 Battalion Operations Officer. The infantry companies and battalions would relay the target coordinates to 4/11 and the 4/11 Operations Officer would assign the targets to the Battery FDCs. Later an ARVN 155 battery located in Quang Ngai was also added on March 5 to support the conflict in the southern part of the battlefield where Bravo 1/7and Golf 2/4 were engaged. It was during this time when the batteries were adjusting fire missions for Bravo 1/7 and Golf 2/4 that a short round landed in the Bravo Company perimeter. Lance Corporal Harry John Stateczny Jr. lost a leg to the short round but could not be evacuated until the next day due to the continuous enemy fire. Lance Corporal Stateczny was finally evacuated the next day and eventually moved to Great Lakes Naval Hospital near his family but died from gangrene on July 3, 1966. It is amazing that there were no other reports of short rounds from the thousands of rounds that were fired on Operation Utah.

Although the battlefield was chaotic, the sky above the battlefield was no less chaotic. On the first day, the area covered a small area of about 2 square miles, and across this airspace were jets strafing, dropping bombs and napalm, helicopters landing troops, dropping supplies and evacuating casualties, and howitzer shells arching through the sky from Binh Son. Somehow the network communications between the different elements provided the necessary coordination. Usually the artillery would check fire to give the helicopters priority to resupply the troops or evacuate the wounded. On the other hand, if the artillery was shooting on an active mission in support of engaged troops, the helicopters would have to wait or return to base until the fire mission was complete. 1st Lieutenant Roach Wrote this letter to his wife Cathy shortly after Operation Utah.

Wednesday, 9 March

My Dearest Cathy,

Well, we have been here a grand total of one week before really undergoing our baptism of fire. Kilo (his battery) is now an initiate of Vietnam as we have fired over two thousand rounds in anger. Don't know whether you've read anything for heard anything about Operation Utah or not [Cathy had not, but as time went on she could connect what she was hearing every morning on the Today Show with the narrative in his letters.] but last Thursday night Kilo was alerted that we were to be committed to the operation which actually began Friday. This was an overnight planned operation ... banking on some hot intelligence from three captured VC. It may have possibly turned out to be the most successful operation of the war thus far, more KIAs, than Starlight and a RAVN (Regular North Vietnamese) now only exists on paper. General Platt (Jonas type from TBS (Jonas Platt was Commanding Officer of The Basic School, Quantico, when most of the Marine Lieutenants on Operation Utah were trained as new second lieutenants)) was the task force commander and Kilo, Mike and Charlie provided the artillery support. Kilo and Mike are credited with seventy percent of the casualties, which totals now (I hear) over a thousand KIAs, and laid down the largest continuous fire barrage for 155 mms Hows since Korea. In two hours between 0500-0700 on Saturday morning Kilo and Mike fired over a thousand rounds a piece supporting an ARVN battalion and 2nd Battalion, 7th Marines who were under heavy attack by the PAVN (Peoples Army of Vietnam). Not only did our fires break up the attack, but they counted for some estimated four hundred KIAs. Of our support General Platt made the comment that he had now found HIS artillery in Kilo and Mike; he loves the 55s and intends to use them in preference to any other artillery support. I can say that we have every right to be proud, because for four full days everyone really put forth a maximum effort.

One of the reasons Operation Utah was such a success is because of the speed with which the intelligence was acted upon. Usually operations are a couple weeks in planning, and by the time they ever get underway everyone knows about them, and the VC make their bird. Starlight was an overnight affair as was Utah. This Operation Double Eagle, however, which received so much publicity, was actually a flop, simply because it surprised no one. Saturday, for example, we will move to our new position and begin firing preparations for Operation Montana, which will probably flop because it's been too long on the planning table. To engage the VC in force it is a necessity to surprise them, catch them completely unawares…

During the night of March 4/5 Marine supporting arms played a large role in staving off the NVA and inflicting heavy casualties after 2/7 consolidated near Chau Nhai (4). This opened up some space for the artillery and air to operate. An Air Force AC-47 arrived on station and dropped flares. Marine jets continued to strike at suspected enemy positions with bombs, rockets, and napalm, while A4s from MAG-1 2 made high altitude, radar-controlled bombing strikes on enemy trail networks leading into the battle area.

Artillery kept pace with the air effort during the night and early morning hours of 4-5 March. Both 155mm howitzer batteries at Binh Son, Batteries K and M, 4th Battalion, 11th Marines, fired in support of the Marines and the ARVN airborne battalion further to the north. The Marine artillerymen expended so many rounds that two ammunition resupply truck convoys from Chu Lai were required to replenish the stock. Once they arrived at Binh Son the trucks backed up to the M109s and the rounds were unloaded directly into the guns.

Just as the second convoy arrived at Binh Son shortly after 0500, the North Vietnamese launched a major attack against the 1st ARVN Airborne Battalion's defensive position near Hill 50. Major Elmer N. Snyder, at that time Task Force Delta operation's officer, asked the artillery liaison officer to call for "…maximum fires on the four grid squares that comprised the battlefield…" In the largest single fire mission yet conducted in the Chu Lai area, the two Binh Son batteries, reinforced by an ARVN 155mm gun battery at Quang Ngai, fired 1,900 rounds in two hours. That required each 155mm howitzer crew to fire more than one round per minute and keep that up for two hours!

If you were in the gun crew inside an M109 mobile howitzer, you would be slinging around heavy 97 lb. howitzer shells, setting fuses, loading propelling charges, all within the stifling and ear-shattering confines of the M109. Although there were gas deflectors on the muzzles, some exhaust would still come back into the M109. It was a Herculean task to fire that many rounds for that many hours!

As 1st Lieutenant Roach was winding down his FDC on 7 March, he was surprised to see Capt. Pete Dawkins and his 1st ARVN Airborne Battalion Commander stop by to thank his FDC and the Gun Line for their support. Dawkins credited the artillery for saving their Battalion and changing the course of battle. While the artillery Marines appreciated this visit from Capt. Dawkins and the ARVN Battalion Commander, they would have gotten a very different reception from the rifle battalions who suffered so many casualties as a result of their misinformation and lack of support.

Except for the short round that hit the Bravo Company 1/7 perimeter, when the ARVN 155s were registering their mission, the fire was extremely accurate. Considering that this was the first engagement of Kilo Battery 4/11, who landed in Vietnam at the end of February, their baptism under fire was extremely successful. They had only a few days to unload their equipment after the sea voyage from Okinawa, unpack, inventory, test and coordinate networks with various command groups like infantry, air and helicopters. The overnight frag orders did not give their planners any time to survey the site at Binh Son for the best firing positions and contingency plans if they were attacked. The men who had just landed after a sea voyage from Okinawa were still acclimatizing to the heat and humidity of Vietnam and were pushed to their maximum physical limits during these four days. Artillery support for Operation Utah was complicated since there were three different target areas at close to maximum range, interaction with jets and helicopters for air space, and coordination with the ARVN battery firing from Quang Ngai in the south and 4/11 firing from the North. Most of the fighting was at close range with no clear front lines which left no margin for error. Capt. Lindauer, who was in Fox Company on the left flank of 2/7 which was most exposed to friendly fire from Binh Son, later was quoted as saying: "You can tell Jim Black (Capt. James O. Black, Commander, Battery M, 4/11) he was right on the money." The same could be said of Kilo Battery. General Platt also had high praise for 4/11's performance on Operation Utah.

The use of supporting arms, artillery and airstrikes, were key to the Marine Corps' success in this battle. The artillery accounted for a significant percentage of the enemy killed and helped save the lives of countless US and allied forces. Unfortunately, the body counts that resulted became the standard for measuring success. This success bolstered the military's belief that supporting arms would help them win the war of attrition. Field artillery was a significant factor in almost every successful battle in Vietnam. However, as we know the war of attrition did not win the war. We were fortunate that we were not on the receiving end of these weapons.

Chapter 17
Corpsman Up!

During the Vietnam War, 10,000 Navy Hospital Corpsman served with their Marine brothers. 645 of them were killed in action and 3,300 were wounded in action. A Marine Infantry Battalion, may have up to two medical officers (MO) and 65 Corpsmen to support 1,000 Marines. When deployed in combat operations, there are usually two corpsmen assigned to each rifle platoon. Corpsmen train as soldiers as well as medical technicians, and serve alongside the Marines and are their first responders when injuries occur. Combat Marines respect their Corpsmen and know that whenever they need medical attention from heatstroke or open sores to the messiest gut shot, "Doc" will be there for them. Doc may also be their last human contact before they die. On Operation Utah, four corpsmen were killed, three of them supporting Hotel Company 2nd Battalion 7th Marines. What follows is taken primarily from the recollections of Gary Watkins who was the only corpsman in Hotel Company who survived Operation Utah.

In Vietnam, the corpsmen did not have any designation like a Red Cross which they wore in previous wars. In modern warfare, the Red Cross would more likely identify them as a valuable asset for targeting. They carried a .45 cal pistol and experienced life in the field like any other grunt. Some carried a rifle, more as a prop, so that a sniper would not single them out as an officer grade target and some corpsmen took on a dual role as rifleman and corpsman.

The main difference between corpsmen and Marines when they went into battle is that they were focused on saving lives rather than destroying life. It is a much greater challenge to bind up a shattered body than to pull a trigger. It is also much more personal. When you are face-to-face with someone who is dying and looking to you for comfort and assurance. They are also more aware of the carnage and gore of war since they worked with it up to their elbows. Often they were called to triage the wounded, making the judgment as to who they should work to save and who was too far gone to care for. Corpsmen were also more exposed to enemy fire since the men who they attended were usually in exposed positions. Enemy soldiers, who saw when someone was hit, would target that area, knowing that other Marines and corpsmen would come to their aid. Some corpsmen would seek an opportunity to engage in combat like Doc Hastriter of India Company who became very proficient with the M20 bazooka and the M72 LAW disposable rocket.

In addition to their combat gear, they carried a medical pack with bandages to control hemorrhaging, treat sucking chest wounds, infuse IV's and morphine to treat pain. With these rudimentary tools, corpsmen were expected to salvage some of the most horrendous wounds that can be inflicted on a human being.

Wounds from high velocity assault rifles like the AK-47 are gruesome. A high velocity bullet creates a blast wave as it travels through the body. It pushes tissues and organs aside in a temporary cavity larger than the bullet itself. Then the tissue bounces back once the bullet passes. Organs are damaged, blood vessels rip, and many victims bleed to death before they reach a hospital. Those who survive long enough are whisked to operating rooms but often the injuries cannot be repaired. Bullets striking bone also cause bone fragments and bullet shards that radiate outward like an exploding grenade, cutting tissue in each fragment's path. Typically, the entry wound appears to be small and may have little bleeding, giving the impression of a minor wound. But the internal trauma and the massive exit wound is much more destructive, particularly if the bullet happened to yaw, tumble or shatter into multiple pieces. I was in a mess line one day with a medical officer when someone dropped a tray of food on the ground. The medical officer commented on how this was like seeing wounded men coming into an OR. How do you pick up the pieces, clean them up and sort it out to how it was before?

At Utah, the NVA, also had a number of heavy 12.7mm machine guns which were used to take down aircraft as well as inflict damage to humans over a mile away. The 12.7mm is equivalent to the US .50 cal Machine gun. The 12.7mm round weighs 46 grams versus 8 grams for the AK-47 rifle. At Utah, an F4 Phantom jet on a napalm run and several helicopters were brought down by the 12.7mm machine guns. Several Marines were also killed by the 12.7mm round. Being hit by a 12.7mm was like being hit by a cannon.

The other weapons that inflicted a tremendous amount of damage were explosive devices like grenades, mortars and land mines. The NVA used 60mm and 82mm Mortars that could also be used to fire US 81mm mortar rounds. Land mines were also embedded around built up positions. While flak jackets afforded some protection against explosion fragments, men would lose chunks of flesh to exposed areas like the arms, legs, and faces. The Marines in Operation Utah wore flak jackets, but flak jackets were not designed to stop assault rifles. The flak jackets proved useful at Utah where the fighting was at close range with grenades and mortars.

A rifleman is looking for someone to shoot and is acutely aware of who is around him and who might be a danger to him; Corpsmen are so focused on going to someone's aid that they often forget that others are shooting at them. An example of this was shown by Hospital Corpsman Robert William Matticks who was attached to Golf Company 2/7 on March 4 when they were caught out in an open rice field by machine guns and automatic weapons fire. The NVA were entrenched in fortified bunkers and an adjoining trench line concealed behind a hedgerow. Observing a wounded Marine lying helpless only about six feet in front of one of the enemy machine gun emplacements, Corpsman Matticks immediately crawled to his side. Completely exposed to the withering fire, he administered first aid and pulled the wounded man to safety. Hearing a call for medical aid from a position on the opposite side of the bunker, he again exposed himself to the murderous enemy fire. With the Viet Cong fire only inches above him, he crawled in front of the machine gun position again, then passed the bunker to reach and give medical assistance to another Marine casualty. His uncommon concern for others at great risk to his own life enabled the wounded men to receive immediate medical care. Any Marine rifleman who would have been able to get as close to the NVA as Matticks did, would have tried to toss a grenade into the bunker to take them out, but Matticks had different priorities. However, for his actions he was awarded a Silver Star.

The corpsmen assigned to Hotel Company 2nd Battalion 7th Marines suffered the greatest casualties during Operation Utah when they were overrun on Hill 37. Gary Watkins and Samuel Orlando were corpsmen assigned to 3rd Platoon of Hotel Company. Their fellow corpsmen—Lawrence Johnson and Daniel Birch—were assigned to 2nd Platoon Hotel Company. Both platoons had been in reserve when they were called up to assault a ridgeline where the NVA were threatening to overrun the battalion's right flank. 3rd Platoon under 1st Lieutenant Harry Ketchum was able to reach the crest of the ridge line on the left and establish a position overlooking the backside of the ridge. 2nd Platoon, led by Staff Sergeant McDermit also reached the crest of the ridge on the right flank but immediately ran into heavy automatic fire and could not find any cover on the right side of the ridgeline. The ground was hard and impossible to dig into for cover. The air was filled with incoming NVA 12.7mm machine gun and AK-47 rounds and exploding 60 MM mortar rounds. In addition, the noise of exploding napalm, the ripping sound of Gatling guns and 500 lbs. bombs from US and South Vietnamese jets made it impossible for the radio operators to communicate on their radios. The lack of communication added to the chaos and confusion of battle. Both platoons took heavy casualties and three of the corpsmen were killed.

Corpsman Daniel Patrick Birch, whose girlfriend in Los Angeles, had recently confirmed the birth of their son was the first to be killed. He had been awarded a Bronze Star the month before. While working with 2nd Platoon, he had taken a direct hit from a North Vietnamese 60 MM mortar round, removing much of the left side of his face, his left forearm, and tore multiple holes in his chest. After tying him back together with combat bandages and a tourniquet, Doc Watkins, along with Maples, a Marine from 3rd Platoon, carried him on a poncho, off the hill, to a medical LZ, below. At the landing zone there already were 18 dead Marines, wrapped in their ponchos, their boots sticking out. They were from Fox Company. Their abandoned gear was scattered around the landing zone. As Maples and Watkins pushed their way through the stalks of a sugar cane field at the base of the hill, toward the landing zone, a medical evacuation chopper was attempting to land. Suddenly the chopper's windshield was exploded by a 12.7mm machine gun, firing from a rice stalk covered bunker, several hundred yards away between the landing zone and 2/7's command and medical position. The windshield-less UH-34, immediately lifted off the landing zone.

Realizing how close they were to the NVA machine gun, Sergeant Brown from Fox Company ordered Doc Watkins to triage the wounded from Hotel and Fox companies and move them to shelter in a grove of coconut palms near 2/7's command post where they had a better chance of being evacuated. Gary protested that he had to return to the hill where the 2nd and 3rd Platoons of Hotel Company were battling for their lives. But he was ordered to carry the Fox Company Commander, Captain Lindauer who was seriously wounded with a left arm that had been shattered by a 12.7mm round. Captain Lindauer also had other wounds in his legs. Gary gathered up 10 other wounded Marines. One of the Marines from 2nd Platoon, had part of his forearm blown off and a sucking chest wound, but somehow despite his grave injuries, assisted Gary and two other Marines in carrying Captain Lindauer to the new medical landing zone. Gary was not sure who the Marine with the missing arm was, but thought he was Lance Corporal Klaus Jurgen Herms who was an immigrant from Gleiwitz, Poland. There was one psychologically wounded marine, who was in a fetal position against a dike being penetrated by 12.7mm tracer rounds which blasted through the paddy dykes like bolts of lightning. Gary told him, "You can join us if you want but we are saddling up."

Gary made one final check on Doc Birch and seeing that he was still alive, but not having the manpower to take him, he gave Birch a shrug and moved off without him. Both men knew that Birch was being triaged, and it was one of the hardest decisions that Gary had to make. Gary led his little band of survivors toward the battalion command post. They hugged the surface of the rice paddy water as close as they could with the 12.7mm rounds snapping by their ears, their boots sucking into the mud in the rice paddies, with the psychologically-wounded Marine staggering behind. They finally made it to the headquarters and medical squad's position, among the coconut palms. However, within minutes, when a medevac chopper attempted to land, eight or ten 60mm mortar rounds came pounding down onto the landing zone, killing several more Marines, including some of the wounded Marines who had helped evacuate the more seriously wounded from the previous landing zone. The Marine with the missing arm and the sucking chest wound was killed by this round of mortars before he could be evacuated. The medical evacuation was suspended for several hours while 2/7 mortars tried to neutralize the NVA Mortars. When Doc Watson was finally able to go back for Doc Birch, Corpsman Birch was dead.

Hospitalman Lawrence Everett Johnson was assigned to 2nd Platoon on Operation Utah along with Doc Birch. Shortly after 2nd Platoon came under heavy mortar and automatic weapons fire, Doc Birch was hit and evacuated, leaving Doc Johnson to cope with the mounting casualties. Doc Orlando came up from the 3rd Platoon to help and the two corpsmen moved from one casualty to another, rendering aid and comfort and supervising the evacuation. When one of the squad leaders was seriously wounded, Johnson attempted to keep the man alive by administering mouth to mouth resuscitation while moving the patient some three hundred yards under fire to the point of evacuation.

2nd Platoon was eventually overrun but was able to consolidate with the 3rd Platoon and repulse the NVA. During the subsequent counter attack, Johnson saw three Marines from 3rd Platoon cut down in a cross fire of automatic weapons. Despite the on-rushing NVA, Johnson attempted to go to their aid, but was struck down by the automatic fire. A squad leader, Sergeant Ruiz, from 3rd Platoon crawled to Johnson's aid and attempted to drag him back. Johnson's last words to Sergeant Ruiz were, "It's alright. Don't be afraid, Sergeant Ruiz."

Many of the Marines who were saved by Johnson remember his calm and reassuring presence as he rendered aid to them. He seemed unconcerned about the bullets and mortars flying around them and made small talk to put them at ease. He seemed unconcerned about his own safety. Even more important than the medical aid, the bandages and morphine, he helped to calm their fears by concentrating on the fact that they were alive and about to be evacuated to safety. His last words to Sergeant Ruiz were indicative of his demeanor: "Don't be afraid, Sergeant Ruiz."

HM3 Lawrence Everett Johnson was posthumously, awarded the Silver Star for his actions on Operation Utah. Doc Johnson had joined the Navy when he was 17 and was a 9 year veteran and was one of the older members of the battalion at age 26. Johnson was married to Shirley Soltis Hayes Johnson who was 19 at the time, and was the father of Corinna Marie Johnson of Binghamton, New York.

Johnson's wife, Shirley, was living with her in-laws while he was overseas. It was 8 March 1966, in the afternoon, she was putting her daughter down for a nap and was removing her shoes. That was when she saw two men in uniform come to her door. They asked to see Mrs. Lawrence Johnson and she knew why they were there. That day, Shirley learned the news of her husband's death by gunshot wounds to the head, near the village of Quang Ngai, on March 4, 1966. He was the fifth man from Broome County to be lost in the Vietnam War and the first married man, according to news reports. Circumstances surrounding Johnson's death troubled Shirley, as details were unclear and often jumbled. Johnson had been scheduled for R&R in Japan and should not have been in combat at the time of his death, she said.

Johnson's father, Everett T. Johnson, was a World War I Veteran, and was in poor health. He cried all the next day and on 10 March, he died of a heart attack at home in Binghamton, less than an hour after calling The Evening Press newspaper to make a statement in honor of his late son.

Reporter Bob Dolan recorded Johnson's tribute to his son:

> He was not a fighter. His duty was to save the lives of all, both friend and enemy. He cried when he left us six months ago. He was shot down that he might no longer minister to the wounded and the sick of our marines in battle.

Everett T. Johnson was a veteran like his son. And so, the grieving family held a double military funeral, with two caskets, draped with American flags, resting side by side.

Samuel Gizzi Orlando joined the Navy when he was 17 and had over 4 years of Naval Service when he was killed on Operation Utah. Doc Orlando and his fellow corpsman and good friend Gary Watkins had the same type of humor and Watkins was like an older brother. They were both a little irreverent, but always there when they were needed. When they first landed in Vietnam, Orlando got in trouble for discharging his .45 cal pistol in the battalion area. He was also in trouble with the 1st Sergeant, who was getting letters from a jewelry store in Oceanside, California claiming that Orlando was late in making payments on a ring he'd bought before he shipped out to Vietnam. Considering everything that was going on, Orlando didn't think that mailing money orders was a high priority. Orlando was interested in all activity surrounding each mission and was constantly asking questions. Orlando had an older brother who had won a Bronze Star in Korea and he talked about him often. Watkins and Orlando always shared a fighting hole at night. What bothered Watkins about Orlando was that he always took his boot off when he slept. Watkins always kept his boots on to avoid having any snakes crawling in his boots or rats crawling up his pant legs. He also wanted to be ready in case they were attacked during the night. Orlando and Gary Watkins had bantered for months about battlefield heroics without any reflection of when and if it came to that, how they would react.

On Operation Utah, Doc Orlando was assigned to 3rd Platoon, Hotel Company along with Doc Watkins. When they were waiting for the helicopters to take them into Utah, His platoon sergeant, Frank Picon, noticed him writing with a stick in the sand and when he looked at what Orlando had written, he saw: "Mrs. Jones your son

189

is dead. He got shot in the head." Frank called him on that and said, "Don't be saying such things!" Orlando passed it off, but Frank wondered ever since if Orlando had had a premonition of what was going to happen to him.

When 3rd Platoon began their advance on their hill objective, Doc Orlando was able to reach the crest of the ridgeline and set up a position overlooking the valley beyond. Unfortunately, the 2nd Platoon on the right flank of 3rd Platoon ran into stiff resistance, and was pinned down by automatic weapons and mortars, taking heavy casualties. Seeing that the 2nd Platoon needed assistance, Orlando left his position of relative safety and moved across the barren hill to aid the 2nd Platoon. 2nd Platoon and 3rd Platoon were separated by a stretch of barren ground that was covered by enemy machine guns and mortars and any attempt to cross that stretch was suicidal. Doc Orlando made that crossing time and time again. He dressed many wounds and helped evacuate casualties making many daring trips across the fire swept hillside. When the 2nd Platoon Corpsman Birch was hit by a mortar and evacuated, the work became even more intense as the casualties continued to mount. On one of the trips back up the hill, he heard the call for more machine gun ammunition and he quickly gathered up the additional load and carried them to the machine gun position which was under intense fire. By this time the 2nd Platoon area was about to be overrun, and the men were told to pass through the 3rd Platoon lines where they could consolidate their remaining resources. Hearing the cries of wounded Marines, Orlando crawled forward to make one more attempt to render aid and was killed by mortar fragments. Dusk had fallen and Hotel Company was ordered to withdraw to their night position. Orlando's body was so far ahead of the perimeter that his body was left on the field of battle.

The next morning, the hill where all the carnage occurred was eerily quiet. The NVA had occupied the ridgeline during the night and Hotel Company was ordered to retake it. They found that the NVA had gathered their dead and wounded and withdrawn. The mission now was to find our missing Marines and corpsmen and bring them home. Fortunately, all the missing men were found, but many of them had been shot multiple times. Gary found Doc Orlando's body lying in a bomb crater. His wallet, watch, and ring were gone. Although he had been hit by mortar fragments his body had also been shot many times. Gary imagines that Orlando would have faced his attackers and cussed them out with his last breath as they shot him. Samuel Gizzi Orlando was awarded the Navy Cross for his actions on March 4, 1966.

During Operation Utah, every unit was heavily engaged and under heavy fire at close range with often less than a few meters separating the combatants. This made it especially hazardous for corpsmen to go to the aid and rescue of their Marines. With Marine and corpsman casualties of 98 killed and 247 wounded, every corpsman distinguished themselves with uncommon valor. Here are just a few of the other corpsmen that were recognized for their heroics.

Hospital Corpsman Third Class James Layton French was serving as a Corpsman attached to Headquarters and Service Company, 2nd Battalion, 7th Marines on 4 March 1966. During Operation UTAH, Hospital Corpsman French was assigned to help organize an aid station site to receive casualties resulting from the vicious battle. For more than twelve hours, while repeatedly subjected to deadly hostile sniper and mortar fire, he worked tirelessly to administer first aid and give comfort to the steady flow of wounded Marines. Exposing himself to enemy fire, he personally carried many patients to helicopter evacuation zones, and on one hazardous trip was painfully wounded in the knee by fragments from an exploding Viet Cong mortar round. Doc French refused treatment and continued to load the evacuees and gave first aid to new casualties.

He boarded a helicopter late that night to provide special care for a severely wounded Marine. Realizing that the battalion was in dire need of medical supplies, he returned to the aid station on the next available flight with the necessary medicines. Still ignoring his own suffering, he remained with his unit and administered aid until he was finally evacuated with the last of the casualties. By his uncommon concern for the welfare of others at his own expense, coupled with exceptional courage and unfaltering dedication to duty, Hospital Corpsman French was awarded the Silver Star.

Hospitalman Tommy Roger Miller was a US Navy Corpsman, age 22, born May 7, 1943 from Laketon, Indiana. During the Vietnam War, Wabash County, Indiana lost sixteen men. The second young man to give his life for his country was Tommy R. Miller.

 Miller was born May 7, 1943, the son of Arden and Genevee Miller and spent most of his life in the sleepy little community of Laketon, Indiana. He went to school in Laketon and graduated from Laketon High School in 1961. There were 29 other people in his graduating class. He attended the United Brethren Church in Laketon. Like many youth in the 1960s he had a decision to make, serve his country or find a way out of it. In January of 1964 he made his decision by enlisting in the United States Navy. In basic training, Miller learned about the history of the Navy: its customs, drills, and basic seamanship, such as tying knots. He endured physical training, fighting fires and marching drills. He marched everywhere from the barracks to the chow hall to class and back to the barracks. In April, he completed basic training and was selected to become a hospital corpsman (HC). Miller packed up his duffel bag and headed to school at Great Lakes. After graduating from Hospital Corpsman School he was stationed at Naval Air Station, Point Mugu near Oxnard, California. In April of 1965 Miller, volunteered to go to Vietnam serving as a hospital corpsman assigned to the 2nd Battalion, 4th Marines (2/4). On March 5, 1966, during Operation Utah, Miller volunteered to assist corpsmen of another unit which was sustaining heavy casualties. He immediately rushed forward to aid a wounded Marine lying in a position exposed to heavy enemy fire. He then observed a wounded corpsman, also exposed to enemy fire from a distance of about 25 meters. He succeeded in reaching the wounded corpsman and began administering first aid when he was struck and mortally wounded by enemy fire. Corpsman Miller was

posthumously awarded a Bronze Star for his action on March 5, 1966.

The Bonds Between Corpsmen

The strongest bond was between the corpsmen as they were Navy and were usually paired up and assigned by teams to different platoons. When Corpsman Tommy Miller was assigned to 2/4 he landed in Chu Lai in May of 1965. He became good friends with Corpsman Michael Hastriter. Before long they were involved in Operation Starlite, their first major engagement. Operation Starlight was followed by Operation Double Eagle on January 28, 1966. It was during this operation that Miller met and struck up a friendship with another hospital corpsman, Carl Dunaway. As Michael Hastriter described it:

> He (Miller) was a very likable guy and he and I, along with other corpsmen, had this fraternity, almost, that we belonged to and we took it very personal when we lost one of them... We knew each other by name on sight. In Operation Double Eagle we were against the PAVN 18th Regiment, 325th Division. That operation scared everyone because the PAVN used Chinese tactics, bugles that were not done since the Korean War and they overran us.

Miller and Dunaway continued their friendship after Operation Double Eagle:

> Our conversations were always more along the lines of our job: How to do this and how to do that. I don't ever recall us talking about our life growing up or even our folks. A lot of our conversations were interrupted by gunfire and interruptions from various sergeants telling us to get up and move.

As a hospital corpsman, Miller had to treat so many other things than they would ever have to think of in the states.

We had guys with mold and fungus which grew under their arms and crotch. Tommy and I didn't get to sleep in a bed for probably six months. We slept on the ground. We wore the same clothes for most of that time also because we just couldn't pack several changes of clothes with us.

On Operation Utah, HC Dunaway was on his last mission. He and Hospital Corpsman Miller were in the third wave but in different choppers.

When we landed a firefight was already going on. I thought we were surrounded. We basically got ambushed as my diary described it. I think I was kneeling, trying to figure out which way to go when I heard someone behind me get hit. I heard my name called out which surprised me. Before I knew it and could turn around, he was thrown down on me. I thought it was just another Marine. I knew he had a head wound and probably dead or damn close to it. I also knew there wasn't anything I could do for him. I cradled his body, you know, not even knowing it was him because his face was so swollen and blue…the noise around me as I remember was so ungodly loud. Hundreds of weapons going off at the same time along with mortars, the choppers, and screaming. I pulled the man around and got him laying across my lap and searched for his dog tags. His face looked so bad. I had his blood down the back of my neck, all over my left side, and covering my lap. I looked at his dog tags and at that moment, it was like the whole world went quiet. I kept looking at his face wondering who this man was. I knew it couldn't have been the same Tommy Miller I knew. But it was. I think it was a few minutes later a couple of Marines pulled me away from there.

The Bonds Between Corpsmen and Marines

The bonds between the Marines and Corpsmen are also very strong even if they didn't know each other by name. Doc Donald Reyerson was the 1st Platoon Corpsman in Lima Company on Operation Utah.

I always knew when I heard "Corpsman Up" that the Marines around me would be giving me covering fire so I could go to work. It sounds funny to say, but I was never afraid, knowing the guys in the platoon had my back.

That Saturday on Hill 50, is still fresh in my memory. We had started around the base of the hill when I heard the first AK-47 fire, and real quick a call for a corpsman came from toward the top of the hill. I started up the hill, working my way through the scrub brush. There were several wounded nearby, and as far as I know I was the only corpsman up there. The first Marine had a really bad head wound and two Marines suddenly were by my side to move him out.

The next Marine had a belly wound, and I was struggling to turn him over when Bartlett (radioman) came to help me. He had a tall whip antenna on the radio which the NVA saw and opened fire. Bartlett was hit in the leg, and I was not, even though I was literally inches from him. Something knocked me forward over the wounded man and then Bartlett fell over me.

Sometime right after Bartlett was moved out I heard another shout for a corpsman. Gary Harlan and Gary Hester had found Lieutenant Cleaver in the underbrush, with him sustaining a serious chest wound. Harlan and Hester stood over me while I worked on Lieutenant Cleaver and they then moved him into the evac choppers.

I heard Dave Ubersox (weapons platoon corpsman) call for help. I was able to find him but it was too hot to stay where we were as grenades were being lobbed back and forth. Dave was able to crawl, and we decided to work our way up to the hilltop where there were some ARVN troops. Partway up the hill I decided to look at Dave's leg wound when he saw that a single NVA had followed us. Dave saw him and yelled "VC! VC! VC!" I began to roll to my left while pulling my .45 which I had in a shoulder holster, knowing that it was probably hopeless. The NVA got off a burst, wounding Dave a second time, and then I heard a long burst from an M14 ending things. The NVA had been so close that when he was shot he fell right at our feet. Doc Ubersox had been shot in the foot as he raised it to ward off the NVA. I don't know where that Marine came from, and I cannot remember his name, but he saved both our lives, without a doubt. I can still picture his face, and I believe he was a squad leader in Lima Company.

Doc Reyerson survived 5 March, and at the end of the day he was ready to eat his C-rations. When he opened his backpack, he found a gooey mess. Sometime during the day a round had shattered the entrenching tool on his backpack and destroyed the C-rations inside: ham and lima beans and beefsteak and potatoes. Since beefsteak and potatoes was his favorite, he picked out the pieces of metal and ate the rest of it. He kept the entrenching tool as a reminder of that day and it still hangs on the wall in his office. Doc Reyerson was always grateful to all the Marines that watched over him in combat.

Thanks to the efforts of the Corpsmen and medical staff of the Navy, of the 278 Marines wounded on Operation Utah, only three men later died of their wounds once they were evacuated. An article in Military Medicine, 165, 5:362, 2000 examined the question "Why Is Marine Combat Mortality Less Than That of the Army?" Data from recent wars, going back to World War II, indicate that a wounded Marine had a 20% lower risk of dying than an Army soldier. During the Vietnam War, one of the hypotheses was that the Navy's combat casualty care was superior to the Army's. During this time a Navy corpsman received months of training compared with only weeks for Army medics.

In addition, corpsmen had the opportunity to use their better training out of necessity. Because Marines were often in intense combat situations where they could not depend on the immediate availability of helicopter evacuation, corpsmen were forced to rely on their better training in battlefield first aid skills rather than the rapid "scoop and run" approach that was the Army's de facto field medical tactic. The extra time they had to care for and console a gravely wounded Marine may have done more to save their life. In fact, the Wound Data and Munitions Effectiveness Team study from the Vietnam War indicates that the Marine evacuation times were almost double those of the Army, and yet the mortality rates for wounded Marines were less. I also believe this is due to the special bond between Marines and Navy Corpsmen in combat situations.

****

A great deal of the information I have gathered about Operation Utah have come from the corpsmen. They seemed to have a broader perspective and awareness of what was going on around them, and afterwards they seemed to be more introspective.

As a Marine who fought in battles and saw men killed and wounded in combat, I have the utmost respect and gratitude for the corpsmen who were the first responders. Although I was fortunate not to need their services in combat, I was comforted that they were there for us. They saw the worst of the carnage and I have always been amazed at how they have been able to cope with these experiences; I am surprised that more have not been devastated by PTSD. Most of the corpsman I've known have gone on to have very successful careers and continued to contribute to society with the same care and concern that they demonstrated in combat.

Doc Donald Reyerson left the Navy and decided to pursue a medical career at age 21. He enrolled at Iowa State University and later was accepted in Iowa University Medical School. During his interview for medical school, his interviewer spent most of the time asking about his Vietnam experience. Reyerson felt that helped him get accepted into the program. He interned at the Mayo Clinic and has been a pediatric physician for over 30 years at the time of this writing.

Chapter 18
"Ski, the Bastard Shot Me!"

I have interviewed many Marines who were wounded in different battles and it is difficult for many to describe what happened, how it felt and what the process of treatment and recovery was like. I found that this was best communicated by a corpsman who was also one of the wounded.

HM3 Bob Ingraham served with 3rd Battalion, 1st Marines. On the second day of Operation Utah. Ingraham was seriously wounded in the ensuing battle for Hill 50. Bob Ingraham is a prolific blogger who has created the Ephemeral Treasures website (https://www.ephemeraltreasures.net) where he describes his experiences in the Vietnam War. What follows is his first hand description of how it feels to be wounded, the process of being treated in the field and the long painful steps of his recovery.

Second LT [Eugene] Cleaver, our platoon leader, was hit by a heavy-caliber shell that almost blew his right arm off at the shoulder. A rifleman had the top of his head blown off by a rifle or machine gun bullet. A 3rd Platoon sergeant sustained a pumping chest wound. Enemy soldiers we couldn't even see tossed grenades over the high, dense brush that surrounded us; a Marine hugging the ground next to me during a grenade attack was put out of action by a piece of shrapnel that pierced his buttocks.

After doing what little I could for LT Cleaver and the sergeant, I was told that a wounded Marine was farther up the hill. I soon found him. His abdomen had been blown open and his intestines were spilling out onto the ground. Amazingly, he was still conscious and seemed relatively calm. I was just beginning to consider what I could do to help him when a Marine further down the hill yelled, "I'm gonna throw a grenade over you guys! I'm gonna get that sniper!" I didn't want to be killed by a Marine grenade, but as I started to hit the dirt I heard a loud gunshot to my right. In the same instant I was slammed to the ground by a bullet. The bullet hit me on the right side of my right leg about 6 inches above the knee. It shattered the femur and blasted out through my inner thigh. It was like a really big sledge hammer had hit me. I don't remember falling; I was just instantly knocked flat. I knew I had been shot. I noticed that my foot seemed to be on backwards. Then I shouted: "Ski, the bastard shot me!" Ski, another corpsman, had been nearby when I was shot.

I had enough strength to lower my fatigue pants to examine the wound. The bullet had left a blue-rimmed hole on my outer thigh. It was about a third of an inch in diameter, roughly the diameter of a 7.62mm M14 or AK-47 round, and was hardly bleeding. (One North Vietnamese soldier who was killed that morning had been using an M14.) On my inner thigh was a patch of mangled flesh a few inches in diameter where the bullet, or what was left of it, had exited my thigh. It looked like fresh hamburger meat. Just a trickle of blood oozed from it; my femoral artery had apparently escaped damage. I could wiggle my toes: I had no major nerve damage. In case I started bleeding heavily, I removed my belt and put it around my thigh to use as a tourniquet, but I was quickly losing strength and couldn't tighten it. Fortunately, I didn't need a tourniquet. I tried to give myself some morphine, which we corpsmen carried in our Unit 1 medical bags, but I was so rattled that I forgot to puncture the seal of the foil syrette. When I tried to inject myself, the tube burst in my hand. It was the only syrette I had.

The battle was still going full blast. Nearby, a hidden rifleman continued to shoot, and I assumed he was the one who had shot me. I could hear him operating his rifle bolt. Rockets and grenades were exploding and the sound of rifle and machine gun fire was constant. It seemed that every time an enemy rifle fired, a Marine screamed. I began to fear a "human wave" attack, so I took out my .45 pistol and held it on my chest, determined to kill the first Vietnamese I saw. Eventually, a Marine crawled up the hill to try to help us: he was shot through the shoulder. So now there were three of us lying there. The Marine with the open abdominal wound kept asking me if he was going to die. I tried to reassure him, but I don't know to this day whether he lived. Another Marine crawled up the hill to help us and was also shot. It wasn't long before I was almost completely incapacitated, not so much by pain but by extreme discomfiture, for want of a better word. The sun was high overhead and intense. My thighs were getting seriously sunburned. (I had not been able to pull my pants back up after lowering them to see my wound.) I was sweating profusely. My skin became ultra-sensitive to touch. Even small bits of debris falling out of the sky from explosions resulted in pain. My entire body began to vibrate. It was as if every cell in my being was charged with electricity. It's hard to describe, but maybe there aren't any words for what I was feeling. Soon I began getting painful cramps in the muscles of not only my wounded leg, but my good leg as well.

A corpsman eventually reached us and managed to put a battle dressing on me. The shooting had slowed by then. Finally, I was half-carried, half-dragged down the hill on my poncho. I screamed every time my butt hit a bump. I don't think I'd been given any morphine. With every bump, I could feel the shattered ends of my femur grating inside my thigh. I feared they would cause more bleeding. At the base of Hill 50, helicopters were starting to arrive to evacuate the wounded. I talked with the Marines. One Marine was crying. His best friend had just been killed before his eyes. I asked someone to take a picture of me, and I took one of him. The picture of me shows me holding my helmet tight to my head. I recall being afraid as bullets were still flying. Eventually I was flown to a nearby field hospital. The corpsmen bandaged my wound more thoroughly, immobilized my leg in a splint, and packed me off to the hospital ship, USS Repose.

I don't remember arriving on the Repose, but recall lying on a gurney in a dark passageway for what seemed an endless period. It must have been late afternoon or early evening when surgeons finally operated on me. My femur was badly fractured. An x-ray shows shattered pieces of bone and fragments of the bullet lodged in my muscles. The exit wound on my inner thigh told just part of the story. The muscle for several inches around the exit wound—and all the way down to the femur—had been turned to pulp by the bullet and had to be excised. Skin and some muscle around the entrance wound had to be trimmed away as well. I received two units of whole blood during the surgery. When I left the OR, I had some new hardware—a threaded steel rod that went completely through my right shin about 6 inches below my knee. Later, it would be used as an anchor point for traction, which would stretch my thigh muscles and hold my femur at its original length while it healed. Following surgery, the wounds were packed with cotton and thoroughly wrapped with bandaging. Next I was encased in plaster from my right foot all the way up to my armpits and down to my left shin. I was ready to be shipped home like a parcel.

I don't recall much about my short time on the Repose. I probably was getting morphine or Demerol regularly; I don't remember being in pain and I slept a great deal. I was probably also on antibiotics at this time. Any gunshot wound is a dirty wound by definition and subject to infection. A bar hung from a frame over my bed that I could chin myself on, but its main purpose was to make it easier for me to use a bedpan. However, it also allowed me to raise myself higher so I could see the ocean through a nearby porthole. The Repose steamed constantly in big circles, or so it seemed to me, but I have been told by a former Repose crewman that the ship sailed back and forth between Chu Lai and Da Nang.

I wrote a letter to my parents a day or two after the surgery. In handwriting even worse than my normal bad scrawl, I described the battle, explained how I was shot, and told them that my recovery would be long. I did not mention that I might lose my leg. I'm not sure that I myself was aware of just how serious my wound was. After 2 or perhaps 3 days on the Repose, I was flown to Danang. The next morning personnel bundled me on board a C-130 Hercules, which flew to Clark Air Force Base Hospital in the Philippines where I would stay overnight. I was able to talk to my parents from the hospital via a telephone-ham radio link. Until that call, they did not know I had been wounded. The next morning I was taken out to the airfield and put on a huge C-141 Starlifter. I recall little about that flight, but remember being in a huge, dark, noisy cavern filled with stretchers. Nurses and medics ran back and forth constantly. I had little pain but infections were raging in my wound and in my bladder. The bladder infection apparently came from a poor procedure when I was catheterized on the Repose. I assumed that most of the wounded on the Starlifter were Marines from Operation Utah, but not until years later would I learn just how bad the casualties were. Historical records are not in full agreement, but it is clear that at least 94 Marines were killed and some 278 were wounded. According to the 3rd Battalion's Combat Operation After Action Report dated 11 March 1966, 42 Marines were killed and at least 100 were wounded. Ten Lima Company Marines had been killed and 20 wounded, including myself.

The aircraft landed in Hawaii and an officer came on board to hand out Purple Hearts. My next memory is being at the hospital at Travis Air Force Base near San Francisco. A day later I had arrived back at the Naval Hospital at Balboa Park in San Diego where I had had my Hospital Corps training. I have fleeting memories of my arrival. I do remember very clearly, however, when corpsmen at Balboa removed my cast and the dressing from my wound. The blood-soaked cotton was firmly stuck to the wound. When the cotton was removed, it felt like flesh was being torn away. As soon as the cast came off, I was put into traction where I would be for the next 111 days. My infections slowly yielded to antibiotics, and skin grafts helped to prevent the formation of excessive scar tissue—but scarcely improved the appearance of my leg! Early in the summer I received another cast that kept my right leg immobilized but at least allowed me to hobble about on crutches. I also got my first liberty and had my first date with my fiancée, Susan Overturf, who had started writing to me when the 3rd Battalion was training in Okinawa. In August, I got a new, smaller cast just covering my right leg, and got my first leave home to New Mexico. Then it was back to San Diego for a few more months. Finally, late in 1966, I was fitted with an ischial weight-bearing brace and told that I would have to wear it for the rest of my life. That meant that I would never again be able to bear weight on my right leg, which could break easily and might not heal a second time. Instead, when I stood or walked, I would literally be "sitting" on the brace, bearing weight not on the leg but on the right ischial tuberosity, my "sit bone." The brace wasn't comfortable, but it gave me a lot of freedom. It was hinged at the knee so I could sit down. The brace was fitted with a special shoe which was permanently attached to it, until I needed new shoes. Very stylish.

I was finally discharged from the hospital in December and flown to the Veterans Administration Hospital in Kansas City, Missouri. Susan was already teaching in Kansas City, Kansas, and I planned to enroll at Kansas City campus of the University of Missouri. My transfer to the VA hospital came with good news. An orthopedic surgeon told me my brace was not necessary and that I should throw it away.

Susan and I were married on 27 December 1966. After our honeymoon, I began taking the brace off only while I was at home in our apartment. I eventually started going out without it. At first I had a deep limp — the muscles in my right leg had atrophied and could not easily support my weight. Soon, however, I was walking almost normally and eventually was able to enjoy hiking, running, and cross country skiing. The greater task I faced, although I did not know it at the time, was the task of putting Vietnam behind me.

I was unaware that combat veterans do not necessarily have the luxury of packaging the past and putting it away in a dusty attic. It turned out that my greatest challenge lay ahead—coping with the psychological trauma of combat. Some 46 years later, I was diagnosed with moderate combat-related Post-Traumatic Stress Disorder, or PTSD, adding a 20% disability rating to my previous 20% rating for my gunshot wound. In 2020, I was receiving about $1,000 a month in disability compensation. I can only guess — and shake my head — at the ongoing cost to American taxpayers for a war that was fought for 10 years to no purpose, a war which decimated its youth, exacerbated the Cold War, and created divisions in American society that last to this day."

****

Doc Bob Ingraham served 37 days in Vietnam before he was seriously wounded and nearly lost a leg to an AK-47. After he returned he attended University and became a teacher. He has also been a journalist and a professional photographer. He now lives in Canada and hosts a widely read website https://www.ephemeraltreasures.net which covers a wide range of interesting topic, including his experiences in Vietnam, and his many interests including astronomy, military history, propeller-driven airliners, philately, and chickens. While Bob Ingraham's narrative ends here, one would assume that he marries and goes on to have an interesting and satisfying career and lives happily ever after, which he does. While he has gone on to live a productive life, the physical effects of his wounds have limited his activities and as he faces his later years, he is limited in the choices he has to better his life such as a hip replacement which is impossible due to the amount of muscle and tissue which he lost when he was wounded.

Part 6
The Home Front

Chapter 19
The Family Bonds

amilies were an important part of most young Marine's lives. Most of us who grew up during that time fondly remember the family as the core of our existence. There were no fast-food restaurants and every evening we sat down as a family and shared our day's experiences around the dinner table. We were not rich, but we did not feel poor. Many of us grew up on a farm or worked in the family business with our parents and spent more time with our parents than we do today. Although we were chauvinistic and related more to our fathers, there was always a special connection to our mothers. I have heard dying Marines call out to their mothers with their last breath.

In 2020 I was contacted by Edward Wetzel who had read my post of my visit to Vietnam in 2016 and wanted to know if I knew his younger brother Chuck Wetzel who was in Hotel Company during Operation Utah. Unfortunately, I did not, since Chuck had only recently joined Hotel Company as a part of the weapons platoon. Ed and I have remained in contact and he has used his engineering skills to help me with validating the map locations for this book.

Ed also shared a memoriam to his brother which he wrote at the request of the New Jersey Vietnam Veterans' Memorial in Holmdel, NJ. Ed's memoriam reminded me about the family ties that many of us experienced and helped me to understand the effects on the family of losing a son and brother to combat. To help you understand what these bonds meant to these young Marines of 1966, I have attached Ed's memoriam as a snapshot into the family life of a young Marine who grew up during the 1950s and 1960s.

Chuck at Chu Lai Beach, December 1965

In Memoriam

Charles Robert Wetzel (Chuck) was born on December 24, 1945, into the small family of Edward Herman Wetzel and Caroline Ostair Wetzel (nee Soders) at Salem Hospital, Salem, New Jersey. His parents took Chuck home from the hospital to the small house they rented in Pennsville, New Jersey. Also, at home was Chuck's two-year-old brother, Edward, Jr. Chuck's mother was a homemaker in a time when most mothers were at home with their children. Chuck's father had enlisted in the US Army at age 16 during the Great Depression when no jobs were available. After some time in the Army, he worked in construction. During World War II he served at US Army training camps in the United States and then was shipped to Okinawa for the planned invasion of Japan just before the end of the war. After leaving the Army, Chuck's father was employed as a structural steel ironworker working on bridges and buildings.

Another brother, Budd, came along in 1947 and still another, Thomas, in 1948. When Chuck was about three years old, his parents moved the family to their new home on Old Wiley Road, Penns Grove, New Jersey that Chuck's father and maternal uncle, Budd, had built themselves. As life turned out for Chuck, this was the only home that he would ever really know.

Soon it was time to start school, and Chuck entered kindergarten at St. James Grammar School in Penns Grove. This was an old-fashioned parochial school where all the teachers and administrators were nuns wearing full habit. At St. James, discipline and responsibility were the most important subjects taught. These learned characteristics would both serve and haunt Chuck and his siblings throughout their lives.

Four Brothers, April 1955, LR - Thomas (age 6), Budd (age 7), Edward (age 11), Chuck (age 9)

Growing up in the Wetzel household in the 1950s was barely controlled chaos. By then there were four boys growing up separated in age by only five years. A sister, Edna May, joined the growing family in 1952, followed by another brother, John in 1954. The house was constantly filled with kids, cats, dogs and constant noise and sibling rivalry. Times were economically hard for the growing Wetzel family. Chuck's father had a seasonable job and was often without work through the winter weather. Hand-me-down clothes from cousins, cardboard patches in shoes with holes, delayed dental care and frustrated desires for the latest toys advertised on the new television programs were reality. Times were especially hard around Christmas when Chuck's father was usually unemployed. The service organizations like the Moose, VFW, and American Legion often helped out with Christmas food baskets and toys for the kids.

Chuck's mother was instrumental in instilling a sense of pride in her young family. She always assured us that other families had it really rough and were indeed poor. We were lucky and should always be aware that there were poor people in the world that we should care about. By the standards of middle-class society in 1950s America, we were indeed poor, but our mother shielded us from that realization.

The material hardships were more than compensated for by the tremendous opportunities for good clean fun in the outdoors. The family had only one car and when Chuck was small, our mother did not drive. Since we lived quite a distance from town out in the country, the children amused themselves with outdoor activities like exploring, swimming, raft building and building tree houses.

At eleven years of age, Chuck joined Boy Scout Troop 3 that was sponsored by the Union Presbyterian Church in Carneys Point, New Jersey. He enjoyed the camping, canoeing, and general good fun associated with Scouting. Camping trips and other activities were often shared with his brothers. Chuck enjoyed Scouting and achieved the third highest Scouting rank, Star Scout.

In 1960, Chuck graduated from St. James Grammar School and then entered St. James High School in Carneys Point. At this time Chuck achieved his full growth at six-feet-tall, about 170 lbs. with dark blond hair and blue eyes. Chuck played football in high school. His football coach said of him:

> Charley was as strong as an ox [...] as quiet as could be and in a sense was the shy type [...] a fine young man who I respected as an athlete for his courage and devotion to his task at hand. Never complaining, just doing his job and a man on the team that never spoke, but you knew all along he was there.

Chuck also worked after school helping out at a small one-man auto repair shop in town. Another brother, Paul, was born in 1962 while

Chuck was still in high school. Chuck graduated from St. James High School on June 8, 1964.

High School Graduation in 1964 with Mother and Father

Not planning on going to college and having no real job prospects, Chuck decided to enlist in the Marine Corps in July 1964, only one month after graduation. Up to this time, Chuck had not traveled more than 100 miles from home, so going to Marine boot camp at Parris Island, South Carolina was an exciting experience. Chuck completed boot camp without incident, was declared a full-fledged Marine and assigned to Camp Lejeune, North Carolina in September 1964. Chuck had only one leave home in November 1964 before his ultimate transfer to Vietnam. During this leave he made a point of visiting all his family and assuring them that he was happy with his decision to join the Marine Corps.

In early December, 1964, Chuck was transferred to Camp Pendleton, California for advanced infantry training. Chuck made several trips with fellow Marines to Los Angeles which he happily described to the family in his letters.

The political situation was heating up in South East Asia and on May 24, 1965, Chuck shipped out on the USS Pickaway from San

Diego, California. The ordinary Marines on the USS Pickaway had no idea where they were going. All they knew was that they had orders to pack their gear, load the ship and head out into the Pacific Ocean. On June 1, 1965, the USS Pickaway landed at Pearl Harbor, Hawaii. The Marines enjoyed three days liberty in Hawaii before boarding ship and heading for Okinawa in the far Pacific. Chuck arrived at Okinawa on June 18, 1965. It is not known whether Chuck knew that his father was on Okinawa only 19 years earlier.

After landing in Okinawa, orders were given to unload all the equipment from the USS Pickaway. Then orders were given to reload all their equipment onto the USS Okanogan. They set sail again into the Pacific Ocean about June 24, 1965. Again, the grunt Marines and probably even the officers on board had no idea what their real destination was to be. Somewhere in the far Pacific orders were received from Washington to proceed to Vietnam.

On July 7, 1965, the 2nd Battalion, 7th Marines aboard the USS Okanogan arrived at Qui Nhon in Vietnam. After an unopposed amphibious landing at Qui Nhon, Chuck's battalion operated roadblocks and checkpoints on National Route 1 and sent its infantry companies on patrol into the hills and valleys around Qui Nhon. The real mission of the unit was to provide security for the buildup of larger forces that the US Army was going to deploy through the port of Qui Nhon. Chuck served as a rifleman on many recon patrols and night ambushes but rarely saw any action or had a glimpse of the enemy. In his letters from this time, he spoke of the boredom, lack of hot food, the sudden terror of night actions, the torment of biting insects and the intense rain. Chuck asked his parents to send him hard candy, insect repellent for the bugs and steel wool to deal with the constant rusting of his rifle.

Chuck was hospitalized with malaria at the 85th Evacuation Hospital near Qui Nhon from about November 4 through December 10, 1965. In letters home during this period Chuck said that he was well cared for but expressed concern that "malaria can sometimes stay with you for the rest of your life." After he was released from the hospital, Chuck rejoined his battalion which had transferred to the Chu Lai enclave around November 12th.

When he rejoined the battalion, Chuck found that his company, Echo, had been transferred to another Marine division, the 4th Marine. Chuck was then reassigned to another company, Hotel

Company, in the battalion. The implication of this reassignment was that Chuck was in a new group of men that did not know him well, so he had to prove himself all over again.

Around the end of January 1966, Chuck volunteered for 60mm mortar training. He became a member of a team of nine men in a mortar section that handled two guns and provided general support to Hotel Company. Since Chuck was a PFC, he was designated as an ammunition carrier. The mortar team trained through about the middle of February and then participated in Operation Double Eagle Phase II. This operation lasted from February 19th through the 28th. Chuck wrote home that he did quite a lot of walking and his company was harassed by snipers all the time. He also wrote that he was "glad their fire wasn't very accurate, if it was, a lot more people would have been hurt."

The exhausted battalion returned to the Chu Lai enclave late in the afternoon of February 28 and the next day was back on the defensive perimeter at the base. Chuck took advantage of this relative down time to write what would be his last letters home on March 2nd. He made sure to answer every letter he had received and wrote a letter to everyone in the family. In all these letters Chuck assured everyone that he was reasonably healthy, proud to be a Marine and expected to arrive home safely in early summer.

Early on the morning of March 4, 1966, the battalion organized a helicopter air lift to a landing zone about nine miles northwest of Quang Ngai City near the small complex of hamlets that were collectively called Chau Nhai. The terrain encountered by the Marines was comparatively flat, unobstructed by obstacles or heavy foliage, dotted with rice paddies crisscrossed by hedgerows and overlooked by several nearby low hills. The first units into the landing zone were met by fierce enemy gunfire. In the course of the landing two helicopters were shot down in the landing zone and another about a mile away. By 1330, all the elements of Hotel Company had arrived and were employed in securing a hilltop overlooking the landing zone from which the enemy was raking the landing zone with heavy weapons fire. Around 1630, Hotel Company was ordered back to the vicinity of the landing zone to aid Fox Company which was desperately engaged with the enemy. Sometime during this brief time period, the war and life ended for

Chuck. The details of his death cannot be determined exactly due to the passage of many years and the chaotic nature of the engagement.

The Wetzel family was later notified of Chuck's fatal injuries via telegram, which partially stated:

I deeply regret to inform you that your son, Private First-Class Charles R. Wetzel, died March 4, 1966, in the vicinity of Quang Ngai, Republic of Viet Nam. He sustained a gunshot wound in the head while participating in an operation against hostile forces.

The telegram was signed by General Wallace M. Green Jr., Commandant of the Marine Corps.

The action of March 4, 1966, was graced several days later with the name Operation Utah. During this operation, the 2nd Battalion, 7th Marines and its attached support units suffered a loss of forty-four men killed in action and one man who died of his wounds. A total of 120 men were wounded, 79 of whom had to be evacuated out of Vietnam for treatment. Chuck's company, Hotel, suffered 21 KIA and at least 31 wounded out of a maximum of 150 men deployed. March 4, 1966 was a very bad day for Hotel Company.

At the time of his death at the age of 20, Chuck was survived by his parents, five brothers, one sister and his maternal grandmother. His older brother, Edward, age 22 was married with one child and a student at Rutgers University. His next younger brother, Budd, age 18 had just graduated from high school and enlisted in the Air Force the previous summer. Thomas, age 17 and sister, Edna May, age 13 were both in high school. John, age 11, was in grammar school and Paul, age 4, had not yet started school.

Chuck's mother was devastated by the loss of her son but had little time to spare for grief. She had to continue to try and maintain a healthy family atmosphere for the young children still at home. Her son's loss in Vietnam was the first casualty from the small town of Penns Grove, NJ. There were tremendous public displays of shock and concern and many people offered what emotional support they could. However, astonishingly at this early point in the Vietnam conflict, she had to endure the taunts of anonymous strangers expressing joy over the loss of her son because they did not support an increasingly unpopular war. In 1984 she had the sad pride of

213

seeing her son's name engraved on the newly completed Vietnam Veterans Memorial Wall in Washington, D.C. She endured it all, died in 1986 and is fondly remembered by her family as a pillar of strength. Chuck's father took his death so hard that it arguably contributed to his early death at 66 years in 1981. To the extent that a father can have a favorite son, Chuck was it. Being a WWII veteran, he was especially devastated by the controversy about the war at home, lack of sympathy about the loss of his son and the sometimes-cruel remarks he and his wife received from ignorant strangers. His basic life beliefs were shattered, he became embittered and couldn't handle the increasing pain caused by a lifetime of hard physical labor.

Members of the Wetzel family continued to serve in the military. Budd completed four years in the Air Force based mostly in the Philippines. Thomas joined the Navy after high school and spent four years on an ammunition ship and aircraft carrier in the Pacific. John enlisted in the Army for three years after high school and was based in Germany. Fortunately, no more Wetzel family members were exposed to the horrors of combat. The small town of Penns Grove was not so fortunate. By the end of the war eleven young men from the area had died in Vietnam from a town no larger than about 5,000 people.

Chuck was posthumously awarded the following military decorations: Purple Heart (U.S), National Defense Service Medal (U.S), Vietnam Service Medal (U.S), Marine Corps Combat Action Ribbon (U.S), Navy Unit Citation (U.S), Presidential Unit Citation (U.S), Gallantry Cross Medal with Palm (RVN), Military Merit Medal (RVN) and the Vietnam Campaign Medal with Date (RVN).

Chuck now lies at eternal rest beside the graves of his parents next to his mother in St. Mary's Cemetery in Salem, New Jersey. As a symbolic homecoming gesture, Chuck's father had arranged that the funeral procession drive by the family home on the way to the cemetery.

Chuck, we all miss you each and every day of our lives. We have all grown old, cynical, and bitter. You will always be young and full of life's joy. Our hope is that your passage was swift and painless. We all live in hope that we will see you once again at the Rainbow Bridge.

214

Notes:
Charles Robert Wetzel, II born on September 9, 1966, was named after the uncle he never had a chance to know. "Charlie" is the son of Chuck's brother, Edward.

Written by: Edward H. Wetzel, Jr., Older Brother, May 25, 2004
Modified: August 13, 2021

The loss of Charles Wetzel was another tragedy of Vietnam. One can only imagine the life that he could have had, what he could have accomplished and contributed to his family and society. Like his older brother I could imagine him returning home, going to college, having a productive career and enjoying a large extended family. The loss of Charles Wetzel was a devastating blow which hastened the loss of his mother and father. I had the pleasure of meeting Chuck's older brother Edward Wetzel and his son Charles Robert Wetzel II when they accepted an invitation to attend a Hotel Company Vietnam Reunion in June 2021. His brother, Edward, read his name during a memorial service to commemorate our fallen comrades. A bell was tolled two times in his honor. I could see that the loss was still fresh in Edward's mind.

Chapter 20
The NVA: Vu Dinh Doan

The NVA also had strong ties to their families. The following is reproduced in part from the People's Army Newspaper dated 17 September 2012, by Tru Trang and Vu Hong and translated by Mai Huong. "Return of a Diary"

On the 28th of March 1966, on Operation Indiana, 21 days after Operation Utah, a Marine, Bob Frazure of 1/7 found a diary on the body of a dead NVA. The NVA's name was Vu Dinh Doan. His diary tells a little of a soldier's life from the perspective of the NVA. Vu Dinh Doan was born in 1937 and was 29 years old when he died in 1966. He was from Hai Duong province, 35 miles from the capital of Hanoi and almost five hundred miles from the former border with South Vietnam. Although the diary does not identify his regiment, which may have been done for security reasons, the place and dates match the history of the 21st regiment which was at Operation Utah. The 21st Regiment was organized in North Vietnam in the summer of 1965 and was formed in the province where he was from, Hai Duong. The 21st Regiment was composed of new recruits, mostly farmers who had never been outside of their local area. The Marines that they were about to face had been training for about a year and were battle-tested before this regiment was formed and infiltrated into South Vietnam in the fall of 1965.

216

The diary records show how, on August 11th 1965, Doan began his journey to South Vietnam.

He records how he crossed into Laos and began his trek down the Ho Chi Minh Trail. The trail was grueling for Vietnamese soldiers—mountains, jungle, and relentless air attacks.

> On this march I have encountered a great deal of problems.
> I ate cold rice gruel, made of leaves. There were great difficulties with food on the trails.

Doan took note of the places he stopped along the way. The place names and the events reflect his honest thoughts, and they come to life through the very personal feelings of a soldier. Vu Ba Con, one of Doan's fellow soldiers, recalls his friend's habit of making notes in his diary. Con recalls that wherever they went, when Doan had a moment of free time he would take out the small notebook to write in it. At some point, this notebook became this soldier's closest friend, one that held his personal secrets. There was nothing particularly grand about what is written. These notes are just a few lines about the feelings of homesickness that suddenly struck him when he stood at the top of a pass and looked out at the mountains and the horizon, or the happiness he felt when he ran into an acquaintance, when he stopped to rest along the route of march, or even during a heavy rainstorm while he was standing guard duty. Those are the things that Doan recounted in his own gentle way.

The translation of the diary helps the reader to understand how the heart of Vu Dinh Doan ached as he thought of home.

> On the 5th Day of the 9th Lunar Month I stood at the top of a pass that was 1,500 meters high. On the 10th day of the 9th Lunar Month, my paternal grandmother's death anniversary, I was standing at the top of a pass that was 1,800 meters high. I sat down at the top of the pass to eat a meal of a rice-ball and salt with Bong, Sao, Con, and Gia...I remembered my life back at home...

The lines are filled with the emotions and feelings of the diary's owner. And those constant feelings of homesickness appear once again.

His friend, Vu Ba Con recalled,

> At that time we all really missed home. However, we spoke of this to one another only occasionally. The rest of the time we kept our feelings inside so that we would not lose our fighting edge. We would just record our feelings in our diaries. During the march we were usually very tired, and no one had time to think about his family. But when we stopped to rest, feelings of homesickness would flood through us. And that was when we would write in our diaries. Everyone kept a diary. Everyone had one or two small home-made notebooks. We kept our notes very short and wrote either in pen or in pencil.

On October 13 the climbing gets even harder as he has to scale a pass that was 2800 meters (7500 feet) high. He says that the sweat was pouring off him and it took eight hours to reach the top and when he reached the top, "I was able to see South Vietnam." After weeks of hauling heavy weapons over mountain peaks, Doan could see where he had come to fight. He thought of his father, and his father's death. That day happened to be the death anniversary of his father which was very important for him due to the Confucian tradition of ancestor worship.

> On 9 January 1966 we marched into Quang Ngai Province. Our march took a total of 15 days. Canh was wounded on 15 January 1966. On 19 January 1966 we stopped to rest for ten days. We ate cold rice with fermented fish sauce at the edge of the jungle tree line in Quang Ngai. My arduous but glorious life…On 1 February 1966 our unit passed our battle resolve. On Tuesday we held the ceremony for us to move out to fight. Our unit consists of 37 men, including an assault unit to destroy enemy tanks …When we read the Army's ten oaths zeal filled us, like a great storm that roils the vast ocean and sky. We swore that we would destroy eight enemy aircraft and five tanks. At exactly 0600 in the evening on 1 February 1966 we moved out for battle.

These lines from the diary paint an image of a time of war.

By the 4th of March, seven months after leaving home, Doan's regiment was northwest of Quang Ngai fighting the US Marines in Operation Utah. Within that regiment he was part of a reserve artillery squad. The name of the Unit, *Hao Doi*, would suggest a reserve or "rear guard" function for that unit. As a rear guard, Doan's job may have been to sacrifice his life, so others could escape. He was the head of the local militia in his village and when he joined the North Vietnamese army he became a squad leader of a .50 caliber machine gun which was considered to be an artillery piece. His only reference to Operation Utah was: "Twelve helicopters arrived and landed troops, then my unit fought all day."

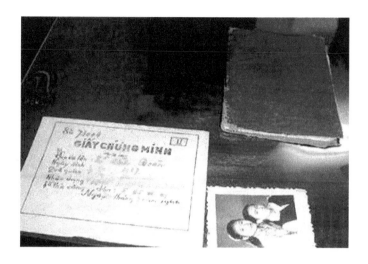

Also in the diary was a photo of two young ladies who were later identified as Ms. Yen and Ms. Nhat. They had become friends with Doan when they were all members of the local guerrilla unit and had given Doan their photo as a memento. On the back of that photo, Doan had written:

> My dear Nhat and Yen. You two gave me this photograph as a memento when I left on 9 June 1965. Now I am living with the people of South Vietnam and I am still trying to stay alive as of 9 March 1966 here in Quang Ngai. If I die, it is for the sake of the Fatherland and for the liberation of South Vietnam. If I live, we will be reunited when our country is reunified and will work together in a unified nation...

This was written just two days after Operation Utah.

The last entry in the diary was on March 21, 1966.

On March 20 1966, The 21st NVA Regiment and the 1st VC Regiment overran an ARVN Outpost northwest of Quang Ngai. The ARVN asked for help and Marine battalions 3/7, 2/4. And 3/5 were called in on Operation Texas which lasted from March 20 to March 25 which cost the Marines 99 KIA and 212 WIA, as costly as Operation Utah.

Doan survived that battle but was killed on Operation Indiana 28 March which was a follow on to Operation Texas. During the month of March the NVA lost 600 killed in action in Utah, 283 in Texas, and 169 in Indiana. Doan was one of many who died that month. The many NVA who were killed in South Vietnam were buried there, near where they were killed. When I visited the area of Operation Utah in 2016, I visited a war cemetery near Hill 85. There were 100s of memorials for the NVA soldiers who fought and died so far from their homes in North Vietnam.

What is common in many of the stories by Vietnamese combatants is the aching sense of homesickness. While homesickness is a common feeling for young men on their first time away from home, most of the Marines and corpsmen experienced this when they went to boot camp. By the time they graduated boot camp and travelled to Okinawa and Vietnam and experienced so many new changes, most of them were over the worst part of homesickness. But for the Vietnamese, they were still in country, eating the same types of food that their mothers and wives cooked, and seeing old people and children that reminded them of the loved ones that they left at home. They were also much more sheltered and naive than the average American teenager who grew up with television and went out with friends, drove cars, dated and competed in sports. Most were country boys from small villages. The biggest difference was that the Marines knew they would be home in thirteen months—God willing—while the Vietnamese did not know when they would be home to see their families and friends. But while they were homesick their bravery was unquestioned.

Bob Frazure found the body of Vu Dinh Doan inside a pit, where it appears he'd been part of a team firing a heavy machine gun. There were two or three drag trails where they had dragged other soldiers away from there. The only reason they didn't drag him away from there was because it just got too hot for them. He was left behind as a rear guard to lay down covering fire and he wasn't going to leave that hill alive. The diary was lying outside of his shirt pocket as though he had taken it out to see it for the last time or he was trying to pass it to someone who would send it home to his family. Bob kept that diary for years after the war until he was able to turn it over to the PBS History Channel who was able to have the diary translated and returned to Vu Dinh Doan's family.

Although Doan had been killed in March of 1966, his family did not know his status until 1975 after the liberation of South Vietnam when one of Doan's friends in the same 21st Regiment, Vu Ba Con, returned home to their village. He brought with him a card that contained some words written by Doan. This *tu-lo-kho* card was given to the children of Doan. (*Tu-lo-kho* is a card game that was played by some North Vietnamese troops). On it was written: "Vu Dinh Doan, killed 7 March 1966 (Western Calendar) at Chop Non Hill, Son Tinh District, Quang Ngai Province."

Vu Ba Con confirmed that it was Doan himself who had written the date of his death on the playing card.

> On the day he died, after lunchtime our unit was informed that enemy troops were moving in behind the sugar cane field and were moving up Chop Non Hill. When he heard the sound of gunfire, Doan grabbed the artillery aiming stake and ran toward our gun. Then he was killed.

During the last moments of his life, he bit the pen to squeeze out a few drops of red ink and wrote on one of the playing cards he always carried with him the date of his death so that later someone might take it and be able to notify his children. He then gave the card to Vu Ba Con. However, it was not until 1975 that Con was finally able to give it to Doan's son, Mr. Son. (There is a difference in the date that was written on the playing card, March 7, compared to March 28 when it was found by Bob Frazure. It may have been that Doan meant to write 27 which would have been the day before Bob found him dead, or he had a premonition that he would die soon and wrote it on March 7. The comment "(Western Calendar)" was inserted by a Vietnamese interpreter but I have no idea how that maps to western calendars).

Doan and his wife, Phuong, fell in love when they were still very young. It was not until they were in their twenties that their first child was born. Their life together did not last very long. After Doan joined the army, his wife had to work hard to support her four children plus Doan's mother and her own mother. Throughout all the years, and even just before she died, she always talked about him and still felt the pain of those years when her husband went off to war. The children also had no mementos of him other than an old shirt of his that was used to keep the children warm when they were young. Son recalled regretfully:

When I reached my adolescent years, all we had was a thick khaki shirt that had belonged to my father. Whenever the weather was cold, my siblings and I would take turns wearing it, until finally it became tattered and simply wore out.

Just before Doan's widow died, she received word that an American veteran wanted to return her husband's diary to her. She was very happy and waited anxiously to see the diary. However, old age caught up with her and she could wait no longer. She died less than a week before US Secretary of Defense Leon Panetta turned the diary over to General Phung Quang Thanh in Hanoi.

At the time of Doan's death in 1966, his son, Son, was one year old. The same age as Mario Ybarra, who was the son of Pfc. Mario Ybarra Sr. of 3/1 who was killed in Operation Utah. Mario Ybarra Jr. worked to have a school named after his father in memoriam. As for Son, it was not until 2001 that he went down to visit the site of the battle to search for his father's grave that the local residents helped him locate. He was able to bring his father's remains home and inter them in a martyr's cemetery near his village. After the war, the Vietnamese government assigned Doan martyr status—an official recognition given to soldiers who died while serving their country. The veterans who knew Doan say that of the 50 young men that had enlisted with Doan from his small farming village, only three survived the war.

In June 2012, the US Secretary of Defense Leon Panetta gave Defense Minister Phung Quang Thanh a number of items that belonged to a People's Army of Vietnam soldier, Vu Dinh Doan, who was killed in a battle in Quang Ngai Province in 1966. Thanks to Bob Frazure, the Marine who recovered these items and kept them since Operation Indiana and PBS Television Network who made this possible.

Members of Doan's family are still living, and he has a surviving son and a daughter.

This is an excerpt from a translated interview with his son in Vietnam:

Hello, I am Vu Dinh Son, a son of martyr Vu Dinh Doan, you pick up my father's diary. On behalf of my family, I would like to say thank you. During the war, I think you were an ethical person.

Bob Frazure is suffering from cancer and could not visit Vietnam to participate in the return of the Diary. He sent this email:

I told my wife how beautiful that country was and I told her about the things I had seen there. I hoped that the family of the Vietnamese martyr will receive the diary. I also hope that they will inform me that they have received this memento of their loved one. Please tell all the Vietnamese people that I no longer have any hate in me and that there is no hate between us, and please tell them that I send them my respects.

Part 7
The Aftermath

Chapter 21
Lessons Learned from Operation Utah

The military planners of Operation Utah must have been very pleased with their apparent victory. The kill ratio was 6 to 1. They had killed 600 of the enemy and there had to be 1200 to 2000 more that were wounded. These wounded would be a drain on their remaining resources. They had destroyed the headquarters of the 21st NVA regiment and essentially annihilated them as a military threat. They were able to display the full capabilities of the world's greatest army with heavy artillery, napalm, 500 pound bombs, thunderous jet air support, and the ability to insert battalions of combat ready troops where the enemy least expected it. The civilian population whose farms and villages we destroyed must have surely been convinced that the NVA and VC could never win this war against such might. The strategy of attrition would surely win the war for South Vietnam. And yet, this same enemy force resurfaced less than a month later and repeated Operation Utah with Operation Texas.

As Operation Utah was the first major engagement between the United States Marine Corps and the North Vietnamese Army, it set the tone for subsequent engagements. I believe that the losses inflicted on both sides solidified the resolve on each side to expand this war. There should have been many lessons learned which could have been used in future engagements. Unfortunately, from my observation, as a former platoon commander during Operation Utah, and subsequent reporting of later engagements, I would say that little was learned and implemented at any level of command. We continued to rip up the country with search and destroy missions and measured our success with body counts. I do not claim to be an expert in military science or national politics. However, there were some obvious lessons that came out of Operation Utah from the participants who were on the other side of that 6-to-1 kill ratio.

The First Lesson: "Platoons, Companies, and Battalions are not interchangeable parts of identical machines."

This is a quote from Lieutenant Colonel Leon N. Utter, Comments on draft MS, dated 13 July 1978 (Vietnam Comment File). The Mix Master program which was used to stagger rotation dates of personnel by rotating companies between battalions was an utter disaster. It broke up battalion unit integrity. Companies were thrown into battle with other companies with whom they have never worked; Command and control, coordination, administrative reporting, logistics support, network communications, coordination with supporting arms, etc., would be abruptly changed. It would have been better to keep the units together and rotate personnel based on normal attrition.

The first Marine battalions that landed in Vietnam in 1965 and 1966 were fortunate in that they had been trained as a unit before landing in Vietnam. Unfortunately, the Mix Master program destroyed the core of that unity. Rotations became even more disruptive later in the year where experienced NCOs were reassigned to new units to lead new troops, instead of training new troops within their existing units. New Marines would arrive and be assigned to a unit where they did not know anyone. Many of the Marines who were in the original battalions had known each other since boot camp and spent years working together through different training assignments. Also, many NCOs and officers were thrown into combat command positions where they had no recent field experience. An NCO who might have been on recruiting duty for the past few years may suddenly be assigned as a platoon sergeant in a rifle platoon where he had no recent combat experience.

Fortunately, some of the high level commanders recognized that the lack of unit integrity had an adverse effect on Operation Utah. Colonel Peatross, the regimental commander of the 7th Marine Regiment observed that it was important that his battalions fight their battles as integral units. Unfortunately, the battalion's day job was to provide perimeter security for the Marine bases; That meant when they were called out for offensive operations, they had to back fill their defensive positions during the operations. When Colonel Peatross's battalions were called out from their positions on the Chu Lai defensive perimeter, Headquarters and Support personnel filled in the gaps left by the infantry. Paymaster personnel logged more time in the Chu Lai defense for the infantry than any other unit. Colonel Peatross later wrote that his 7th Marines had two distinct advantages over other regiments during his tour in Vietnam. "We had one regimental commander and no changes in battalion commanders, and these units were always together..." Unfortunately, the battalions remained in name only as the rifle companies were rotated about.

Colonel Leon Utter, who commanded the 2nd Battalion, 7th Marines during this period, reinforced Colonel Peatross's observations on the importance of unit integrity.

> Platoons, companies, and battalions are not interchangeable parts of identical machines [...] As a battalion commander, I was frequently directed to provide a platoon or company to someone else's headquarters for operations. My answer was, invariably, Assign me the mission and let me take my own people! While this required the replacement of my own people on the line - we went to the field as 2/7. We knew each other, how to communicate; we had our common experience and lessons learned and mistakes made; we could anticipate one another. While we frequently distressed administrators and logisticians by wanting to fight as a unit, it is my not-too-humble opinion that our tactical successes proved, repeatedly, the validity of the concept and justification of the effort.

Colonel Leon N. Utter, Comments on draft MS, dated 13 July 1978 (Vietnam Comment File)

The Second Lesson: Commit at least the same number of troops as the opposition in any operation and do not rely on supporting arms to make up the difference.

In Operation Utah, the commanders suspected that they would be attacking an NVA Regiment on their home ground and they committed only one understaffed Marine battalion and one understaffed ARVN Airborne Battalion, a force of 1000 men under a split command, against a fresh NVA regiment and an adjunct of VC troops which could have totaled over 4000 men! I assume that they thought our training and supporting arms would make up for the difference. To make matters worse, they also took one rifle company away from the Marine Battalion to provide security for the artillery that was situated six miles to the north of the battle area; this essentially took that rifle company out of the fight. There were also no reserve forces planned at the beginning, so when the enormity of the engagement became apparent, reinforcements could not be inserted until the next day. Supporting arms was not effective against the enemy fortifications. Although the artillery fired a lot of rounds, they were not where we needed them because they were placed to the north in Binh Son, on the other side of the enemy forces, which meant they could not fire on the enemy without possible splash-over into friendly positions. It would have been more effective for the artillery to be southeast of us in Quang Ngai and fire over us into the enemy forces. Airstrikes were better at targeting and were more effective than stationary artillery. Airstrikes saved Bravo Company 1/7 when they were surrounded at the landing zone near An Tuyet (1) and were running out of ammo. While the bombardment did little to destroy enemy fortifications, the sound of screeching jets, the bombardment, strafing and napalm explosions, must have been unnerving to the enemy. However, the best supporting arms cannot make up for a lack of boots on the ground.

Third Lesson: Do your own reconnaissance before committing to an operation.

With all the intelligence technology and special reconnaissance resources available to the US forces, none of it seems to have been used in preparation for Operation Utah even though we were facing a suspected regimental size force. Even if intelligence was developed, none of it was shared with the company level units who were committed to battle. When we reached the battlefield, we discovered weapons that we had not faced before, 12.7mm heavy machine guns that could take down helicopters and jet aircraft, as well as devastate attacking ground forces. The equivalent to .50 cal machine guns essentially chewed up the paddy dykes that were our primary means of cover. We also encountered recently dug entrenchments and networks of tunnels, protected by mines and booby traps.

At the unit level we had no warning that we could possibly be facing NVA regulars until we saw the green uniforms with camouflage and their AK-47's. These were not the VC in black pajamas with rusty, old mausers. Since most of the fortifications looked new to us, an aerial reconnaissance should have seen some signs of this activity since most of the area was open rice paddies and small villages. There should have been thousands of new people in the area with recently trampled trails, cooking fires or smoke, and tailings from the tons of dirt that must have been excavated. Perhaps some of us would have used more caution in attacking NVA regulars in fortified positions, and used more airstrikes before advancing. This would have saved lives. If there were signs of fortifications, we should have had a contingent of engineers to remove boobytraps and destroy fortifications with the first wave that landed on 4 March. Fortunately, engineers were included in the battalions that came the next day on 5 March. In Lieutenant Colonel P.X. Kelly's After Action Report, he recommended that a helicopter be made available for the battalion commander to do a reconnaissance of the battle area prior to launching an assault.

A good idea, but if the information does not get down to the small unit leaders prior to the assault, it wouldn't do much good. Attacking fortified positions means that the NVA were well supplied with ammunition, since their supply depots were there and they were not limited in ammunition as were the Marines who had to carry everything in on their backs. The brass on the NVA shell casings that were found on Operation Utah were still bright and shiny and they had tons of it cached in their tunnels. If we had known we would have loaded up with more ammo before we boarded the helicopters. A normal combat load would be seven magazines but many of the more experienced Marines carried two or three bandoliers (sixty rounds per bandolier) of M14 ammo. We would have probably had each Marine carry extra ammo for the machine guns and mortars as well.

Lieutenant Colonel Young of 3/1 noted the difference in engagement between the VC on Operation Double Eagle where they had to aggressively pursue the enemy and the NVA on Operation Utah who fought from well-fortified positions with heavy weapons.

"Accordingly, the most obvious lesson learned from Operation Utah, as well as recent operations conducted, was the requirement to be prepared for either type of VC contact by fully exploiting all information collection assets—i.e., scouts, higher, adjacent, and subordinate units, recent aerial reconnaissance to include photography, infrared, camouflage detection, etc.—in order to ensure proper and timely interpretation of VC contacts. This problem, while not without solution, does require extensive and careful, weighted consideration and study with the most immediate solution being more effective use of the aforementioned information collection agencies and the indoctrination and education of troop leaders, at all levels, so that indications of enemy intentions are properly interpreted at the lower levels, as well as higher level, with immediate and appropriate action being initiated on the lowest level possible and coordinated and controlled at the higher levels. "

The Fourth Lesson: Unity of Command with the ARVN forces

The South Vietnamese government recognized that the ARVN could not defeat the VC, let alone the NVA, so they asked for US military help and when that arrived they let the Americans do their fighting. The United States became so dominant that it was impossible for the ARVN to continue the war once the Americans left.

It was painfully obvious to the Marines that the ARVN were not there to fight and their reports were worse than inaccurate, they were misleading. On the initial assault in Operation Utah, the ARVN's job was to secure the landing zone. However, as soon as they landed, they moved off the landing zone, and the 2/7 Marines landed in a hot landing zone which they expected to be secure. Luckily, the NVA did not exploit their early advantage when only 20 Marines from Fox Company were able to land in the first wave. When the ARVN ran into resistance near Hill 50, the Marines altered their direction of attack to relieve enemy pressure on the ARVN's right flank. This exposed the Marines' left flank and when the ARVN were requested to move up and fill the gap, the ARVN commander refused, leaving a Marine platoon cut off from the rest of the battalion.

In Lieutenant Colonel Utter's 2/7 After Action Report, he states in constrained terms:

> Liaison with the 2nd ARVN Division must be made to determine what is necessary to improve the present

battlefield command structure in U.S/ARVN coordinated operations. If our American advisors are to fulfill their missions of adequately preparing the Vietnamese military in the art of war, so that one day they may stand alone, why then do they fail to emphasize now one of the cardinal principles of war - unity of command? How can the Vietnamese commander learn this principle if we didn't show him what it will do for him? What assurance is there that when he works alongside other ARVN units; under whose operational control he may not be, that he will understand his responsibility to quickly respond to requests from a fellow commander that would exploit a tactical advantage? The importance of his understanding now may well be the difference between victory or defeat.

The ARVN continued to provide inaccurate and misleading reports as to their location and the location of enemy troops. They falsely reported that they had secured the village of Chau Nhai (3) and Hill 50. This proved to be wrong when Mike Company 3/1 was ambushed in the open rice paddies near Chau Nhai (3) and Lima Company 3/1 walked into an ambush when they went to join up with the ARVN on Hill 50. On Hill 50 the ARVN could be seen on the top of the Hill motioning the Marines forward, while the NVA were waiting in ambush just below the crest of the Hill. Another mistake may have been made when depending on the ARVN forces to provide blocking positions on the west and east of the encirclement on March 6. The NVA and VC escaped the encirclement by heading to the west through the ARVN blocking forces. During Operation Utah the Marines suffered 98 dead and 278 wounded while the ARVN had 30 killed and 120 wounded. It was obvious who bore the brunt of this battle.

While we knew after the first few joint operations that the ARVN forces would not be self-sufficient without our support, we continued building up the ARVN forces. The United States created a South Vietnamese military that was built in the image of its own: One that was based on the use of massive supporting arms firepower and endless supplies. It was a rich nation's military. By 1970 the ARVN had the world's fourth largest army. But in 1972 we began withdrawing combat forces and the Paris Peace Accords in 1973 ended US involvement in Vietnam. As soon as that happened the Peace Accords were broken and the eventual outcome was the defeat of the ARVN and the capture of Saigon on April 30 1975. This experience was repeated in Afghanistan where, after 20 years of support, the Afghan armed forces collapsed in a matter of days after the United States announced they were leaving.

Conclusion

There are other issues and lessons to be learned on a broader political, social and economic scale. But that is not the purpose of this book. When the die was cast and decisions were made, the Marines were committed to carry them out. Our sacrifices in Operation Utah did not alter the outcome of the Vietnam War.

Regardless of what decisions the politicians and the generals made, when we were in Operation Utah, we fought for one another, and those of us who survived will always remember and honor our brothers.

Chapter 22
Connecting the Dots

In the early 1960's when most of us in Operation Utah had signed up to join the Marine Corps or volunteered to go to Vietnam, it was a decade full of promise. We had a new President, John F. Kennedy and his First Lady, who made people of all races, creeds and nationalities feel welcome and included in their vision of a better world. He was a Navy hero who fought in harm's way and stood up to the Russians and inspired us with the audacious goal to land an American on the moon in that decade and bring him back.

At that time we thought that the world was so modern with fast automobiles, television, and jet airplanes. We learned about the world around us through the newspapers and *Life Magazine* or news reels at the movie theaters. Our view of the world was very simplistic. It was a clear choice between democracy and communism and it was a clear duty for us to fight for our country just like our fathers and uncles. Most of us were volunteers, eager to fight and even die for our country and our way of life.

However, things were changing rapidly while we were signing up for the Marine Corps and going through our initial training to become efficient "green killing machines." Most of us knew nothing about Vietnam or the political machinations that were being played out in that country. We did not know that the Joint Chiefs of Staff and the CIA were urging Kennedy to commit troops to Vietnam as early as the end of 1961.

In a nationally televised speech from the Oval Office, on June 11, 1963, President Kennedy called for the end of racial discrimination and the full and complete integration of the nation's Black minority into the life of the nation. The issue was a moral one, he said, as old as the Scriptures and as clear as the American Constitution. Congress needed to enact, as soon as possible, sweeping legislation that would finally guarantee equal rights and equal opportunities to all Americans.

In November of 1963, President Kennedy was assassinated in Dallas and the 1960's turned ugly. There were race riots and more assassinations. The South Vietnam leader Ngo Dinh Diem was also assassinated in a coup in 1963 and the political situation in Vietnam deteriorated even further. However, the young Marines were still inspired by Kennedy's vision and dedicated to our country's service. Even as we struggled through the first year of the Vietnam War with lack of supplies and difficult lessons learned, morale remained high.

However, the attitude at home was changing as the daily evening TV news showed unfiltered footage of the war as it was being fought and the growing list of casualties. Protests against the war seemed to focus less upon the immorality of war than on the criminality of the men who fought that war. Instead of being honored as heroes, our returning veterans were being called "baby killers." This was especially hard on the parents who had to bury their sons while protestors demonstrated against the war. Their sons had not burned their draft cards, nor sought deferments, nor ran away to Canada. They did what they thought was right. However, it was not just the protestors. Controversy about the war was prevalent at home. There was often a lack of sympathy about the loss of their son and the sometimes cruel remarks received from ignorant strangers as described by a brother of one of those killed. Their basic life beliefs were shattered and many became embittered while trying to cope with the increasing pain of their loss.

Next to Afghanistan, the Vietnam War was the longest running war that cost over 58,000 American and 4 to 5 million Vietnamese lives on both sides. Vietnam is now unified and is one of the fastest growing economies in South East Asia. In my previous job with Hitachi Data Systems, I did business with companies in Vietnam and worked with our colleagues there. Most of the people I worked with in Vietnam were born after the Vietnam War and seemed to have a friendly attitude to Americans despite the tremendous loss of life that their country suffered. When I shared that I fought in the "American War," the Vietnamese I met seemed to become more receptive to me. They are able to differentiate between the perpetrators of the war and the ones who had to fight it, unlike the attitude that seemed to prevail in the United States. My Vietnamese colleagues and friends in the United States have made many contributions to society and most have prospered despite the hardships they faced when they fled the fall of South Vietnam. How would life have been different if the war had not happened?

The experiences of the Marines who survived Operation Utah are probably much different from those who came after. These young men went off to war with the heroic images of World War II that were captured in films like *Sands of Iwo Jima* or *Battle Cry*, and they expected to come home to the cheers of grateful, patriotic, crowds. They shipped out as a unit who trained together and had many shared experiences which bound them together as a band of brothers.

The troops that followed were committed piecemeal. They joined units as individuals where they did not know anyone. They came in on a transport that was also used to carry out the body bag of the person they were replacing. They also had in their minds the images of the nightly news of the latest casualties rather than the Hollywood images of World War II movies. The new replacements were also more involved in the racial tensions, student protests, and the drug culture of the 1960s. The morale of the troops that followed us deteriorated and some returned psychologically devastated, bitter, drug-addicted people, who had a hard time re-adjusting to society due to the divisive nature of the Vietnam War and society as a whole. I would say that this was not true of our fate. Most of us returned and had successful careers, whether it was in the military, the corporate world, driving a truck or the family farm. Because we had been together as a unit and faced combat together, our after war experience was more like that of the World War II veterans—minus the homecoming parades. Although, this is changing as we approach our final years and we become more introspective.

Contemporary research on long-term effects of combat exposure have shown that high-combat veterans were more likely than low- or moderate-combat veterans to report that their military service enhanced their ability to cope with adversity. When comparing clinical ratings of psychological functioning during adolescence to those in midlife, only high-combat veterans experienced a significant increase in resilience, with low- and moderate-combat veterans experiencing no significant increase. I found that to be true in my own life. Whenever I faced stressful situations in my private or public life, I asked myself "what's the worst that can happen?" and found that I already had faced the worst and was able to move forward.

However, that study also found that these positive effects experienced through midlife declined with increasing age. Combat veterans are more likely to confront and rework their wartime memories in an attempt to find meaning and coherence, particularly as they navigate later-life changes like aging, retirement, loss of loved ones, and decline in health. Psychologists have identified this as Later-Adulthood Trauma Reengagement (LATR). LATR is viewed as a normal, developmental process like a life review. It can lead to either positive or negative outcomes depending on one's intrapersonal and social/environmental resources. Someone with very good resources (good self-esteem, social support, etc.) is more likely to come to acceptance of their own experience and someone without those resources is more likely to encounter distress.

Our physical health is also more likely to decline further. Most of us are suffering the increasing physical effects of the war thanks to Agent Orange which was unique to Vietnam. Former athletes like Nick Grosz, and Jim Nor are hobbled by cancer, and Parkinson's and other diseases caused by Agent Orange. Those who suffered traumatic wounds from high velocity weaponry that was introduced in Vietnam, like Corpsman Bob Ingraham, (who described being wounded in Chapter 18) have endured a lifetime of pain and medical treatments. There is also an increasing number of veterans who are experiencing PTSD as we are affected by LATR. Fortunately the VA has been very supportive and most of us are on some level of disability. I hope that this book will help my fellow veterans come to terms with LATR in a positive way.

Operation Utah left a lasting impression on all of us who were there. It also changed our perception on life and the course of our lives. The following is an example of how this affected Gary Watkins who contributed so much to this book. Gary was a self-described goof-off and high school dropout when he entered the Navy. His experiences re-focused his life and he went on to earn two master's degrees and had a successful international career. He was instrumental in developing a memorial for the KIAs in Hotel Company 2/7 during the Vietnam War and is a major contributor to Hotel Company 2/7 reunions. Here is how Gary Watkins processed his Vietnam experience.

Gary Watkins 1966

I deactivated from the Navy Reserve by the end of June. Although Duke University would give me a year of credit toward a two-year degree for ER Assistant training (because of my work as a corpsman in Vietnam), the last thing I could imagine doing was getting the smell of blood on my hands. Even if it would take me fifteen years after obtaining a second MFA degree from Columbia to earn an ER Assistant's salary, I have never regretted that decision.

Still, for two years after my Vietnam tour, I considered American war policy as having a positive impact on Vietnam. Around both the Qui Nhon and Chu Lai Bases, there were civil development programs putting in wells, building schools and dams and stretches of new hamlets.

Then, one day traveling with my brother, I was stopped in my tracks, remembering the extraordinary violence that I had personally witnessed in eight major combat operations.

Even after that experience, I still had very conflicting feelings about America's Vietnam War. I finally connected the dots of the war violence with the breaking up of the student demonstrations on the San Jose State campuses when I attended a massive demonstration on the Washington Mall in November 1969. I had been a San Jose College student the previous year, during the 1968 assassinations of

Martin Luther King and Bobby Kennedy, and the violence and burnings in Detroit, Newark, Los Angeles and Washington, as well as at the Democratic Chicago Convention. I went to the Mall (in Washington DC) just to see if I could make some meaning of all this. Witnessing the hundreds of thousands of seemingly ordinary people, families, streaming down the avenues, some of what the speakers were saying began to penetrate and I came away from the Washington Monument that day thinking something's not right.

I still held all of my thoughts and feelings about the military and about death in the war—the Marines and corpsmen I had zipped up in body bags, the napalm-burnt North Vietnamese soldier I had ordered shot (by Odem, a Marine rifleman who several hours later was mortally wounded), along with the Vietnamese lives that I had failed to make an extra effort to save at arm's length.

But something happened to me in 1991. Coming out of jury duty onto 5th Avenue, I found myself crossing the Vietnam Veterans straggling at the tail end of the Desert Storm ticker tape parade. It just smacked me in the face. I stood there, weeping, until I found myself saying with confidence: "Guys, I'm coming back to get you. Don't know how this is going to work out, but you're coming home!"

It took two tries and eight years, to get the stone moving up that hill, but in February, 1999, I was standing in that gutted, 500-bomb crater on Hill 37. I had climbed the hill through a heavy grove of young, twenty-foot eucalyptus trees behind a local teenager I had hired to guide me and my driver. The top of the hill was still littered with blown up bits from a Marine Corps' backpack radio. Near the top, the young Vietnamese boy scooped up an unexploded, 60mm, North Vietnamese mortar round and tossed it over his head. It landed right in front of me as if to fully remind me exactly what it would take to bring the H-2/7 Marines and corpsman who I had bagged and tagged during Operation Utah back to the "World." As the below photos document, it would take, until May 2015 and July 2017, respectively, to complete that final journey, with the massive help of all the 1965-1970, H-2/7 Reunion Marines who have met every other year since 1996.

Good afternoon sir, The Battalion has put up your plaque. The plaque will be the first thing Marines see as they make their way up the steps in 2/7. Thanks to all of you who contributed and sacrificed which allowed mine and future generations of Marines to continue to fight and win wars.

1st Sergeant Foster, 2BLT 7th Marines (July, 2017)
2BLT 7th Marines Headquarters, Twentynine Palms, Ca

Part 8
The Tribute

Chapter 23
Gone But Not Forgotten

The purpose of this book is to honor all the Marines and corpsmen who gave the ultimate sacrifice during Operation Utah. Gary Watkins helped to build a memorial for the KIAs in Hotel Company 2/7. That was his company. There were many other Marines and Corpsmen who suffered the same fate and had similar stories in the other companies that fought in Operation Utah. This chapter lists each of these Marines and Corpsman with as much detail as I could glean from their online tributes. These online tributes are primarily taken from The Wall of Faces Vietnam Veterans Memorial Fund (VVMF).

Someone once said that the death of one man is a tragedy, but the death of a thousand men is a statistic. The virtual Wall of Faces tries to keep each man's life and legacy remembered by featuring a page dedicated to honoring every person whose name is inscribed on the Vietnam Memorial Wall in Washington DC. VVMF is committed to finding a photo to go with each of the more than 58,000 names on The Wall. They are closing in on that goal and as of the writing of this book they are only missing 200 pictures. VVMF also provides an online forum which allows family and friends to share memories, post pictures, and connect with each other. I have drawn a lot of the stories in this book from this forum. More importantly the wall of faces helps us to look at their faces and see them as individuals rather than a list of names, or as a statistic.

In this chapter, I include the pictures of all the men who died in Operation Utah since the pictures often speak more than words can describe as we look into their youthful faces. This is also a tribute to the aged survivors who are now in their 70s and 80s. We can look into the faces of our fallen brothers and remember them and remember how we were at that age when we went off to war. As survivors many of us went on to have children of our own, we can now appreciate the sense of loss that their parents must have felt and taken to their grave.

While the official records list 98 Marines killed in Operation Utah I include the names of those who died at a later date due to wounds suffered during that battle. Sergeant John Henry Eaglin from India Company 3/1 died of his wounds on 11 April 1966. Corporal Russell Edward Metzger from India Company 3/1 died of his wounds on 4 June 1966 and Lance Corporal Harry John Stateczny from Bravo Company 1/7, died from his wounds on July 3, 1966. All three suffered their wounds on Operation Utah on 5 March, 1966. There is a total of 101 men listed in this chapter. Since the names on the Wall are listed by the date of their death, 98 of the 100 Marines and Corpsmen who were killed in Operation Utah are listed on the Vietnam Veterans Memorial wall Panel 05E. The three others who died of their wounds at later dates are on panels 06E and 08E. They represent the 58,281 others whose names are listed on the Vietnam War Memorial in Washington DC. I have left a tribute on each of 101 names from Operation Utah and others that I knew who were killed in action in Vietnam. I encourage all who knew any of the Vietnam veterans on this wall to visit the VVMF website and leave a tribute so we can learn more about these men and honor their sacrifice.

The Marines who were killed in action (KIAs) are listed below by Battalion and by Company. Rather than list them alphabetically in one list, I identify them with the units that they fought and died with, with their friends and comrades. It also helps to correlate their stories back to the chapters that I wrote about each company.

3rd Battalion 1st Marine Regiment

On March 4, the 3rd Battalion was hastily called on to assist 2/7 who was heavily engaged in a battle with the 21st NVA Regiment in Quang Ngai Province on Operation Utah. 3/1 was helicoptered into a blocking position north of the battle area the evening of March 4, and was assigned the mission of assaulting the NVA Regimental Headquarters which was entrenched in fortified positions on Hill 50. All three rifle companies—India, Lima, and Mike Companies—were heavily engaged in an eight-hour battle rooting out the NVA and VC from a complex of tunnels and well prepared defensive positions before they were able to take Hill 50 and the villages that were at the base of Hill 50. 3/1 suffered heavy casualties with 45 KIA. India Company suffered the most KIA with 20 followed by Mike Company with 15 and Lima Company with 10.

India Company 3rd Battalion 1st Marine Regiment

India Company was initially in reserve when 3/1 began its assault on Hill 50 on March 5, 1966. However, when Mike Company ran into entrenched resistance from NVA that were dug in at Chau Nhai (3) at the Base of Hill 50, India company was called in for assistance to clear Chau Nhai (3) and passed through Mike company to continue the assault on Hill 50. India Company suffered 20 KIA, the most of any Rifle Company in Operation Utah.

Sergeant Robert Brown (31) was born 17 January 1935 in Plaquemine, Iberville Parish, Louisiana and died 5 March, 1966, in Quang Ngai, Vietnam. Robert was a squad leader and died as a result of a gunshot wound to the chest from hostile rifle fire while leading an assault on Hill 50. Sergeant Robert Brown was awarded the Bronze Star Medal for valor for his exemplary courage under fire. He is survived by his wife, Eleanor L. and two children; Robert Jr. and Brigit Karen Brownlee all of Oceanside, California and his parents; Mr. & Mrs. Thomas Brown of Plaquemine, Louisiana. He sailed from Okinawa on the USS Paul revere and made the beach landing on Operation Double Eagle I on 28 January 1966 with India Company, 3rd Battalion, 1st Marines Regiment, 3rd Marine Division. On 4 March 1966, he had just received a letter from his wife with photos of his baby that was born after he left. He had written her a letter before he boarded the helicopter that morning, not knowing it would be his last. Sergeant Robert Brown is honored on the Vietnam Veterans Memorial wall Panel 05E line 114.

Corporal Albert Cabanayan (21) was born on February 07, 1945 to Mr. and Mrs. Jose Cabanayan in Kahului, Maui, Hawaii. He was very popular in high school. He was an active student, active in band and well-liked. He was one of those students that was destined to be called "most likely to succeed." He sailed from Okinawa on the USS Paul Revere and made the beach landing on Operation Double Eagle I on 28 January 1966 in Quang Ngai Province with India Company, 3rd Battalion, 1st Marine Regiment, 3rd Marine Division. He died on 5 March 1966 from hostile rifle fire on Operation Utah near Hill 50, Chau Nhai (3), Quang Ngai Province. He was found next to the body of his fellow Hawaiian, Lance Corporal Robert Lani Nueku, where they made their last stand together. Albert was the first Maui Marine to die in Vietnam. His sister, Sylvia Cabanayan, while a student at the University of Hawaii, helped to organize an R&R program for wounded servicemen at Tripler Hospital in Maui. Corporal Albert Cabanayan had served 2 year in the Marine Corps and is honored on the Vietnam Veterans Memorial Wall Panel 05E, Line 114.

Pfc. Steven Anthony Church (20) was born 6 March 1945 in Los Angeles, California and died one day before his birthday on 5 March 1966. He is survived by his mother, Kathryn M. Church of 17300 Pacific Highway South, Seattle, Washington and his father; William A. Church of 11126 Ruthelen Avenue, Los Angeles, California. Steven enlisted in the Marines 5 February, 1963 at a recruiting office in Seattle. After graduation from Boot Camp and Infantry Training Regiment, he joined India Company, 3rd Battalion, 1st Marine Regiment, 3rd Marine Division. Steven sailed from Okinawa on the USS Paul Revere and made the beach landing on Operation Double Eagle I on 28 January 1966 in Quang Ngai Province with India Company. Steven had already been awarded a Purple Heart Medal for wounds which he suffered in a previous operation. During the helicopter assault into the landing zone on 5 March 1966, he was wounded in the leg but was able to continue the assault. Later that day, Steven died as a result of gunshot wounds to his chest. He would have been 21 years old the next day. Pfc. Steven Anthony Church is buried at Evergreen-Washelli Memorial Park, Seattle Washington and is honored on the Vietnam Veterans Memorial Wall Panel 05E, Line 116.

 **Corporal Leland Francis Dixon (31)** was born 9 March 1934 in Gulfport, Harrison County, Mississippi, USA. He had the rank of corporal with 10 years of service. Occupation or specialty was rifleman. Corporal Dixon sailed from Okinawa on the USS Paul Revere and made the beach landing on Operation Double Eagle I on 28 January 1966 in Quang Ngai Province with India Company, 3rd Battalion, 1st Marine Regiment, 3rd Marine Division. On 5 March 1966, Corporal Leland died through hostile action, small arms fire. near Chau Nhai (3) east of Hill 50, in Quang Ngai province during Operation Utah. Corporal Leland Francis Dixon is honored on the Vietnam Veterans Memorial Wall, Panel 05E, Line 115.

 **Sergeant John Henry Eaglin (24)** was born 7 March, 1942. He was the son of Mr. and Mrs. Paul Eaglin sailed from Okinawa on the USS Paul Revere and made the beach landing on Operation Double Eagle I on 28 January 1966 in Quang Ngai Province with India Company, 3rd Battalion, 1st Marine Regiment, 3rd Marine Division. On 5 March 1966, during Operation Utah, Sergeant Eaglin was gravely wounded by hostile small arms fire and was evacuated to the Navy

Hospital ship Repose where he died on 11 April from his wounds. He was married just shortly before he shipped out for Vietnam and is survived by his wife, Mrs. John H. Eaglin of Corpus Christi, Texas. Sergeant Eaglin and his wife had a daughter during the three months that he was in Vietnam. John was an honor graduate of Blessed Sacrament High School in 1960 and enlisted in the Marine Corps on June 9, 1960. Sergeant John Henry Eaglin is buried at Live Oak Cemetery, Beaumont, Texas and is honored on the Vietnam Veterans Memorial Wall, Panel 06E, Line 99.

Lance Corporal Thomas Kenneth Emmons (20) was born in Denver, Colorado 29 November, 1945. Thomas was the son of John B. Emmons and Agatha L. Emmons of Denver Colorado. He enlisted in the US Marine Corps on July 15, 1963 in Denver. He sailed from Okinawa on the USS Paul Revere and made the beach landing on Operation Double Eagle I on 28 January 1966 in Quang Ngai Province with India Company, 3rd Battalion, 1st Marine Regiment, 3rd Marine Division. Corporal Emmons was killed by multiple hostile gunshot wounds on 5 March, 1966 while assaulting Hill 50 on Operation Utah. Lance Corporal Emmons is buried at Ft. Logan National Cemetery, in Denver, Colorado and is honored on the Vietnam Veterans Memorial Wall, Panel 05E, Line 116.

Corporal Roy Gonzales, Jr. (26) was born on August 16, 1939. According to our records Texas was his home or enlistment state and Bexar County was included within the archival record. We have San Antonio listed as the city. Corporal Ray Gonzales was stationed at Marine Barracks, Naval Air Station in Corpus Christi, Texas from 1963 to 1966 where he was part of the color guard detail which attended military funerals of our fallen heroes from the Corpus Christi area. In the later part of February 1966 he was sent to Vietnam

248

where he joined India Company 3rd Battalion, 1st Marine Regiment and served as a rifleman. Gonzales was killed by hostile small arms fire while assaulting Hill 50 on Operation Utah. Roy is buried at Fort Sam Houston National Cemetery and is honored on the Vietnam Veterans Memorial Wall, Panel 05E, Line 117.

Pfc. William Richard Graham (19) was born in Cheverly, Prince Georges County, Maryland, on May 29, 1946. Pfc. Graham was the son of Betty and Ellis Graham of Lortan, Virginia. He attended Mount Vernon High School. He enlisted in the Marine Corps in 1965 and joined India Company, 3rd Battalion, 1st Regiment after graduation from boot camp and Infantry Training Regiment. He sailed from Okinawa on the USS Paul Revere and made the beach landing on Operation Double Eagle I on 28 January 1966 in Quang Ngai Province with India Company. Pfc. Graham was killed on 5 March 1966 by hostile small arms while assaulting Hill 50 on Operation Utah. Pfc. Graham is interred at Arlington National Cemetery, Arlington, Virginia and is honored on the Vietnam Veterans Memorial Wall, Panel 05E, Line 126.

Pfc. Ronnie Elmon Hall (22) was born on November 25, 1943. Fort Wayne Indiana is listed as his home state. He was the son of Mr. and Mrs. Harry E. Hall of Fort Wayne, Indiana. He joined the Army in September 1961 and later transferred to the Marine Corps. He joined India Company, 3rd Battalion, 1st Marine Regiment in 1965. He sailed from Okinawa on the USS Paul Revere and made the beach landing on Operation Double Eagle I on 28 January 1966 in Quang Ngai Province with

India Company. While trying to pull a wounded Marine from the line of fire during Operation Utah on 5 March, 1966, Pfc. Hall was wounded by hostile fire near Hill 50 and later died on 28 march 1966 as a result of those wounds. Pfc. Hall is interred at Lindenwood Cemetery, Fort Wayne, Indiana and is honored on the Vietnam Veterans Memorial Wall, Panel 06E, Line 056.

Pfc. Danny Trent Higgs (20) was born 18 Feb 1946 in Battle Creek, Calhoun County, Michigan. Danny the son of Fines F. Higgs and Marie E. Higgs of Battle Creek Michigan enlisted in the US Marine Corps on April 28 1965 in Detroit, Michigan. After graduation from boot camp and Infantry Training Regiment, he joined India Company, 3rd Battalion, 1st Marine Regiment. He sailed from Okinawa on the USS Paul Revere and made the beach landing on Operation Double Eagle I on 28 January 1966 in Quang Ngai Province with India Company. Pfc. Higgs died of multiple fragmentation wounds while assaulting Hill 50 on 5 March 1966 during Operation Utah. Pfc. Higgs is interred at Reese Cemetery, Springfield, Calhoun County, Michigan and is honored on the Vietnam Veterans Memorial Wall, Panel 05E, Line 126.

Pfc. Fred Howard Horton (18) was born on July 15, 1947. Colorado was his home or enlistment state and Denver listed as the city. He enlisted in the Marine Corps in 1965. After graduation from boot camp and Infantry Training Regiment, he joined India Company, 3rd Battalion, 1st Marine Regiment. He sailed from Okinawa on the USS Paul Revere and made the beach landing on Operation Double Eagle I on 28 January 1966 in Quang Ngai Province with India Company. Pfc. Horton died on

5 March 1966 from small arms fire while assaulting Hill 50 during Operation Utah. He is interred at Fort Logan National Cemetery, Denver, Colorado and is honored on the Vietnam Veterans Memorial Wall, Panel 05E, Line 118.

 **Lance Corporal Frederick George Lynch, Jr. (21)** was born February 28, 1945. He was from Philadelphia, Pennsylvania. He was the son of Frederick G. Lynch Sr. and Helen T. Lynch of Philadelphia. "Fred" Lynch had a keen sense of humor and a deep love for his family. He attended Father Judge and Frankford high schools before enlisting in the Marine Corps in 1962 at the age of 17 during the Cuban missile crisis. The 21-year-old Lance Corporal, a messenger, was assigned to India Company of the 3rd Battalion, 1st Marines, 1st Marine Division. He sailed from Okinawa on the USS Paul Revere and made the beach landing on Operation Double Eagle I on 28 January 1966 in Quang Ngai Province with India Company. Lance Corporal Lynch was killed by hostile small arms fire while attacking an enemy position with grenades near Hill 50. He died in Quang Ngai Province, Vietnam, on 5 March 1966, with only 45 days remaining on his four-year enlistment. Survivors include his parents and three sisters. Lance Corporal Lynch is interred at Holy Sepulchre Cemetery, Cheltenham, Pennsylvania and is honored on the Vietnam Veterans Memorial Wall, Panel 05E, Line 119.

Corporal Russell Edward Metzger (23) was born on 04 April 1943. His Home town was North Highlands, California. Corporal Metzger joined the Marine Corps in September 1961 and was due to finish his enlistment on September 5, 1965. His last assignment was with India Company, 3rd Battalion, 1st Marine Regiment. However, anyone with an enlistment date of 1 September 1965 and later was extended to go with India Company to Vietnam. Corporal Metzger sailed from Okinawa on the USS Paul Revere and made the beach landing with India Company on Operation Double Eagle I on 28 January 1966 in Quang Ngai Province. He was wounded on 5 March 1966 by a fragmentation grenade while assaulting Hill 50 on Operation Utah. He later died of his wounds on 4 June 1966. Corporal Metzger is interred at Pacific Crest Cemetery, Redondo Beach, California and is honored on the Vietnam Veterans Memorial Wall, Panel 08E, Line 7.

Pfc. Alan Craig Mulford (19) was born 25 March, 1946 in San Juan, San Juan Municipality, Puerto Rico. Alan was born in Puerto Rico and later moved to Seattle and was adopted by his stepfather as his son. Pfc. Mulford died 20 days before his 20th birthday and is survived by his parents, Kenneth W & Marcia Mulford of Seattle, Washington. After graduation from boot camp and Infantry Training Regiment, he joined India Company, 3rd Battalion, 1st Marine Regiment. He sailed from Okinawa on the USS Paul Revere and made the beach landing on Operation Double Eagle I on 28 January 1966 in Quang Ngai Province. Alan died of multiple gunshot wounds to the body from hostile small arms fire, on 5 March 1966 while assaulting enemy positions on Hill 50 during Operation Utah. He is interred at Willamette National Cemetery, Portland, Oregon and is honored on the Vietnam Veterans Memorial Wall, Panel 05E, Line 121.

Lance Corporal Robert Lani Nueku (22) was born on October 15, 1943. Hawaii was his home or enlistment state and Honolulu County included within the archival record. We have Nanakuli listed as the city. He is survived by his mother Emmaline Kanakaole of Nanakuli. He was drafted into the Marine Corps and entered via Selective Service. He served as a rifleman with 1st Marine Division, 3rd Battalion, 1st Marines, India Company. He sailed from Okinawa on the USS Paul Revere with India Company and made the beach landing on Operation Double Eagle I on 28 January 1966 in Quang Ngai Province. Lance Corporal Nueku died through hostile action from small arms fire on 5 March 1966, while assaulting Hill 50 on Operation Utah. He was found next to the body of his fellow Hawaiian, Corporal Albert Cabanayan where they made their last stand together. He is interred at the National Memorial Cemetery of The Pacific, Honolulu, Hawaii and is honored on the Vietnam Veterans Memorial Wall, Panel 05E, Line 121.

Pfc. David Louis Sabec (20) was born 31 August, 1945 Dayton, Ohio. David was the son of Lawrence Sabec and Betty J. Sabec of Vandalia, Ohio. He enlisted in the US Marine Corps on May 3, 1965 in Cincinnati OH. After graduation from boot camp and Infantry Training Regiment, he joined India Company, 3rd Battalion, 1st Marine Regiment. He sailed from Okinawa on the USS Paul Revere and made the beach landing on Operation Double Eagle I on 28 January 1966 in Quang Ngai Province. He had only arrived in Vietnam a few short months but saw heavy combat receiving several leg wounds. He died on 5 March 1966 while assaulting Hill 50 during Operation Utah. David was a star athlete at Vandalia-Butler High School, graduating in 1963. Local residents, headed by Dwight Elkins, Sabec's baseball coach, started a drive to erect new lights, dedicated to Sabec, at the

253

football field. Pfc. Sabec is interred at Dayton Memorial Park Cemetery, Dayton, Ohio and is honored on the Vietnam Veterans Memorial Wall, Panel 05E, Line 123.

Pfc. Charles Sherlee Satcher (19) was born 10/11/1946 from Vallejo, California. He enlisted in the US Marine Corps in 1965. After graduation from boot camp and Infantry Training Regiment, he joined India Company, 3rd Battalion, 1st Marine Regiment. He sailed from Okinawa on the USS Paul Revere and made the beach landing on Operation Double Eagle I on 28 January 1966 in Quang Ngai Province. Pfc. Satcher was killed by hostile small arms fire on 5 March 1966 on Operation Utah during the assault on Hill 50. He was shot in the leg and was pinned down in a manioc field. Several of his platoon went to his aid but were pinned down by fire and could not move him. Although they tied a tourniquet around his leg, he tore it off and bled to death. Pfc. Satcher is honored on the Vietnam Veterans Memorial Wall, Panel 05E, Line 123.

Pfc. Royce Glenn Scoggins (18) of McKinney, Texas, was born 2 October, 1947, and joined the Marines in March 15, 1965 at the age of seventeen. Pfc. Scoggins was the son of Mrs. Eula Mae Mitchell of Tioga and Glenn Scoggins of McKinney. After graduation from boot camp and Infantry Training Regiment, he joined India Company, 3rd Battalion, 1st Marine Regiment. As a machine gunner. He sailed from Okinawa on the USS Paul Revere and made the beach landing on Operation Double Eagle I on 28 January 1966 in Quang Ngai Province. On Saturday 5 March, 1966, Pfc. Scoggins was killed in action near Hill 50 on Operation Utah as he operated his M60 machine gun in a heated battle. He was killed while providing covering fire as his platoon tried to recover a wounded Marine. Pfc. Scoggins is interred in the City Cemetery at Tioga, Texas, and his name is listed on the WALL, the Vietnam Veterans Memorial, in Washington, DC, at Panel 5E, Row 124.

Pfc. Mario Ybarra (22) was born 1 May, 1943, in San Benito, Texas. Son of Fidela Gonzalez and Felipe Ybarra, 1961 graduate of Weslaco High School. He enlisted in the Marine Corp in 1962. He was married to Manaen Hernandez and had a son Mario G. Ybarra, Jr. who was born March 13, 1965 and was one years old when he attended his father's funeral. Pfc. Ybarra sailed from Okinawa on the USS Paul Revere and made the beach landing on Operation Double Eagle I on 28 January 1966 in Quang Ngai Province with India Company, 3rd Battalion 1st Marine Regiment, 1st Marine Division. Pfc. Ybarra was killed by hostile gunfire on 5 March 1966, during Operation Utah, while going to the aid of a wounded Marine. Pfc. Mario Ybarra Elementary School in Weslaco, Texas was named in his honor. Pfc. Ybarra is interred at Highland Memorial Park Cemetery, Weslaco, Texas and is honored on the Vietnam Veterans Memorial Wall, Panel 05E, Line 127.

Pfc. Charles Louis Zoog (22) was born 2 August, 1943 in Washington, Washington County, Pennsylvania. Charles enlisted in the Marines 10 July, 1963 at a Pittsburgh Recruiting Office. He sailed from Okinawa on the USS Paul Revere and made the beach landing on Operation Double Eagle I on 28 January 1966 in Quang Ngai Province with India Company, 3rd Battalion, 1st Marine Regiment, 3rd Marine Division. Pfc. Zoog was killed on 5 March 1966 by a gunshot wound on Operation Utah during the assault on Hill 50. Pfc. Zoog is survived by his parents, Henry Jerome G. and Mary E. Zoog of Hickory. Pennsylvania. Charles is buried at Forest Lawn Gardens, Canonsburg, Washington County, Pennsylvania and is honored on the Vietnam Veterans Memorial Wall, Panel 05E, Line 127.

Lima Company 3/1

On 5 March, 1966 Lima Company was participating in Operation Utah with an ARVN unit in the area northwest of Quang Ngai City in a complex of villages known as Chau Nhai. Operation Utah was to be a coordinated attack against the 21st NVA. They were ambushed and came under heavy fire from the NVA that were entrenched on and around Hill 50. Despite being ambushed, the aggressive efforts of Lima Company cleared Hill 50 and produced 33 NVA KIA with a possible additional 55 KIA. Friendly casualties were 10 KIA and 20 WIA.

Lance Corporal James Jerome Bradley (20) was born on November 10, 1945 and was from New York City. Lance Corporal Bradley was the husband of Angela R. Bradley of New York City, and father of a son, Mark. He was the son of Joseph M. and Nora R. Bradley, from the Bronx, New York. Lance Corporal Bradley was in 3rd Platoon, Lima Company, 3rd Battalion, 1st Marine Regiment. Lance Corporal Bradley struggled to enlist in the Marine Corps. He was rejected twice, once for curvature of the spine and again for asthma. He was quiet and always ready to give a hand when needed. He sailed from Okinawa on the USS Paul Revere and made the beach landing on Operation Double Eagle I on 28 January 1966. He met his fate 37 days later on 5 March 1966 and paid the ultimate sacrifice on Operation Utah. Lance Corporal Bradley was killed in action from multiple fragmentation wounds suffered near Hill 50. He is interred at Gate of Heaven Cemetery, Hawthorne, New York and is honored on the Vietnam Veterans Memorial Wall, Panel 05E, Line 113.

Pfc. Thomas William Edwards (19) was born on September 20, 1946 and was from Binghamton, New York. He was a rifleman assigned to Lima Company, 3rd Battalion, 1st Marine Regiment. He sailed from Okinawa on the USS Paul Revere and made the beach landing on Operation Double Eagle I on 28 January 1966. On 5 March 1966, he died through hostile action, small arms fire near Chau Ngai 3 east of Hill 50 during Operation Utah. Thomas is buried at Calvary Cemetery, Johnson City, NY. and is honored on the Vietnam Veteran's Memorial in Washington DC. His name is inscribed at VVM Wall, Panel 05e, Line 115

Pfc. Joseph George Evan, Jr. (20) was born 2 April, 1945 and was from Uniontown, Fayette County, Pennsylvania. He was the son of Mr. & Mrs. Joseph Evans. He enlisted in the Marine Corps on 15 April 1962 a few days after turning 17. He sailed from Okinawa on the USS Paul Revere and made the beach landing on Operation Double Eagle I on 28 January 1966 in Quang Ngai Province. When he arrived in Vietnam he was with H&S Company of the 3rd Battalion, 1st Marines, and was later transferred to Lima Company 3rd Battalion, 1st Marines as a rifleman. Pfc. Evan died as a result of multiple fragmentation wounds on 5 March 1966 near Hill 50. He is interred at Saint Joseph's Roman Catholic Cemetery, Hopwood, Pennsylvania and is honored on the Vietnam Veterans Memorial Wall, Panel 05E, Line 116.

Lance Corporal Philip Fitch (20) He was born on 9 May, 1945 and was from Cincinnati, Ohio. He was the son of James and Vera Turner Fitch and enlisted in the Marine Corps July, 1963, at the age of 17.

Lance Corporal Fitch was a machine gunner in Lima Company, 3rd Battalion, 1st Marine Regiment. He sailed from Okinawa on the USS Paul Revere and made the beach landing on Operation Double Eagle on 28 January 1966. Lance Corporal Fitch died on 5 March 1966 from hostile small arms fire while assaulting Hill 50 during Operation Utah. He is interred at Flagg Spring Cemetery, Newton, Ohio and is honored on the Vietnam Veterans Memorial Wall, Panel 05E, Line 114.

Pfc. Rickey Dean Garner (18) was born 26 November, 1947 and was from Paris, Texas. Rickey was the son of Dahlia B. Garner, dear brother of Peggy S. Renfro of Dallas Texas, and the son of Roy Garner. He enlisted in the US Marine Corps on March 22, 1965 in Dallas. After graduation from Boot Camp and the Infantry Training Regiment, he was assigned to Lima Company, 3rd Battalion, 1st Marines, 3rd MARDIV (Rein) FMF. He sailed from Okinawa on the USS Paul Revere and made the beach landing on Operation Double Eagle I on 28 January 1966. On Operation Utah on 5 March 1966, while serving as a runner in the Second Platoon, Pfc. Garner was taken under heavy fire on Hill 50. Observing a group of five North Vietnamese soldiers in a trench about 20 yards from where he stood, he charged the trench, firing his automatic as he ran. As a result of his daring conduct he succeeded in destroying the enemy positions and saving two of his wounded comrades, but sustained wounds which resulted in his death.

Pfc. Garner's courageous actions on Hill 50 accounted for a number of enemy casualties and contributed materially to his company's success in securing the position. Pfc. Garner was posthumously awarded a Silver Star for his conspicuous gallantry and intrepidity in action. Pfc. Garner is interred at Laurel Land Memorial Park, Dallas, Texas and is honored on the Vietnam Veterans Memorial Wall, Panel 05E, Line 116.

Staff Sergeant Leonard Ashby Hultquist (30) was born 1 October, 1935 in Omaha, Nebraska. Leonard rebuilt his life and gained a new family at Boys Town. He was helped through Father Flanagan's dream. He attended school there and with his brothers prepared to make positive contributions in our society. He was married to Nancy M. Hultquist, and had three daughters, ages 3, 5, and 6, at the time of his death. The Boys Town Class of 54 held a dedication ceremony for Staff Sergeant Hultquist on June 24, 2000 at the Veterans Memorial in Boys Town, Nebraska. Melody Green, his middle daughter, gave a speech. Though she never had the opportunity to know her father, Melody learned a great deal about him as a Marine and as a husband through the many letters that he wrote to his wife and the many letters of condolences from his fellow Marines. He was a Platoon Sergeant in Lima Company, 3rd Battalion, 1st Marine Regiment. He sailed from Okinawa on the USS Paul Revere and made the beach landing on Operation Double Eagle I on 28 January 1966. On 5 March 1966, Staff Sergeant Hultquist was killed by hostile small arms fire while leading his men on an assault on Hill 50 during Operation Utah. He is interred at Fort McPherson National Cemetery, Maxwell, Nebraska and is honored on the Vietnam Veterans Memorial Wall, Panel 05E, Line 118.

Pfc. Jose Enrique Laguer (20) was born on 12 January, 1946 in Aguadilla, Aguadilla Municipality, Puerto Rico. Jose is the son of Herminia V. Laguer of Brooklyn New York and Enrique Laguer who predeceased him. He enlisted in the US Marine Corps on July 22, 1964 in New York City. In Vietnam, he was assigned to and served with the Weapons Platoon, Lima Company, 3rd Battalion, 1st Marines, 3rd MARDIV (Rein) FMF. He sailed from Okinawa on the USS Paul Revere and made the beach landing on Operation Double Eagle I on 28 January 1966. On 5 March 1966, Pfc. Laguer was killed by hostile rifle fire during the assault on Hill 50 on Operation Utah He is interred at Long Island National Cemetery, East Farmingdale, New York and is honored on the Vietnam Veterans Memorial Wall, Panel 05E, Line 120.

Pfc. Jerry Emmet Parks (22) was born on 21 June, 1943 and was from Grand Rapids, Michigan. He is survived by his wife, Katherine; one son, Scott Richard; his parents, Claude and Bernice Parks, of Grand Rapids. He enlisted in the Marine Corps in May, 1965. In Vietnam, he was assigned to and served with the Weapons Platoon, Lima Company, 3rd Battalion, 1st Marines, 3rd MARDIV (Rein) FMF. He sailed from Okinawa on the USS PAUL REVERE and made the beach landing on Operation Double Eagle I on 28 January 1966. Pfc. On 5 March 1966, Parks was killed by multiple fragmentation wounds on Operation Utah while he was assaulting Hill 50. He is interred at Rosedale memorial Park, Tallmadge, Michigan and is honored on the Vietnam Veterans Memorial Wall, Panel 05E, Line 122.

Corporal Jimmy Pineda Sanchez (23) was born on 8 June, 1942 in Brownsville, Texas. His parents, Mr. & Mrs. Carlos Sanchez, were deceased. He was survived by his wife Sonia Q Sanchez of Los Angeles. He enlisted in the Marines 29 July, 1963 at the Los Angeles Recruiting Office. He sailed from Okinawa on the USS Paul Revere and made the beach landing on Operation Double Eagle I on 28 January 1966 with Lima Company, 3rd Battalion, 1st Marine Regiment, 3rd Marine Division. On 5 March 1966, Jimmy was a fireteam leader on Operation Utah and exposed himself to hostile fire as he laid covering smoke for the rescue of another fire team with two wounded Marines. During this action he suffered a gunshot wound to the chest and was killed. Corporal Sanchez was posthumously awarded a Silver Star for his conspicuous gallantry and intrepidity in action. Corporal Sanchez is interred at Rose Hills Memorial Park, Whittier, California and is honored on the Vietnam Veterans Memorial Wall, Panel 05E, Line 123.

Sergeant David Shields (27) was born on May 16, 1938 in Glasgow, Scotland. His home is listed as Rutherford, New Jersey. He was survived by his parents Mr. and Mrs. Joseph Shields. Sergeant Shields emigrated to the United States in 1962 and enlisted in the Marine Corps in May 1963. Before coming to the United States he was a sailor. He sailed from Okinawa on the USS Paul Revere and made the beach landing on Operation Double Eagle I on 28 January 1966. with Lima Company. 3rd Battalion, 1st Marine Regiment, as a machine gunner. On 5 March 1966, Sergeant Shields was killed by hostile small arms fire during the assault on Hill 50 during Operation

Utah. He is interred at Long Island National Cemetery, New York and is honored on the Vietnam Veterans Memorial Wall, Panel 05E, Line 124.

Mike Company 3rd Battalion 1st Marine Regiment

On March 4, 1966, Operation UTAH was launched under the command of Task Force Delta in the Son Thinh District of Quang Ngai Province where the Marines would encounter elements of the 21st NVA Regiment. With units pre-positioned the night before, the Marines moved forward on their search and destroy mission at first light on 5 March, 1966. With little contact in the morning hours, Mike Company got heavily engaged with the enemy in the vicinity of Chau Nhai (3) by 1100 hours with the battle continuing into the afternoon. Mike Company engaged and aggressively assaulted the enemy fortified positions and by approximately 1330 hours were able to penetrate the enemy positions which came at a cost of fifteen Marines killed and forty-six wounded in the action. Enemy resistance slackened with nightfall and when the Marines again began their attack at daybreak on 6 March they found the NVA had withdrawn. The position turned out to be an extensive tunnel and underground bunker complex for the NVA 21st Regiment.

Sergeant Charles Eugene Anderson (24) was born on 23 July, 1941 and was from Spokane, Washington. He was survived by his wife Judith Anderson, his two sons, and his mother Gladys Anderson, all of Spokane. He enlisted in the Marine Corps in 1960. Sergeant Anderson was well loved and respected by the men that he trained in Camp Pendleton and Okinawa. When 3/1 was being formed up in Camp Pendleton, he was assigned to Mike Company 3/1. When 3/1 was preparing to leave for Okinawa and Vietnam, he made an effort to ensure that all his men were able to take leave before shipping out. Sergeant Anderson arrived in

Vietnam and made the assault landing on Operation Double Eagle I on 28 January 1966. Sergeant Anderson was killed on 5 March 1966 by hostile small arms fire while assaulting enemy positions in Chau Nhai (3) on Operation Utah. He is interred at Riverside Memorial Park, Spokane, Washington and is honored on the Vietnam Veterans Memorial Wall, Panel 05E, Line 112.

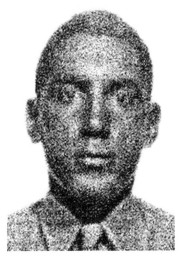

Corporal Anibal Felipe Aviles, Jr. (19) was born 11 April, 1946 in Mayaguez, Puerto Rico and moved to New York, New York with his mother Celeste Aviles. His father; Anibal Felipe Aviles Sr is in Corozal, Puerto Rico. Anibal enlisted in the Marines 17 April, 1963, six days after his 17th birthday. He arrived in Vietnam and made the assault landing on Operation Double Eagle I with Mike Company, 3rd Battalion,1st Marine Regiment, on 28 January 1966. On 5 March 1966 Corporal Aviles was killed by hostile small arms fire while assaulting enemy positions Chau Nhai (3) on Operation Utah. He is interred at Long Island National Cemetery, East Farmingdale, New York and is honored on the Vietnam Veterans Memorial Wall, Panel 05E, Line 113.

Sergeant David Leon Baumgardner (26) was born on March 21, 1939 and was from El Cajon, California. He had enlisted in the Marine Corps in 1958 and served during the Vietnam War. He had the rank of Sergeant. Occupation or specialty was rifleman. Sergeant Baumgardner served with 1st Marine Division, 3rd Battalion, 1st Marines, Mike Company. He arrived in Vietnam and made the assault landing on Operation Double Eagle I with Mike Company on 28 January 1966. On 5

March 1966 Sergeant Baumgardner was killed due to multiple fragmentation Wounds while assaulting enemy positions in Chau Nhai (3) during Operation Utah. He is interred at Mount Calvary Cemetery, Topeka, Kansas and is honored on the Vietnam Veterans Memorial Wall, Panel 05E, Line 112.

Sergeant Charles Ellis Crutchfield (22) was born on January 13, 1944 and was from Kinmundy, Illinois. Sergeant Crutchfield joined the Marine Corp in 1963 and joined Mike Company, 3rd Battalion, 1st Marine Regiment in August 1965. He arrived in Vietnam and made the assault landing on Operation Double Eagle I with Mike Company on 28 January 1966. On 5 March 1966 Sergeant Crutchfield was killed by multiple fragmentation wounds while assaulting enemy positions in Chau Nhai (3) during Operation Utah. He is survived by his father, Ed, of Salem, Illinois and his mother Arizona, of Brush, Colorado. He is interred at Phillips Cemetery, Omega, Illinois and is honored on the Vietnam Veterans Memorial Wall, Panel 05E, Line 117.

Corporal Henry James Doster (19) was born on 7 March, 1946 in Buffalo, New York. Henry was the husband of Jo Ann S. Doster of Buffalo, and the son of Elsie M. Doster of Spencer New York and Junior M. Doster of Buffalo. He enlisted in the US Marine Corps on April 11, 1963 in Buffalo New York. He arrived in Vietnam and made the assault landing on Operation Double Eagle I on 28 January 1966 with Mike Company 3rd Battalion, 1st Marine Regiment. On 5 March 1966 Corporal Doster was killed in action from a hostile gunshot wound while assaulting enemy positions in Chau Nhai (3) during Operation Utah. He is interred at Forest Lawn Cemetery, Buffalo, New York and is honored on the Vietnam Veterans Memorial Wall, Panel 05E, Line 115.

Pfc. Charles Lee Edwards (18) was born 15 March, 1947, in Memphis, Tennessee. Charles the son of James W. Edwards and Frances W. Edwards of Memphis enlisted in the US Marine Corps on July 14 1964 in Memphis TN. He arrived in Vietnam and made the assault landing on Operation Double Eagle I with Mike Company. 3rd Battalion, 1st Marine Regiment on 28 January 1966. On 5 March 1966, Pfc. Edwards was killed in action from a hostile gunshot wound while assaulting enemy positions in Chau Nhai (3) during Operation Utah. FC Edwards is interred at Memorial Park Cemetery, Memphis, Tennessee and is honored on the Vietnam Veterans Memorial Wall, Panel 05E, Line 115.

Pfc. Louis Peter Hernandez (18) was born on June 2, 1947 and was from San Bernardino, California. He was the son of Mr. and Mrs. John Hernandez of San Bernardino. Enlisted in the US Marine Corps in 1965. After Boot Camp and Infantry Training Regiment he was assigned to Mike Company, 3rd Battalion, 1st Marine Regiment, 1st Marine Division as a rifleman He arrived in Vietnam and made the assault landing on Operation Double Eagle I with Mike Company on 28 January 1966. Pfc. Hernandez was killed in action on 5 March 1966, when he sustained wounds from small arms fire while assaulting enemy positions in Chau Nhai (3). Pfc.

Hernandez is interred at Mountain View Cemetery in San Bernardino, California and is honored on the Vietnam Veterans Memorial Wall, Panel 05E, Line 117.

Pfc. Thomas Alvin Jennings (21) was born 18 January, 1945 and was from Robinson, Crawford County, Illinois. Thomas was the son of Robert G. Jennings and Martha Jennings of Palestine, Illinois. Although Tom won a starting position in football at Eastern Illinois University, he left school to enlist in the US Marine Corps on April 30, 1965 in Indianapolis IN. After Boot Camp and Infantry Training Regiment he was assigned to Mike Company, 3rd Battalion, 1st Marine Regiment, 1st Marine Division as a rifleman He arrived in Vietnam and made the assault landing on Operation Double Eagle I with Mike Company on 28 January 1966. Pfc. Jennings was killed in action from a hostile gunshot wound. On 5 March 1966, while assaulting enemy positions in Chau Nhai (3) during Operation Utah. Pfc. Jennings is interred at Palestine Cemetery, in Palestine, Illinois and is honored on the Vietnam Veterans Memorial Wall, Panel 05E, Line 118.

Corporal William David McCuen, Jr. (21) was born on April 2, 1944 and was from Philadelphia, Pennsylvania. He was a 1962 graduate of Northeast Catholic High School and was the son of Mr. and Mrs. William D. McCuen of Philadelphia. The 21-year-old corporal had worked as a drill sergeant before being assigned to Vietnam. He was a rocket launcher, ammunition carrier and squad leader in Mike Company of the 3rd Battalion, 1st Marines, 1st Marine Division. He arrived in Vietnam and made the assault landing on Operation Double Eagle I with Mike Company on 28 January 1966. Corporal McCuen died from hostile small arms fire in Quang Ngai Province on 5 March 1966 while assaulting enemy positions in Chau Nhai (3) during Operation Utah. He is interred at Holy Sepulchre Cemetery, Cheltenham, Pennsylvania and is honored on the Vietnam Veterans Memorial Wall, Panel 05E, Line 121.

Pfc. Charles Adam Mc Gee (18) was born 19 Aug 1947 and was from Alton, Madison County, Illinois. He was the son of Mr. and Mrs. Thomas McGee of Alton. He enlisted in the Marine Corps in February 1965 and took his basic training at San Diego, California. He was assigned to Mike Company, 3rd Battalion, 1st Marine Regiment as a machine gunner. He arrived in Vietnam and made the assault landing on Operation Double Eagle I with Mike Company on 28 January 1966. Pfc. McGee died from a hostile gunshot wound while assaulting enemy positions in Chau Nhai (3) during Operation Utah on 5 March 1966. He is interred at Oakwood Cemetery, Upper Alton, Pennsylvania and is honored on the Vietnam Veterans Memorial Wall, Panel 05E, Line 121.

Pfc. Joel Rodriquez (22) was born 11 March, 1943, Rio Grande City, Starr County, Texas. He was the son of Cecilo and Antonia P. Rodriguez of Rio Grande City, Texas. He enlisted in the Marines 22 March, 1965, at the San Antonio Recruiting Office. After Boot Camp and Infantry Training Regiment he was assigned to Mike Company, 3rd Battalion, 1st Marine Regiment, 1st Marine Division as a rifleman Joel arrived in Vietnam and made the assault landing on Operation Double Eagle I with Mike Company on 28 January 1966. Pfc. Rodriquez was shot in the head and body and was downed in the killing zone of an enemy machine gun during the assault on Chau Nhai (3) on Operation Utah. He was rescued by Pfc. Danny Hernandez but died as a result of his wounds on 5 March 1966. He is interred at Rio Grande City Cemetery, Rio Grande City, Texas and is honored on the Vietnam Veterans Memorial Wall, Panel 05E, Line 124.

Private James Herbert Rowden (21) was born 26 June, 1944 in Medford, Oregon. He was the son of Mr. and Mrs. Harvey Rowden, who lived near McKee Bridge, Oregon. His wife, I. Juanita, and two small children live at the Resmore Mobile Court and Apartments in Talent, Oregon. He attended Medford High School prior to entering the Marine Corps in June, 1962. He left for Viet Nam 26 Aug, 1965 and was assigned to Mike Company, 3rd Battalion, 1st Marine Regiment, 1st Marine Division as a rifleman. James died as a result of multiple fragmentation wounds on 5 March 1966 on Operation Utah. He is interred at Memory Gardens Memorial

Park, Medford, Oregon and is honored on the Vietnam Veterans Memorial Wall, Panel 05E, Line 123.

The Rowdens were notified in February 1968 that their second Marine son, John, 21, had also been killed while fighting on 10 Feb, 1968. John had enlisted because he thought his dead brother would have wished it, the parents explained. They had another son, Douglas who received his draft notice and would be automatically exempted from military service if he were the only remaining son, but the Rowdens also have a younger son, Malcolm, 10 years old.

"I feel we have donated enough to the Vietnam cause," Rowden said, still shocked by notification of John's death. In 1968 James's younger brother John was buried next to him, followed by his father, Harvey, who was a Navy Veteran. The younger brothers Douglas and Malcolm were granted exemptions.

Pfc. Clyde Edward Trievel (19) was born 12 December, 1946 Reading, Berks County, Pennsylvania. Clyde was the son of Clyde E. Trievel Sr. and Mae Trievel of Boyertown, Pennsylvania and enlisted in the US Marine Corps in June 1965 after graduation from Boyertown High School in Reading, Pennsylvania. After Boot Camp and Infantry Training Regiment he was assigned to Mike Company, 3rd Battalion, 1st Marine Regiment, 1st Marine Division as a rifleman He arrived in Vietnam and made the assault landing on Operation Double Eagle I with Mike Company on 28 January 1966. Clyde died as a result of Hostile small arms fire on 5 March 1966 while assaulting enemy positions in Chau Nhai (3) during Operation Utah. He is interred at Friedens Church Cemetery, Oley, Berks County, Pennsylvania and is honored on the Vietnam Veterans Memorial Wall, Panel 05E, Line 125

Pfc. Richard Allen Wagner (18) was born on January 6, 1948 and was from Stockton, California. Pfc. Wagner enlisted in the Marine Corps in 1965 at the age of 17. After Boot Camp and Infantry Training Regiment he was assigned to Mike Company, 3rd Battalion, 1st Marine Regiment, 1st Marine Division as a rifleman He arrived in Vietnam and made the assault landing on Operation Double Eagle I with Mike Company on 28 January 1966. Richard died as a result of Hostile small arms fire on 5 March 1966 while assaulting enemy positions in Chau Nhai (3) during Operation Utah. He is interred at San Joaquin Catholic Cemetery, Stockton, San Joaquin County, California, and is honored on the Vietnam Veterans Memorial Wall, Panel 05E, Line 125

Pfc. Kerry Lee Williams (18) was born 2 July, 1948 and was from Philadelphia, Pennsylvania. He was the son of Louise Stanley of Philadelphia. The Benjamin Franklin High School graduate worked as a stock boy before joining the Marine Corps in August 1965. After Boot Camp and Infantry Training Regiment, the 18-year-old PFC was sent to Viet Nam, where he was assigned to Mike Company of the 3rd Battalion, 1st Marines, 1st Marine Division. Kerry died as a result of Hostile small arms fire on 5 March 1966, while assaulting enemy positions near Chau Nhai (3) during Operation Utah, less than a month after arriving in Viet Nam. He is interred at Arlington National Cemetery and is honored on the Vietnam Veterans Memorial Wall, Panel 05E, Line 125

Golf Company 2nd Battalion 4th Marines

On March 4, Operation UTAH was launched under the command of Task Force Delta in the Son Thinh District of Quang Ngai Province

270

where the Marines would encounter elements of the 21st NVA Regiment. The 2nd Battalion 4th Marines made a Helicopter assault the morning of 5 March in which several helicopters were shot down by .50 cal machine guns. They then proceeded on a search and destroy mission. Golf Company got heavily engaged with the enemy in the vicinity of An Tuyet, Quang Ngai Province until 1100 hours of the next day 6 March, 1966.

Pfc. Kenneth Edward Beauregard (19) was born December 24, 1946 and was from New Bedford, Massachusetts. He was the son of Victor J Beauregard. He arrived in Vietnam in July 1965 with India Company, 3rd Battalion 7th Marine Regiment which was redesignated Golf Company 2nd Battalion, 4th Marine Regiment in October 1965. Kenneth was a rifleman and died as a result of small arms fire on 5 March, 1966 during Operation Utah near An Tuyet in Quang Ngai Province. He is interred at Sacred Hearts Cemetery, New Bedford, Massachusetts and is honored on the Vietnam Veterans Memorial Wall, Panel 05E, Line 113.

Sergeant Antonio Jiminez (28) was born January 9, 1938 and was from Waco, Texas. He arrived in Vietnam in July 1965 with India Company, 3rd Battalion 7th Marine Regiment which was redesignated Golf Company 2nd Battalion, 4th Marine Regiment in October 1965. Sergeant Jiminez was a Platoon Sergeant when he was killed as a result of small arms fire on 5 March 1966 during Operation Utah near An Tuyet In Quang Ngai Province. He is interred at Waco Memorial Park, Waco, Texas and is honored on the Vietnam Veterans Memorial Wall, Panel 05E, Line 119.

Pfc. Darrell Lee Johnson (19) was born on 7/28/1946 and was from Phoenix, Arizona. He was the son of Mr. and Mrs. Weldon B. Johnson of Phoenix. Darrell attended Central High School and enlisted in the Marine Corps in 1964. When Pfc. Johnson arrived in Vietnam he was assigned to Golf Company, 2nd Battalion, 4th Marine Regiment, 3rd Marine Division, Third Marine Amphibious Force as a rocket assault man. Darrell died as a result of a gunshot wound to the side of the abdomen from hostile small arms fire on 5 March 1966 on Operation Utah near An Tuyet in Quang Ngai Provence. He is interred at Greenwood Memory Lawn Cemetery, Phoenix, Maricopa county, Arizona and is honored on the Vietnam Veterans Memorial Wall, Panel 05E, Line 119.

Corporal Conrad Alan Sipple (22) was born on 3 November 1943 and was from Salem, Indiana. He was the son of Mr. and Mrs. Alan Sipple of Salem. Corporal Sipple arrived in Vietnam in July 1965 with India Company, 3rd Battalion 7th Marine Regiment which was redesignated Golf Company 2nd Battalion, 4th Marine Regiment in October 1965. He was assigned as a squad leader in 1st Platoon, Golf Company, when he was killed on 5 March 1966 near An Tuyet on Operation Utah.

The Navy Cross was presented to Corporal Sipple for extraordinary heroism as a squad leader with Golf Company, Second Battalion, Fourth Marines, Third Marine Division (Reinforced), Fleet Marine Force, in the Republic of Vietnam. On 5 March, 1966. The company was engaged in operations against insurgent communist forces in the vicinity of An Tuyet, Quang Ngai Province,

272

when Corporal Sipple's platoon came under extremely heavy small-arms and automatic weapons fire from Viet Cong forces entrenched on a commanding ridgeline. Numerous casualties were inflicted on the platoon and many fell in areas exposed to annihilating fire. With full knowledge of the hazards involved and with complete disregard for his own safety, Corporal Sipple braved the fierce, hostile fire repeatedly to assist in the evacuation of wounded Marines. Oblivious to the unrelenting fusillade of automatic weapons fire, he braved the storm alone on two occasions to assist wounded comrades to safety. On two other occasions, he returned into the vicious enemy fire to assist others in the evacuation of seriously wounded comrades who had to be carried bodily from the extremely hazardous area. On his fourth sally into the furious hail of enemy fire, he was mortally wounded. Through his outstanding initiative and inspiring valor in the face of great personal risk he saved his comrades from further injury or possible loss of life. He gallantly gave his life in the cause of freedom. Corporal Sipple died as a result of small arms fire on 5 March. He is interred at Crown Hill Cemetery, Salem, Indiana. Sipple Road in Camp Pendleton, California is named after Corporal Sipple. He is honored on the Vietnam Veterans Memorial Wall, Panel 05E, Line 124.

Corporal Joseph George Stoudt (20) was born 8 December, 1945 and was from Berks County, Pennsylvania. Joe was born in Pottstown and was a member of Immaculate Conception Roman Catholic Church, Birdsboro. He was the son of Mr. and Mrs. Earnest W. Stoudt of Douglasville. He was a 1963 graduate of Daniel Boone High School, where he played center on the varsity football team. After graduation, Joe worked at Allura Corporation, near Birdsboro, before enlisting in the Marine Corps. He arrived in Vietnam in July 1965 with India Company, 3rd Battalion 7th Marine Regiment which was redesignated Golf Company 2nd Battalion, 4th Marine Regiment in October 1965. On 5 March 1966, Corporal Stoudt was a machine gun team leader on Operation Utah when he was hit in the chest and killed while leading his machine gun team in an attack against heavy automatic weapons fire near An Tuyet in Quang Ngai Province. He is interred at Immaculate Conception Cemetery, Birdsboro, Pennsylvania and is honored on the Vietnam Veterans Memorial Wall, Panel 05E, Line 125.

 **Lance Corporal Michael Linn Bianchini (19)** was born 10 December, 1946 and was from San Francisco, California. He was the son of Mr. and Mrs. Joseph Bianchini of San Francisco. In Vietnam, he was a member of H&S Company Raider Platoon as a fireteam leader in 2nd Battalion, 4th Marine Regiment, 3rd Marine Division. Lance Corporal Michael Lynn "Linn" Bianchini had been awarded a Bronze Star with a V for Valor and a Purple Heart on December 25, 1965. On 5 March 1966 his company was engaged in operations against insurgent communist forces in the vicinity of An Tuyet, Quang Ngai Province during Operation Utah. Lance Corporal Bianchini's raider platoon came under extremely heavy small-arms and automatic weapons fire from Viet Cong forces entrenched on a commanding ridgeline. Lance Corporal Bianchini was killed by a booby trap that was tripped by another Marine and was awarded his second Purple Heart. He is interred at Golden Gate National Cemetery, San Bruno, San Mateo County, California and is honored on the Vietnam Veterans Memorial Wall, Panel 05E, Line 113.

HM Tommy Roger Miller (22) was born May 7, 1943, the son of Arden and Genevee Miller and spent most of his life in the sleepy little community of Laketon, Indiana. He went to school in Laketon and graduated from Laketon High School in 1961. There were 29 other people in his graduating class. He attended the United Brethren Church in Laketon. Like many youth in the 1960s he had a decision to make, serve his country or find a way out of it. In January of 1964 he made his decision by enlisting in the US Navy. On 5 March 1966 Tommy was assigned as a corpsman in Golf Company 2/4 when he was shot in the head shortly after landing in a helicopter assault near An Tuyet in Quang Ngai Province during Operation Utah. He is interred at Pleasant Hill Cemetery, North Manchester, Wabash County, Indiana and is honored on the Vietnam Veterans Memorial Wall, Panel 05E, Line 120.

Bravo Company, 1st Battalion, 7th Marine Regiment

On March 4, Operation UTAH was launched under the command of Task Force Delta in the Son Thinh District of Quang Ngai Province where the Marines would encounter elements of the 21st NVA Regiment. B Company 1st Battalion 7th Marines along with two Companies from 2nd Battalion 4th Marines made a helicopter assault the morning of 5 March near An Tuyet, Quang Ngai Province, in which several helicopters were shot down by hostile .50 cal machine guns. While the two companies from the 4th Marines moved north to support another battalion, Bravo Company stayed at the landing zone to protect the downed helicopters. Isolated in a rice field in no man's land, an under-strength infantry rifle company of 165 young Marines fought one of the most intense battles in the Vietnam War against an estimated five hundred or more elite North Vietnamese soldiers. Surrounded by an NVA battalion and under almost constant fire and pressure throughout the day and night,

Bravo Company fought for its life and were only able to survive with airdrops of critical ammunition supplies.

Pfc. John Henry Bell (21) was born 7 Mar 1944 Olmsted, Pulaski County, Illinois. Pfc. Bell is the son of Mr. Henry & Mrs. Ethel (nee Edmonds) Bell of Peoria, Illinois, and he is a 1962 graduate of Woodruff High School, and joined the Marines on March 10, 1965. Pfc. Bell left a 10-month-old son, John Adrian Bell. Pfc. Bell arrived in Vietnam in November 1965 and served as a rifleman in the area of Quang Ngai Province of South Vietnam with Bravo Company of the 1st Battalion of the 7th Marine Regiment of the 1st Marine Division. Pfc. Bell was killed on 5 March 1966 by hostile small arms fire near An Tuyet in Quang Ngai Province on Operation Utah. He is interred at Springdale Cemetery and Mausoleum, Peoria, Illinois and is honored on the Vietnam Veterans Memorial Wall, Panel 05E, Line 112.

Corporal Roy John Higgins, Jr. (24) was born June 25, 1941 in Belleview, Illinois and was from Maricopa County, Arizona. He was the son of Anna M. Higgins of Phoenix. He arrived in Vietnam in November 1965 and served as the machine gun squad leader in Bravo Company, 1st Battalion, 7th Marines. He re-enlisted in the US Marine Corps on 29 December 1965 while he was in Vietnam. Corporal Higgins was killed on 5 March 1966 by hostile small arms fire near An Tuyet in Quang Ngai Province during Operation Utah. He is interred at Saint Francis Cemetery, Phoenix, Maricopa County, Arizona and is honored on the Vietnam Veterans Memorial Wall, Panel 05E, Line 118.

Corporal Mario Clayton Kitts (19) was born 26 Aug 1946 in Bastian, Bland County, Virginia. Mario was the son of Lucille M. Curry of Monticello, Indiana and Clayton H. Kitts of Des Moines, Iowa. He enlisted in the US Marine Corps on December 27, 1963 in Indianapolis, Indiana. He arrived in Vietnam in November 1965, and was serving with Bravo Company, 1st Battalion, 7th Marines, as a machine gunner on Operation Utah when he was killed on 5 March 1966, by hostile small arms fire near An Tuyet in Quang Ngai Province. He is interred at Lucasville Cemetery, Lucasville, Ohio and is honored on the Vietnam Veterans Memorial Wall, Panel 05E, Line 119.

Sergeant Charles Frederick Setzenfand (24) Charles was the son of Mr. Charles A. Setzenfand and Mrs. Beverly B. Setzenfand of Butler Pennsylvania. He had re-enlisted in the US Marine Corps on April 10, 1964 in Camp LeJeune North Carolina. He arrived in Vietnam in November 1965 and was serving as a squad leader with Company B, 1st Battalion, 7th Marines. in Vietnam. Sergeant Setzenfand was killed on 5 March 1966 by hostile small arms fire near An Tuyet in Quang Ngai Province on Operation Utah. He is interred at Butler County Memorial Park and Mausoleum - Butler, Pennsylvania and is honored on the Vietnam Veterans Memorial Wall, Panel 05E, Line 123.

**Pfc. Gary Ercil Sooter (19)** was born on December 17, 1946 in Ulman, Missouri. His home of record is Independence Missouri. He is the son of Mrs. Robert Root of Independence; his father, Ercil Sooter of Ulman. He made his home with his grandparents, Mr. and Mrs. Alvin Sooter, for about four years. He helped care for Mr. Sooter during the long illness preceding his death. He entered the service on December 30, 1964. He arrived in Vietnam in November 1965 and was a rifleman in Bravo Company, 1st Battalion, 7th Marines when he was killed on 5 March 1966. Bravo Company came under repeated infantry attacks and a heavy barrage of accurate enemy mortar fire while guarding some downed helicopters. Realizing the seriousness of the situation, Pfc. Sooter exposed himself continually to intense small-arms and destructive mortar fire to cover and defend approaches to his platoon's position. Later that night, observing the enemy attempting to penetrate on his left, he again fearlessly ran through a heavy volume of mortar and automatic weapons fire to block the advancing Viet Cong. While blocking the initial attempted enemy penetration, he continued to expose himself, without regard for his own safety to intense enemy fire until he fell mortally wounded. As a result of his courageous actions and heroic initiative, many of the enemy were killed and the attempted penetration of his platoon's position was prevented. Pfc. Sooter was posthumously awarded the Silver Star for his heroic actions. His sister, Marjorie Garner, wrote a book about his life, *Tribute to a Hero*. He is interred at Woodlawn Cemetery, Independence, Missouri and is honored on the Vietnam Veterans Memorial Wall, Panel 05E, Line 124.

Lance Corporal Harry John Stateczny Jr was born on 8/11/1945. He is survived by his father, Harry Stateczny Sr., and two sisters, Helena Stateczny and Jacquiline Muellenbach of Chicago, Illinois. Harry was born and raised in Chicago and was known as "Buddy" to his friends, because he was everyone's friend. Always the life of the party. He just wanted to enjoy life and have a good time. Harry enlisted in the Marines 3 March, 1965, at a Chicago recruiting office. Harry arrived in Vietnam in November 1965, and served as a rifleman in Bravo Company, 1st Battalion, 7th Marine Regiment, 1st Marine Division. On 5 March 1966 while participating in Operation Utah, Bravo Company engaged enemy forces near An Tuyet, 8 kilometers north northwest of the Quang Ngai. During the fire fight, Harry received multiple fragmentation wounds to his right leg and left thigh and was medevac to a Naval Hospital for treatment. Harry was later transferred to the Naval Hospital, at Great Lakes, Illinois, 13 April 1966 for further treatment and to be near his family. He died on 3 July 1966 as a result of cardiac arrest, due to an infection from shrapnel wounds he sustained on Operation Utah on March 5, 1966. He is honored on the Vietnam Veterans Memorial Wall Panel 8E, Line 12.

2nd Battalion 7th Marine Regiment

On March 4, 1966, 7th Marine Regiment experienced its greatest one day loss of life during the Vietnam War when 42 of their own were killed in action. The list of KIA included one officer, one sergeant, and three corporals. The rest of the 37 killed were lance corporals, and PFCs, with an average age of 20 and less than 3 years in the Marine Corps. They came from all over the United States, including two immigrants. Only five were married and they were mostly the older NCOs and officers. Of the four companies from 2/7, there were 12 KIA in Fox Company, 4 in Golf Company, 18 in Hotel Company, and 9 in H&S company. The heaviest casualties were suffered by 2nd Platoon, Hotel Company, when the NVA overran their position.

Fox Company 2nd Battalion 7th Marines

Fox Company 2/7 led the assault into Operation Utah on 4 March 1966. They were heavily engaged when they changed direction to support the ARVN forces engaged on Hill 50. When the ARVN forces failed to support Fox Company's left flank, they lost contact with their 1st Platoon and suffered heavy casualties.

Second Lieutenant Donald Richard Lumley was born December 30, 1936, and was from Knoxville, Tennessee. He was the son of Mr. and Mrs. Harry C. Lumley and the husband of Karolee Lumley of Sacramento, California. Before he entered the service he had a promising baseball career. In 1956, Lumley joined the Marine Corps for three years where he played baseball. After he left the Marine Corps he played minor league ball and served as the freshman baseball coach at the University of Tennessee in Knoxville. 2nd Lieutenant Lumley was an eight-year veteran of the US Marine Corps who was recalled to active duty and was commissioned as a 2nd Lieutenant in January 1965. In August of 1965 he joined Hotel Company 2nd Battalion, 1st Marine Regiment in Camp Pendleton. He arrived in Vietnam in November 1965 and at the end of February 1966, his company was re-designated Fox Company 2nd Battalion, 7th Marine Regiment under the command of Captain Jerry Lindauer. He served with Fox Company, as the Platoon Commander of their 1st platoon. On 4 March 1966. 2nd Lieutenant Lumley, age 29, was killed in action dying from enemy gunshot wounds when his platoon was cut off on Operation Utah near Hill 50. 2nd Lieutenant Lumley is interred at East Lawn Elk Grove Memorial Park, Elk Grove, California and is honored on the Vietnam Veterans Memorial on Panel 05E, Line 107.

Sergeant Donnell Dean McMillin was the son of Mr. and Mrs. John M. McMillin of Adrian, Missouri. and the husband of Dorothy L. McMillin of Mena, Arkansas. Sergeant McMillin was an eight-year veteran of the US Marine Corps. Sergeant McMillin was a Marine rifleman, age 25, born November 3, 1940. Sergeant McMillin arrived in Vietnam in November 1965 with Hotel Company 2nd Battalion, 1st Marine Regiment and the company was re-designated Fox Company 2nd Battalion, 7th Marines on 1 March, 1966.. Sergeant McMillin was killed in action on 4 March 1966, dying from enemy gunshot wounds during Operation Utah near Hill 50. Sergeant McMillin is interred at Pinecrest Memorial Park, Mena, Polk County, Arkansas and is honored on the Vietnam Veterans Memorial on Panel 05E, Line 109. For his heroic actions that day Sergeant McMillin was awarded the Silver Star.

CITATION: The President of the United States of America takes pride in presenting the Silver Star (Posthumously) to Sergeant Donnell D. McMillin (MCSN: 1813597), United States Marine Corps, for conspicuous gallantry and intrepidity in action while serving with Company F, Second Battalion, Seventh Marines, FIRST Marine Division (Rein.), FMF, in the Republic of Vietnam on 4 March 1966. The company came under extremely heavy automatic weapons fire from an estimated Viet Cong regiment which was well entrenched on its front and flank. As his platoon maneuvered toward the enemy, Sergeant McMillin, completely disregarding his own personal safety, made his way through intense enemy fire to some of his men who could not advance. Ignoring the vicious fire and demonstrating courage and authority in the face of grave danger, he led these men out of their covered position and across a fire-swept rice paddy toward the enemy. Immediately after this movement, the leader of the second platoon was seriously wounded and Sergeant McMillin, with full knowledge of the hazard involved, unhesitatingly and with complete disregard for his own personal safety, went to his aid. In doing so, he was mortally wounded. With bold initiative and uncommon courage, Sergeant McMillin was an inspiring example to his men as he upheld the highest traditions of the Marine Corps and the United States Naval Service. He gallantly gave his life in the cause of freedom.

 **Corporal Bruce Davis** was the son of Isam Davis and Georgia E. Davis of Gilbert, Louisiana. He enlisted in the US Marine Corps on April 30, 1963 in Shreveport, Louisiana. Corporal Davis was a Marine rifleman, age 20, born August 2, 1945. Corporal Davis arrived in Vietnam in November 1965 with Hotel Company 2nd Battalion, 1st Marine Regiment and the company was re-designated Fox Company 2nd Battalion, 7th Marines on 1 March 1966. On 4 March 1966, Corporal Davis was killed in action dying from enemy gunshot wounds during Operation Utah near Hill 50. Corporal Davis is interred at Oakley Cemetery, Franklin Parish, Louisiana and is honored on the Vietnam Veterans Memorial on Panel 05E, Line 101. Corporal Davis was presented with the Silver Star Medal posthumously "For conspicuous gallantry and intrepidity in action."

CITATION: The President of the United States of America takes pride in presenting the Silver Star (Posthumously) to Corporal Bruce Davis (MCSN: 2035575), United States Marine Corps, for conspicuous gallantry and intrepidity in action while serving with Fox Company, Second Battalion, Seventh Marines, first Marine Division (Rein.), FMFPac, in connection with combat operations against the enemy in the Republic of Vietnam on 4 March 1966. During an operation in Quang Ngai Province, his company came under heavy frontal and flanking fire from a well-entrenched Viet Cong force. As a Squad Leader in the reserve platoon, Corporal Davis was given the mission of assisting the left flank platoon in holding off an enemy assault and evacuating wounded Marines. He unhesitatingly led his squad through intense fire against an enemy unit that was attempting to envelop the company's flank. Through his aggressive leadership and skilled deployment of his squad, the enemy assault was repulsed without a single friendly casualty. His men succeeded in killing twenty Viet Cong in the process. Again maneuvering his squad in order to make contact with the left flank platoon, one of his members was seriously wounded. When he attempted to reach the wounded Marine he was met by a large volume of fire. Corporal Davis, with complete disregard for his own personal safety, moved through the intense fire to the side of his comrade and gave him aid. While attempting to remove the wounded Marine, Corporal Davis was mortally wounded. His bold initiative, aggressiveness, and uncommon ability as a leader of men were in keeping with the highest traditions of the Marine Corps and of the United States Naval Service. He gallantly gave his life for his country.

 **Lance Corporal Allen Charles Bailey** was the son of Mr. and Mrs. Hayden L. Bailey of Omaha, Nebraska. He enlisted in the US Marine Corps on April 29, 1963 in Omaha, NE. Lance Corporal Bailey was a Marine Machine Gunner, age 20, born August 31, 1945, from Omaha, NE. Lance Corporal Bailey arrived in Vietnam in November 1965 with Hotel Company 2nd Battalion, 1st Marine Regiment and his company was re-designated Fox Company 2nd Battalion, 7th Marine Regiment on 1 March 1966. On 4 March 1966, Lance Corporal Bailey was killed in action, dying from enemy gunshot wounds during Operation Utah near Hill 50. Lance Corporal Bailey is interred at Westlawn-Hillcrest Memorial Park, Omaha, Nebraska and is honored on the Vietnam Veterans Memorial on Panel 05E, Line 099.

Private First Class Ronald William Goddard was the son of Jack W. Goddard (Deceased) and Mildred A. Goddard of Seattle, Washington. He enlisted in the US Marine Corps on October 6, 1964. Pfc. Goddard was a Marine anti-tank assaultman, age 18, born June 20, 1947, from Seattle, WA. Pfc. Goddard arrived in Vietnam in November 1965 with Hotel Company 2nd Battalion, 1st Marine Regiment and his company was re-designated Fox Company 2nd Battalion, 7th Marine Regiment on 1 March 1966. On 4 March 1966, Pfc. Goddard was killed in action dying from enemy gunshot wounds while trying to rescue a wounded Marine. Pfc. Goddard is interred at Washington Memorial Park, SeaTac, King County, Washington and is honored on the Vietnam Veterans Memorial on Panel 05E, Line 102. Pfc. Ronald W. Goddard was presented with the Bronze Star Medal with a Combat V, posthumously "For heroic achievement on March 4, 1966."

Pfc. David Michel Hann was a Marine rifleman, age 19, born December 30, 1946, from Santa Monica, California. Pfc. Hann arrived in Vietnam in November 1965 with Hotel Company 2nd Battalion, 1st Marine Regiment and his company was re-designated Fox Company 2nd Battalion, 7th Marine Regiment on 1 March 1966. On 4 March 1966, Pfc. Hann was killed in action dying from enemy gunshot wounds during Operation Utah near Hill 50. Pfc. Hann is interred at Fort Rosecrans National Cemetery, San Diego, San Diego County, California and is honored on the Vietnam Veterans Memorial on Panel 05E, Line 103.

Private First Class Harry Philip Helt, Jr. was the son of Harry P. Helt Sr. and Elizabeth Helt of Staten Island, New York. He enlisted in the US Marine Corps on June 24, 1964. Pfc. Helt was a Marine rifleman, age 21, born September 10, 1944, from New York, New York. Pfc. Helt arrived in Vietnam in November 1965 with Hotel Company 2nd Battalion, 1st Marine Regiment and his company was re-designated Fox Company 2nd Battalion, 7th Marine Regiment on 1 March 1966. On 4 March 1966, Pfc. Helt was killed in action dying from enemy gunshot wounds during Operation Utah near Hill 50. Pfc. Helt is interred at Moravian Cemetery, New Dorp, New York and is honored on the Vietnam Veterans Memorial on Panel 05E, Line 103.

Private First Class Robert Berg Labbe was the son of Helen K. Labbe of Salem, OH and Gerald R. Labbe. He enlisted in the US Marine Corps on September 1, 1964 in Cleveland, Ohio. Pfc. Labbe was a Marine rifleman, age 19, born November 23, 1946, from Salem, Oregon. Pfc. Labbe arrived in Vietnam in November 1965 with Hotel Company 2nd Battalion, 1st Marine Regiment and his company was re-designated Fox Company 2nd Battalion, 7th Marine Regiment on 1 March 1966. On 4 March 1966, Pfc. Labbe was killed in action, dying from enemy gunshot wounds during Operation Utah near Hill 50. Pfc. Labbe is honored on the Vietnam Veterans Memorial on Panel 05E, Line 106.

Lance Corporal Michael Anthony Shands was the husband of Carol Shands, the son of Elmer E. Shands and Frances L. Shands all of Rosemead, California. He enlisted in the US Marine Corps on September 1, 1964 in Seattle, WA. Lance Corporal Shands was a Marine anti-tank assaultman, age 20, born July 3, 1945, from Issaquah, WA. Lance Corporal Shands arrived in Vietnam in November 1965 with Hotel Company 2nd Battalion, 1st Marine Regiment and his company was re-designated Fox Company 2nd Battalion, 7th Marine Regiment on 1 March 1966. Lance Corporal Shands was killed 4 March 1966 when Fox Company was maneuvering across some open rice paddies and came under intense enemy fire during Operation Utah near Hill 50. Lance Corporal Shands is interred at Rose Hills Memorial Park, Whittier, California and is honored on the Vietnam Veterans Memorial on Panel 05E, Line 109.

Lance Corporal Alfred John Smith was a Marine rifleman, age 20, born November 3, 1945, from Houston, Texas. Lance Corporal Smith arrived in Vietnam in November 1965 with Hotel Company 2nd Battalion, 1st Marine Regiment and his company was re-designated Fox Company 2nd Battalion, 7th Marine Regiment on 1 March 1966. On 4 March 1966 Lance Corporal Smith was in the first wave of a helicopter assault on the area near Hill 50 during Operation Utah and was killed from enemy gunshot wounds while maneuvering across a field of fire. Lance Corporal Smith is interred at Saint Cyril & Methodius Catholic Cemetery, Damon, Texas and is honored on the Vietnam Veterans Memorial on Panel 05E, Line 109.

Private First Class Cresencio Paul Sanchez was the son of Eddie Sanchez of Wilmington, California, and the dear brother of Lydia Sanchez. He had two years of prior service in the US Army before he enlisted in the US Marine Corps on October 21, 1964 in Albuquerque, New Mexico. Pfc. Sanchez was a Marine rifleman, age 20, born December 21, 1945, from Roswell, New Mexico. Pfc. Sanchez arrived in Vietnam in November 1965 with Hotel Company 2nd Battalion, 1st Marine Regiment and his company was re-designated Fox Company 2nd Battalion, 7th Marine Regiment on 1 March 1966. On 4 March 1966, Pfc. Sanchez was killed in action dying from enemy gunshot wounds during Operation Utah near Hill 50. Pfc. Sanchez is honored on the Vietnam Veterans Memorial on Panel 05E, Line 109.

Private First Class Delbert Leroy Trube, Jr. was the son of Delbert Leroy Trube, Sr. and Betty A. Chambers Trube of Burdick, Kansas. Pfc. Trube was a Marine Machine Gunner, age 18, born August 18, 1947, from Burdick, Kansas. Pfc. Trube arrived in Vietnam in November 1965 with Hotel Company 2nd Battalion, 1st Marine Regiment and his company was re-designated Fox Company 2nd Battalion, 7th Marine on 1 March 1966. On 4 March 1966, Pfc. Trube was killed in action, dying from multiple fragmentation wounds from an enemy explosive device during Operation Utah near Hill 50. Pfc. Trube is honored on the Vietnam Veterans Memorial on Panel 05E, Line 110.

Golf Company 2nd Battalion 7th Marines
On 4 March, 1966 Golf Company was engaged in a fierce firefight during Operation Utah. They were able to destroy two enemy Machine gun emplacements and held the center of the line for 2/7 until they were able to consolidate to night positions at Chau Nhai (4).

Private Gary Charles Allen was the son of Mary R. Tyler of Pleasant Hill, California and William I. Allen Jr. With his Twin brother Larry and older brother William, he left school to enlist in the Marine Corps in 1963. Gary had been active in Concord Boy Scouts and was a Varsity Guard on the Pleasant Hill High School Football team. Private Allen was a Marine rifleman, age 20, born December 22, 1945, from Pleasant Hill, California. Private Allen arrived in Vietnam on 6 July 1965 with Golf Company, 2nd Battalion, 7th Marines. On 4 March 1966, Private Allen was killed in action from multiple fragmentation wounds from an enemy explosive device while assaulting an enemy position on Operation Utah. Private Allen is interred at Queen of Heaven Cemetery, Lafayette, Contra Costa County, California and is honored on the Vietnam Veterans Memorial on Panel 05E, Line 097.

Lance Corporal Heriberto Armenta was born in Cananea, Mexico. His parents came to California when he was still a boy. He enlisted in the US Marines on February 12, 1964 in Los Angeles, California. Lance Corporal Armenta was a Marine rifleman, age 19, born June 6, 1946, from Los Angeles, California. Lance Corporal Armenta arrived in Vietnam on 6 July 1965 with Golf Company, 2nd Battalion, 7th Marines, 1st Marine Division (Rein), III

MAF, FMFPac. On 4 March 1966, Lance Corporal Armenta was killed in action dying from multiple fragmentation wounds from an enemy explosive device as he was assaulting an enemy machine gun position during Operation Utah. Lance Corporal Armenta is interred at Calvary Cemetery, Los Angeles, Los Angeles County, California and is honored on the Vietnam Veterans Memorial on Panel 05E, Line 098.

Lance Corporal Lester Robert Atherden was a Marine Machine Gunner, age 21, born September 6, 1944, from Milford, Connecticut. Lance Corporal Atherden arrived in Vietnam on 6 July 1965 with Golf Company, 2nd Battalion, 7th Marines, 1st Marine Division (Rein), III MAF, FMFPac. On 4 March 1966, Lance Corporal Atherden was killed in action dying from enemy gunshot wounds as he was assaulting an enemy position during Operation Utah. Lance Corporal Atherden is interred at Saint Michael's Cemetery, Stratford, Connecticut and is honored on the Vietnam Veterans Memorial on Panel 05E, Line 100.

Lance Corporal Isiah Baker, III was the son of Mazerine M. Miller and Isiah Baker Jr. (Deceased) of New Orleans, Louisiana. He enlisted in the US Marine Corps on April 8, 1963 in New Orleans, Louisiana. Lance Corporal Baker was a Marine rifleman, age 23, born November 26, 1942, from New Orleans, Louisiana. Lance Corporal Baker arrived in Vietnam on 6 July 1965 with Golf Company, 2nd Battalion, 7th Marines, 1st Marine Division (Rein), III MAF, FMFPac. On 4 March 1966, Lance Corporal Baker was killed in action, dying from enemy gunshot wounds while assaulting an enemy position during Operation Utah. Lance Corporal Baker is interred at Mount Olivet Cemetery and Mausoleum, New Orleans, Louisiana and is honored on the Vietnam Veterans Memorial on Panel 05E, Line 099.

Hotel Company 2/7

Hotel Company suffered the most casualties on 4 March, 1966 when they were overrun on Hill 37. They managed to beat back the attack and later consolidated with the rest of the battalion at Chau Nhai (4). Three of the four corpsmen assigned to Hotel Company were killed.

Pfc. Richard Graham Allen was the son of Sergeant 1/C Ronald I. Allen of HQ Co. USAG-SAS Engineer Section on active duty and Margaret M. Lutes of Long Beach, California. He enlisted in the US Marine Corps on February 26, 1964 in Los Angeles, California. Pfc. Allen was a Marine rifleman, age 19, born January 28, 1947, from Long Beach, California. Pfc. Allen arrived in Vietnam on 6 July 1965 with Hotel Company, 2nd Battalion, 7th Marines, 1st Marine Division (Rein), III MAF, FMFPac. On 4 March 1966, Pfc. Allen was killed in action dying from enemy small arms fire while assaulting Hill 37. Pfc. Allen is interred at Sunnyside Cemetery, Long Beach, Los Angeles County, California and is honored on the Vietnam Veterans Memorial on Panel 05E, Line 098.

Pfc. Stephen Paul Alsted was a Marine rifleman, age 19, born April 19, 1946, from Des Moines, Iowa. Pfc. Alsted arrived in Vietnam on 6 July 1965 with Hotel Company, 2nd Battalion, 7th Marines, 1st Marine Division (Rein), III MAF, FMFPac. On 4 March 1966, Pfc. Alsted was killed in action dying from enemy small arms fire while assaulting Hill 37 during Operation Utah. Pfc. Alsted is interred at Laurel Hill Cemetery in Des Moines and is honored on the Vietnam Veterans Memorial on Panel 05E, Line 098.

Lance Corporal Raymond Blanchette was the son of Raymond A. Blanchette and Marie Gaboriau Blanchette of Tolland, Connecticut. He enlisted in the US Marine Corps on September 25, 1962 in Hartford, Connecticut. Lance Corporal Blanchette was a Marine rifleman, age 21, born May 22, 1944, from Tolland, Connecticut. Lance Corporal Blanchette arrived in Vietnam on 6 July 1965 with Hotel Company, 2nd Battalion, 7th Marines, 1st Marine Division (Rein), III MAF, FMFPac. On 4 March 1966, Lance Corporal Blanchette was killed in action, dying from enemy gunshot wounds while assaulting Hill 37 during Operation Utah. Lance Corporal Blanchette is interred at Saint Bernard's Cemetery, Rockville, Connecticut and is honored on the Vietnam Veterans Memorial on Panel 05E, Line 099.

Lance Corporal Rupert Sadler Carven, III was the son of Rupert Sadler Carven Jr. and Dorothy Veronica Durant Carven of Newton, MA. He enlisted in the US Marine Corps on November 1, 1962 in Boston, MA. Lance Corporal Carven was a Marine rifleman, age 24, born December 27, 1941, from Newton, MA. Lance Corporal Carven arrived in Vietnam on 6 July 1965 with Hotel Company, 2nd Battalion, 7th Marines, 1st Marine Division (Rein), III MAF, FMFPac. On 4 March 1966, Lance Corporal Carven was killed in action, dying from enemy gunshot wounds while leading his fire team in an assault on hill 37 during Operation Utah. Lance Corporal Carven is interred at Holyhood Cemetery, Brookline, Massachusetts and is honored on the Vietnam Veterans Memorial on Panel 05E, Line 100.

Lance Corporal John Jay Edwards was the son of Ralph F. Edwards Jr. and Jacqueline T. Edwards of Dillsburg, Pennsylvania. He enlisted in the US Marine Corps on August 31, 1964 in Philadelphia, Pennsylvania. Lance Corporal Edwards was a Marine rifleman, age 20, born February 25, 1946, from Lock Haven, Pennsylvania. Lance Corporal Edwards arrived in Vietnam in January 1966 and was assigned to Hotel Company, 2nd Battalion, 7th Marines, 1st Marine Division (Rein), III MAF, FMFPac. On 4 March 1966, Lance Corporal Edwards was killed in action from enemy gunshot wounds while clearing a night position on the defensive perimeter during Operation Utah. Lance Corporal Edwards is interred at Saint Mary's Cemetery, Wilkes-Barre, Pennsylvania and is honored on the Vietnam Veterans Memorial on Panel 05E, Line 102.

Pfc. William Johnson was the son of Hattie "B" Johnson of Dallas, Texas and Floyd Johnson of Frisco, Texas. He enlisted in the US Marine Corps on February 10, 1964 in Dallas, Texas. Pfc. Johnson was a Marine rifleman, age 20, born December 11, 1945, from Dallas, Texas. Pfc. Johnson arrived in Vietnam on 6 July 1965 with Hotel Company, 2nd Battalion, 7th Marines, 1st Marine Division (Rein), III MAF, FMFPac. On 4 March 1966, Pfc. Johnson was killed in action dying from enemy small arms fire while assaulting Hill 37 during Operation Utah. Pfc. Johnson is interred at Sand Flat Pioneer Cemetery, Athens, Texas and is honored on the Vietnam Veterans Memorial on Panel 05E, Line 105.

Lance Corporal Andrew Lalone Hastings was the son of LaVerne E. Signaigo of Lamay, MO. and Andrew C. Hastings deceased. He enlisted in the US Marine Corps on August 31, 1964 in Philadelphia, Pennsylvania. Lance Corporal Hastings was a Marine rifleman, age 22, born August 6, 1943, from Lemay, Missouri. Lance Corporal Hastings arrived in Vietnam on 6 July 1965 with Hotel Company, 2nd Battalion, 7th Marines, 1st Marine Division (Rein), III MAF, FMFPac. On 4 March 1966, Lance Corporal Hastings was killed in action dying from enemy gunshot wounds while assaulting Hill 37 on Operation Utah. Lance Corporal Hastings is interred at Resurrection Cemetery, Affton, Missouri and is honored on the Vietnam Veterans Memorial on Panel 05E, Line 102.

Lance Corporal Klaus Jurgen Herms was the son of Walter B. Herms and Hildegard M. Herms of Covina, California. He enlisted in the US Marine Corps on February 10, 1964 in Los Angeles, California. Lance Corporal Herms was a Marine rifleman, age 20, born June 28, 1945, in Gleiwitz, Poland, his family emigrated to the United States and settled in San Dimas, California. Lance Corporal Herms arrived in Vietnam on 6 July 1965 with Hotel Company, 2nd Battalion, 7th Marines, 1st Marine Division (Rein), III MAF, FMFPac. On 4 March 1966, during Operation Utah, Lance Corporal Herms was severely wounded while assaulting Hill 37 but managed to help carry a wounded officer to an medivac landing zone. He was killed when a enemy mortar round exploded in the landing zone just as he was about to be evacuated. Lance Corporal Herms is interred at Forest Lawn Memorial Park, Covina, Los Angeles County, California and is honored on the Vietnam Veterans Memorial on Panel 05E, Line 104.

Corporal Henry James Hooper was the Son of Mr. Henry Thomas Hooper and Mrs. Carrie Bell Beville. Corporal Hooper was a Marine rifleman, age 23, born February 6, 1943, from Reidsville, North Carolina. Corporal Hooper arrived in Vietnam on 6 July 1965 with Hotel Company, 2nd Battalion, 7th Marines, 1st Marine Division (Rein), III MAF, FMFPac. On 4 March 1966, Corporal Hooper was killed in action dying from enemy gunshot wounds while leading his squad in an assault on Hill 37 during Operation Utah. Corporal Hooper is interred at Reidlawn Cemetery in Reidsville, North Carolina and is honored on the Vietnam Veterans Memorial on Panel 05E, Line 104. For his heroic actions that day Corporal Hooper was awarded the Bronze Star with the Combat V for Valor.

Lance Corporal William John Hrinko was the son of John J. Hrinko and Anna Hrinko of Worthington, Ohio. He enlisted in the US Marine Corps on February 29, 1964 in Cincinnati, Ohio. Lance Corporal Hrinko was a Marine rifleman, age 22, born March 9, 1943, from Worthington, OH. Lance Corporal Hrinko arrived in Vietnam on 6 July 1965 with Hotel Company, 2nd Battalion, 7th Marines, 1st Marine Division (Rein), III MAF, FMFPac. On 4 March 1966, Lance Corporal Hrinko was wounded while assaulting Hill 37 and was later killed by a mortar explosion when he was being evacuated by helicopter. Lance Corporal Hrinko is interred at Union Cemetery, Columbus, Ohio and is honored on the Vietnam Veterans Memorial on Panel 05E, Line 104.

Pfc. Thomas Patrick Johnston (20) was born 27 December 1945 and was from Philadelphia, Pennsylvania. He was the son of Mr. and Mrs. Thomas E. Johnston of Philadelphia. He arrived in Vietnam on 6 July 1965 with Hotel Company, 2nd Battalion, 7th Marines as a rifleman. On 4 March 1966, Operation Utah was launched in Quang Ngai Province where the Marines would encounter elements of the 21st NVA Regiment. Pfc. Johnston survived the fierce battle on 4 March but was killed by small arms fire on 5 March during the mop up. He is interred at Beverly National Cemetery, Beverly, New Jersey and is honored on the Vietnam Veterans Memorial Wall, Panel 05E, Line 119.

Private First Class Lewis Albert Kimmel, Jr. was the son of Technical Sergeant Lewis A. Kimmel Sr. USAF stationed at Tan Son Nhut AFB Air Force Base in Saigon, Vietnam and Pearl E. Kimmel of Camarillo, California. He enlisted in the US Marine Corps on February 15, 1963 in Port Hueneme, California. Pfc. Kimmel was a Marine rifleman, age 21, born May 23, 1944, in Camarillo, California. Pfc. Kimmel arrived in Vietnam on 6 July 1965 with Hotel Company, 2nd Battalion, 7th Marines, 1st Marine Division. On 4 March 1966, Pfc. Kimmel was killed in action dying from enemy small arms fire while assaulting Hill 37 on Operation Utah. His father Technical Sergeant Lewis Kimmel Sr. escorted his son's body back to Camarillo California. Pfc. Kimmel is interred at Ivy Lawn Cemetery, Ventura, California and is honored on the Vietnam Veterans Memorial on Panel 05E, Line 105.

Private First Class Franz Joseph Kolbeck was the son of Charlotte Kolbeck and Joseph F. Kolbeck (deceased) of Deerfield, Illinois. He won all state honors in Football in High School. Those who knew him described him as a gentle giant. He enlisted in the US Marine Corps on August 9, 1963 in Chicago, Illinois. Pfc. Kolbeck was a Marine rifleman, age 21, born October 3, 1944, from Deerfield, Illinois. Pfc. Kolbeck arrived in Vietnam on 6 July 1965 with Hotel Company, 2nd Battalion, 7th Marines. On 4 March 1966, Pfc. Kolbeck was killed in action, dying from enemy small arms fire while assaulting Hill 37 during Operation Utah. Pfc. Kolbeck is interred at Memorial Park Cemetery, Skokie, Illinois and is honored on the Vietnam Veterans Memorial on Panel 05E, Line 106.

Private First Class Vinford Franklyn Michael was the son of Mr. and Mrs. Joseph Michael of the Bronx, New York, the husband of Sandra R. Michael, the father of Vinford F. Michael, Jr. and the brother of Lance Corporal Victor Michael serving with H&HS-2, MWHG-2 in Cherry Point, North Carolina. He enlisted in the US Marine Corps on June 26, 1964 in New York, New York. Pfc. Michael was a Marine rifleman, age 20, born January 30, 1946, from New York, New York. Pfc. Michael arrived in Vietnam on 6 July 1965 with Hotel Company, 2nd Battalion, 7th Marines, 1st Marine Division. On 4 March 1966, Pfc. Michael was killed in action dying from enemy small arms fire while assaulting Hill 37 during Operation Utah. Pfc. Michael had been in Vietnam for 242 days. Pfc. Michael is interred at Long Island National Cemetery and is honored on the Vietnam Veterans Memorial on Panel 05E, Line 107.

Private First Class Henry Duane Odom was the son of William Aaron Odom (Deceased) and Georgia Elizabeth Taylor Odom of Eldorado, Oklahoma. Pfc. Odom was a Marine rifleman, age 19, born August 27, 1946, from Eldorado, Oklahoma. Pfc. Odom arrived in Vietnam on July 6, 1965 with 3rd Platoon, Hotel Company, 2nd Battalion, 7th Marines, 1st Marine Division. On 4 March 1966, Pfc. Odom was killed in action dying from multiple fragmentation wounds when he went to support his friends in 2nd Platoon who were being overrun on Hill 37 during Operation Utah. Pfc. Odom had been in Vietnam for 242 days. Pfc. Odom is interred at Eldorado Cemetery, Eldorado, Oklahoma and is honored on the Vietnam Veterans Memorial on Panel 05E, Line 108.

Lance Corporal Peter Gary Scavuzzo was the son of Lorraine Scavuzzo (Deceased) and William R. Scavuzzo of Toms River, NJ and brother of William R. Scavuzzo of Bayonne, NJ. Lance Corporal Scavuzzo was a Marine rifleman, age 19, born October 10, 1946, from Toms River, NJ. Lance Corporal Scavuzzo arrived in Vietnam on 6 July with Hotel Company, 2nd Battalion, 7th Marines, 1st Marine Division. On 4 March 1966, Lance Corporal Scavuzzo was killed in action, dying from enemy small arms fire as he was assaulting Hill 37 on Operation Utah. Lance Corporal Scavuzzo is interred at Saint Gertrude Cemetery, Colonia, New Jersey and is honored on the Vietnam Veterans Memorial on Panel 05E, Line 107.

Lance Corporal Robert Lee Smith, Jr. was the son of Robert A. and Annie M. Smith of Newport News, VA. He enlisted in the US Marine Corps on June 19, 1964 in Richmond, VA. Lance Corporal Smith was a Marine Machine Gunner, age 20, born July 31, 1945, from Newport News, VA. Lance Corporal Smith arrived in Vietnam on 6 July 1965 with Hotel Company, 2nd Battalion, 7th Marines, 1st Marine Division. On 4 March 1966, Lance Corporal Smith was killed in action while assigned to 1st Platoon Hotel Company, as they rescued a platoon from Fox Company during Operation Utah. He died from multiple fragmentation wounds from an NVA Grenade. Lance Corporal Smith is interred at Warwick River Mennonite Church Cemetery, Newport News, Virginia and is honored on the Vietnam Veterans Memorial on Panel 05E, Line 110.

Pfc. Charles Robert Wetzel (20), born December 24, 1945, from Penns Grove, New Jersey. He was the son of Edward H. Wetzel and Caroline S. Wetzel of Penns Grove, New Jersey. Pfc. Wetzel was a Marine rifleman. He arrived in Vietnam on 6 July 1965 with Fox Company, 2nd Battalion, 7th Marines, 1st Marine Division. After recovering from malaria in December 1965, he was reassigned to Hotel Company 2nd Battalion 7th Marines as a 60mm Mortar man. On 4 March 1966, Pfc. Wetzel was killed in action, dying from enemy small arms fire while assaulting Hill 37 during Operation Utah. Pfc Wetzel is interred at Saint Mary's Cemetery, Salem, New Jersey and is honored on the Vietnam Veterans Memorial on Panel 05E, Line 111.

Hospitalman Third Class Daniel Patrick Birch was a US Navy Corpsman, age 20, born February 28, 1946, from Los Angeles, California. HM3 Birch arrived in Vietnam on 6 July 1965 with Headquarters and Service Company, 2nd Battalion, 7th Marines, 1st Marine Division (Rein), III MAF, FMFPac. He was attached to Hotel Company for operational purposes. On 4 March 1966, HM3 Birch was killed in action dying outright from multiple fragmentation wounds from an enemy explosive device during Operation Utah. HM3 Birch is interred at Long Island National Cemetery, East Farmingdale, Suffolk County, New York and is honored on the Vietnam Veterans Memorial on Panel 05E, Line 99.

Lance Corporal William Wesley Brown was the son of Corlis R. Brown of Indian Harbour Beach, Florida and Thelma Brown (Deceased). He enlisted in the US Marine Corps on January 30, 1964 in Shreveport, Louisiana. Lance Corporal Brown was a Marine rifleman, age 19, born September 7, 1946, from Shreveport, Louisiana. Lance Corporal Brown arrived in Vietnam on 6 July 1965 with Headquarters and Service Company, 2nd Battalion, 7th Marines, 1st Marine Division. He was attached to Hotel Company for operational purposes. On 4 March 1966, Lance Corporal Brown was killed in action, dying from enemy small arms fire while assaulting Hill 37 on Operation Utah. Lance Corporal Brown is honored on the Vietnam Veterans Memorial on Panel 05E, Line 099.

Private First Class Michael Anthony Gilson was the son of Carl A. Sr. and Josephine M. Brady Gilson of Sacramento, California. He enlisted in the US Marine Corps on January 28, 1964 in San Francisco, California. Pfc. Gilson was a Marine Field Radio Operator, age 20, born January 21, 1946, from Sacramento, California. Pfc. Gilson arrived in Vietnam on 6 July 1965 with Headquarters and Service Company, 2nd Battalion, 7th Marines, 1st Marine Division. On 4 March 1966, Pfc. Gilson was killed in action, dying from enemy small arms fire as he assaulted Hill 37 during Operation Utah. Pfc. Gilson is honored on the Vietnam Veterans Memorial on Panel 05E, Line 103.

Corporal Johnny Ray Holloway was the son of Loane W. Bevill and Anderson B. Holloway (deceased) of Okolona, Mississippi. He enlisted in the US Marine Corps on August 1, 1962 in Memphis, TN. Corporal Holloway was a Marine Mortarman, age 20, born July 14, 1945, from Okolona, Mississippi. Corporal Holloway arrived in Vietnam on July 1965 with Headquarters and Service Company, 2nd Battalion, 7th Marines, 1st Marine Division as a member of the Battalion 81mm Mortar Platoon. On 4 March 1966, Corporal Holloway was killed in action, dying from enemy small arms fire near Chau Nhai (4) during Operation Utah. Corporal Holloway is honored on the Vietnam Veterans Memorial on Panel 05E, Line 104.

Pfc. Joseph Samuel Herron was the son of Tucker and Margaret Herron of Jackson, Mississippi. He enlisted in the US Marine Corps on May 2, 1964. Pfc. Herron was a Marine anti-tank assaultman, age 21, born May 28, 1944, from Jackson, Mississippi. Pfc. Herron arrived in Vietnam on 6 July 1965 with Headquarters and Service Company, 2nd Battalion, 7th Marines, 1st Marine Division. On 4 March 1966, Pfc. Herron was killed in action, dying from enemy small arms fire while assaulting Hill 37 during Operation Utah. Pfc. Herron is honored on the Vietnam Veterans Memorial on Panel 05E, Line 104.

Hospitalman Lawrence Everett Johnson was the son of Everett Tyler Johnson and Madeline Mildred Johnson, the husband of Shirley Soltis Hayes Johnson and the father of Corinna Marie Johnson all of Binghamton, New York. He enlisted in the US Navy on May 29, 1957 in Albany, New York. HM3 Johnson was a US Navy Corpsman, age 26, born August 15, 1939, from Binghamton, New York. HM3 Johnson arrived in Vietnam on 6 July 1965 with Headquarters and Service Company, 2nd Battalion, 7th Marines, 1st Marine Division, and was attached to Hotel Company for operational purposes. On 4 March 1966, HM3 Johnson was killed in action dying from enemy gunshot wounds on Hill 37 during Operation Utah. HM3 Johnson is interred at Vestal Hill Memorial Cemetery, Vestal, New York and is honored on the Vietnam Veterans Memorial on Panel 05E, Line 105. For his heroic actions that day HM3 Johnson was awarded the Silver Star.

CITATION: The President of the United States of America takes pride in presenting the Silver Star (Posthumously) to Hospital

Corpsman Third Class Lawrence Everett Johnson (NSN: 5140638), United States Navy, for conspicuous gallantry and intrepidity while serving as a Corpsman attached to the Second Battalion, Seventh Marines, FIRST Marine Division, on 4 March 1966, during Operation UTAH in the Republic of Vietnam. With casualties mounting when his platoon was subjected to heavy enemy mortar and automatic weapons fire shortly after the company had secured the high ground dominating the right flank of the battalion's zone of action, Hospital Corpsman Third Class Johnson, in the face of intense fire, unhesitatingly moved from one casualty to another, rendering aid and comfort and supervising the evacuation. When one of the squad leaders was seriously wounded, Hospital Corpsman Third Class Johnson attempted to keep the man alive by administering mouth to mouth resuscitation while moving the patient some three hundred yards under fire to the point of evacuation. During a later enemy counterattack, he observed another wounded Marine to his front and, despite the onrushing enemy, attempted to reach the victim but was struck down by enemy fire. In sacrificing his own life to save the lives of others, Hospital Corpsman Third Class Johnson displayed outstanding courage and a selfless devotion to duty, in keeping with the highest traditions of the United States Naval Service.

Pfc. Frank Lopez, Jr. was the son of Eustolia Lopez of Detroit, Michigan and Frank "D" Lopez. He enlisted in the US Marine Corps on February 12, 1964. Pfc. Lopez was a Marine Field Radio Operator, age 20, born September 22, 1945, from Detroit, Michigan. Pfc. Lopez arrived in Vietnam on 6 July 1965 with Headquarters and Service Company, 2nd Battalion, 7th Marines, 1st Marine Division (Rein), III MAF, FMFPac. On 4 March 1966, Pfc. Lopez was killed in action, dying from multiple fragmentation wounds from an enemy explosive device while going to the aid of a fallen officer. In 2001 the Officer that he tried to save, 1st Lieutenant Pete Amish.

was able to recognize, Pfc. Lopez's heroic action with a posthumous award of a Bronze Star with a V device for Valor. Pfc. Lopez is honored on the Vietnam Veterans Memorial on Panel 05E, Line 106.

Hospitalman Samuel Gizzi Orlando was a US Navy Corpsman, age 21, born August 1, 1944, from Birmingham, Michigan, with over 4 years Naval service. HM Orlando arrived in Vietnam on 6 July 1965 with Headquarters and Service Company, 2nd Battalion, 7th Marines, 1st Marine Division, and was attached to Hotel Company for operational purposes. On 4 March 1966, HM Orlando was killed in action, dying from multiple fragmentation wounds from a hostile explosive device while going to the aid of wounded Marines on Hill 37. HM Orlando is interred at Arlington National Cemetery, Arlington, Virginia and is honored on the Vietnam Veterans Memorial on Panel 05E, Line 108. For his extraordinary heroism that day Hospitalman Orlando was awarded the Navy Cross.

CITATION: The President of the United States of America takes pride in presenting the Navy Cross (Posthumously) to Hospitalman Samuel Gizzi Orlando (NSN: 5910304), United States Navy, for extraordinary heroism on 4 March 1966, while serving as a Corpsman in Hotel Company, Second Battalion, Seventh Marines, First Marine Division (Reinforced), Fleet Marine Force, during Operation UTAH in the Republic of Vietnam. Upon learning that additional corpsmen were needed when one of the platoons of his company was particularly hard hit by intense automatic weapons and heavy mortar fire and was sustaining heavy casualties, Orlando unhesitatingly left his position of relative safety and moved across a barren hill, in the face of intense fire, to the wounded Marines. Exercising outstanding professional skill and resourcefulness, he dressed many wounds and helped evacuate casualties, making several daring trips across the fire-swept area. During one of these trips, when he heard a call for more machine-gun ammunition, he quickly acquired the necessary rounds and carried them to the machine-gun position which was in critically short supply. Hearing the cries of a wounded Marine during an ensuing enemy counterattack, Orlando crawled forward in a courageous attempt to render aid but was mortally wounded by enemy fire at the moment he reached his objective. In sacrificing his own life while saving the lives of many of his comrades, Orland displayed the highest degree of courage and self-sacrifice. His heroic and inspiring efforts were in keeping with the highest traditions of the United States Naval Service.

Private First Class Thomas Wardrop, III was the son of Thomas Jr. and Mary J. Wardrop of Huntington, IN. He enlisted in the US Marine Corps on February 12, 1964. Pfc. Wardrop was a Marine Field Radio Operator, age 21, born February 6, 1945, from Huntington, IN. Pfc. Wardrop arrived in Vietnam on 6 July 1965 and was assigned to Headquarters and Service Company, 2nd Battalion, 7th Marines, 1st Marine Division, and was attached to Fox Company for operational purposes. Pfc. Wardrop was killed in action on 4 March 1966, dying from enemy gunshot wounds while going to the aid of a wounded officer near Hill 50 during Operation Utah. Pfc. Wardrop is interred at Mount Hope Cemetery, Huntington, Indiana and is honored on the Vietnam Veterans Memorial on Panel 05E, Line 111. For his heroic actions that day Pfc. Wardrop was awarded the Bronze Star with the V device for Valor.

CITATION: For heroic achievement in connection with operations against the enemy while serving as a Forward Air Control Team Radio Operator, 2nd Battalion, 7th Marines, 1st Marine Division, Republic of Vietnam, March 4, 1966. While advancing during Operation Utah, the entire battalion came under extremely heavy fire from the well-entrenched 21st North Vietnamese Army Regiment near the Chau Nhai hamlets. In some of the most intense fighting of the war, the rifle company to which Pfc. Wardrop's three-man team was attached was pinned down and immediately sustained numerous casualties requiring medical evacuation. While simultaneously requesting close air support and maneuvering across the fire-swept terrain to locate a helicopter landing zone, the forward air control officer was seriously wounded. Reacting immediately, Pfc. Wardrop, while still carrying his heavy radio equipment and with complete disregard for his own safety, exposed himself, without hesitation, to enemy fire and went to the aid of the wounded officer. Pfc. Wardrop was mortally wounded attempting to shield the wounded officer from the unrelenting fusillade. His heroic action was directly responsible for saving the officer's life. His exceptional performance of duty as a radio operator under the most adverse conditions helped initiate the airstrikes and medical evacuations that undoubtedly saved the lives of scores of Marines, contributing to the accomplishment of the battalion's mission. He gallantly gave his life in the service of his country. Pfc. Wardrop's unswerving devotion to duty and heroic actions were an inspiration to all who observed him and were in keeping with the highest traditions of the Marine Corps and the United States Naval Service. The Combat Distinguishing Device is authorized. For the President, J. L. Jones, Commandant of the Marine Corps.

HQ Company HQ Battalion, 3rd Marine Division

Corporal Lester Arthur Wesighan was the son of Lester W Wesighan of Vernon, NJ and his mother; Wilma Denison of Branchville, NJ. He enlisted in the US Marine Corps and was assigned to HQ Company HQ Battalion, 3rd Marine Division as a Correspondent. He was born on April 22, 1941. While Corporal Wesighan was at Operation Utah as a correspondent, he was killed while going to the aid of a fallen Marine on 4 March 1966. Lester studied to become a Presbyterian minister. While going to college, he worked for a publishing company in NYC. He was a poet and was to be discharged in Sept. 1966 and to come home to NJ to a job on the NJ Herald, Sussex Co, NJ. Corporal Wesighan is honored on the Vietnam Veterans Memorial on Panel 5E, line 111.

Summary of KIAs by Unit

3rd Battalion 1st Marines
India 3/1	20 KIA
Lima 3/1	10 KIA
Mike 3/1	15 KIA

2nd Battalion 4th Marines
Golf 2/4	5 KIA
H&S 2/4	2 KIA
Bravo 1/7	6 KIA

2nd Battalion 7th Marines
Fox 2/7	12 KIA
Golf 2/7	4 KIA

Hotel 2/7	18 KIA
H&S 2/7	8 KIA

H&S 3MAR DIV.	1 KIA

This quote was left on the memorial page for Pfc. Frank Lopez and is one of the reasons I felt compelled to write this book.

"Someone once said, 'Death is not final until you are forgotten.' While I breathe all of you will live on and your sacrifices for our freedom will be remembered. Let me just say, 'Thank you and Semper Fidelis' from an old comrade and a grateful nation."

Postlude

I visited the Operation Utah area in August of 2016. I had been a keynote speaker at a company event in Danang and I took the opportunity to visit the battlefield. A good friend and colleague of mine from Singapore, Pratuysh Kare, accompanied me. I had difficulty finding the site since the Chau Nhai cluster of villages no longer exist on any current maps. Today, most Vietnamese were born years after the war and have never heard of Chau Nhai and the battles that occurred there. After the war the government had built an irrigation and drainage canal through the area, replanted trees, and paved the roads and renamed it Son Tinh district.

In 1966 the hills were barren since the primary fuel was charcoal and for centuries, wood cutters had chopped down the trees near the villages to make charcoal. Now the primary fuel is propane or electricity and the jungle has reclaimed the hills and erased the contours of the grounds we fought over so many years ago. Cars now travel across paved roads that were once dirt paths that we patrolled so cautiously, looking for land mines. My iPhone pinged from a Pokemon Go alert while I was climbing a jungle covered hill. Where we once carried backpack radios and juggled radio frequencies to make contact, we now had access to the world in our iPhone.

During my visit, my Vietnamese travel agent put me in contact with a Mr. Tu who was a Viet Cong veteran and a former resident of Chau Nhai (3). Mr. Tu had been a general in the Viet Cong Army and seemed to be well respected by the local people that we met. Since he did not speak any English, we communicated through my driver who spoke pretty good English but had no knowledge of the war or the area we were in. We visited some sites, but nothing looked familiar. Some of the earlier books that mentioned Operation Utah had my company, Hotel 2/7, on Hill 85, so I was looking in the wrong area. Hill 85 was much taller than the hills I remembered. I could not locate Hill 50 and did not know about Hill 37 at that time. (Hill 37 was identified by my friend Ed Wetzel, the older brother of

Pfc Charles Wetzel, who used GPS coordinates from my iPhone photos, grid coordinates from After Action Reports, and Google Earth to help me map out the locations for this book) Although the area was still very rural, the area was over grown with vegetation making it very difficult to find any familiar landmarks.

After several hours of visiting different locations around the area, Mr. Tu invited us to his home for tea. Mr. Tu showed me several citations which he and his wife had received from General Giap. His wife had also been an officer in the VC Army. Their family altar had pictures of General Giap and Ho Chi Minh which indicated their fealty to these Vietnamese Communist leaders. He confirmed that he had lived in Chau Nhai (3) during Operation Utah and had participated in that battle. Later when I checked the GPS location of this picture of Mr. Tu and his wife, I found that his house was located where 2/7 had set up their night perimeter on 4 March 1966. In Chau Nhai (4).

I felt a little strange drinking tea with a former enemy who had inflicted so much carnage on my fellow Marines. I am sure that Mr. Tu had suffered even more losses, since I had been in Vietnam for only thirteen months while he had been involved for the duration. I guess I thought about all the Marines who died there while I was drinking tea and having a friendly conversation with someone who was our enemy at that time. However, I felt very connected to Mr. Tu and his wife despite our different backgrounds. We had been here before on these same grounds.

Earlier, Mr. Tu took me to a large military cemetery near Hill 85 where hundreds of soldiers were interred. While I had always suspected that the casualty count for NVA killed at Operation Utah may have been overstated, seeing this large cemetery confirmed that a great many NVA had been killed here. The local VC would bury their dead in family plots so I knew that these dead were all NVA who had travelled from their homes in North Vietnam to fight and die in this area. Vu Dinh Doan's son probably found his remains in this cemetery. I burned incense and said a prayer for them as I prayed also for our Marines; So many young lives that ended too soon.

When I told my Marine Corps friend, Hank Barnett about my visit to the scene of Operation Utah and my visit with our former enemy, he asked me an interesting question. He asked me if my new Vietnamese friend would say who won the battle of Operation Utah. It did not occur to me to ask that question. In terms of the way that the score was kept, by "body count", the Marines were the winners as proclaimed by the official After Action Reports and publications like Life Magazine, Stars and Stripes, and the Marine Corps Gazette.

But as Hank and I knew; and as everyone who was there would know. There were no winners in Operation Utah. As soon as we left the NVA and VC came back and repaired the tunnels and bunkers and the Marines came back to fight the NVA and VC again and again for Operation Texas, then for Operation Indiana, then Nevada, then Hot Springs, then …

The military cemetery in Son Tinh, near hill 85 and a few panels on the Vietnam Wall In Washington DC are all that are left to memorialize the sacrifices on both sides at Operation Utah. Unfortunately, when our generation passes away the names will just become statistics unless there is a written record that the families can access for their family history. A good source for them are the online tributes that are posted on the Wall of Faces Vietnam Veterans Memorial Fund (https:// www.vvmf.org/wall-of-faces) website. This book was written to also provide a memorial to those who fought in Operation Utah.

Addendum on Awards

"One of the most important things we can all do for veterans is to honor the service of those who have gone above and beyond the call of duty."

—Defense Secretary Leon E. Panetta

During the narrative of Operation Utah, I have mentioned various awards that were given for heroic action by a number of the Marines and Corpsmen in this battle. In this chapter, I describe these awards so that you can share in America's time-honored tradition of recognizing the acts of valor performed by Soldiers, Sailors, Airmen and Marines. Unfortunately, in the confusion of battle, the transfer of individuals and units, and the evacuation of wounded personnel, many awards were lost in the shuffle. I hope that this book will inspire some of the readers, especially the veterans, to pursue awards for our comrades. It is not too late as long as witnesses are alive. I include some stories of awards that were given years after Operation Utah and the process for pursuing awards for actions that deserve recognition.

Awards for Valor

The **Medal of Honor** (MOH) is the United States government's highest and most prestigious military decoration that may be awarded to recognize American soldiers, sailors, marines, airmen, Space Force guardians, and coast guardsmen who have distinguished themselves by acts of valor. The medal is normally awarded by the President of the United States, but as it is presented "in the name of the United States Congress," it is often referred to as the *Congressional Medal of Honor*.

The **Navy Cross** is the United States Navy and United States Marine Corps' second-highest military decoration awarded for sailors and marines who distinguish themselves for extraordinary heroism in combat with an armed enemy force.

The **Silver Star Medal (SSM)** is the United States Armed Forces' third-highest military decoration for valor in combat. The Silver Star Medal is awarded primarily to members of the United States Armed Forces for gallantry in action against an enemy of the United States.

The **Bronze Star Medal (BSM)** is a United States Armed Forces decoration awarded to members of the United States Armed Forces for either heroic achievement, heroic service, meritorious achievement, or meritorious service in a combat zone. When the medal is awarded by the Navy, Marine Corps, or Coast Guard for acts of valor or meritorious service in combat, the Combat "V" is authorized for wear on the medal.

The **Republic of Vietnam Gallantry Cross**, also known as the Vietnamese Gallantry Cross or Vietnam Cross of Gallantry is a military decoration of the former Government of South Vietnam. It was awarded for accomplishing deeds of valor or displaying heroic conduct while fighting the enemy.

 The **Purple Heart** is awarded in the name of the President of the United States to any member of the Armed Forces of the United States who, while serving under competent authority in any capacity with one of the US Armed Services after April 5, 1917, has been wounded or killed.

During Operation Utah, there were no Medal of Honors awarded. There were four Navy Crosses awarded, three to Marines and one to a Navy Corpsman. There were also a number of Silver Stars, Bronze Stars, and Vietnamese Crosses of Gallantry awarded for heroic action along with Purple Hearts that were awarded to those who were wounded and KIA. The records are not complete enough to name all the recipients, so I only mention those that I was able to find. If any of the readers of this book have information about awards that I did not recognize please forward the information to me and I will add them to future publications of this book. Silver Star Awards and Navy Crosses can be found by entering the recipient's name on the https://valor.militarytimes.com/hero website.

I find it unusual that there were no Medal of Honors awarded during Operation Utah. Certainly each of the Navy Cross winners would have qualified and some of the Silver Star awards would also qualify in my opinion. There is currently an effort to upgrade the Silver Star award for Pfc. Danny Hernandez to a Medal of Honor which is being sponsored by several Veterans and VFW Organizations who have seen the citation and believe that it is more than comparable to other MOH Awards.

During my research for this book, I came across many stories of heroism and leadership which were not recognized by medals or awards. An example are the many men who were killed while trying to go to the aid of a fellow Marine or Corpsman. All of these acts were heroic and should have been recognized by more than a Purple Heart. There was also the question of fairness and consistency.

The highest awards that were awarded as a result of actions during Operation Utah were four Navy Crosses. These Navy Cross was awarded to:

Gunnery Sergeant Talmadge A. Downing M Company 3/1
Weapons Plt Sergeant assaulted several enemy positions

Lance Corporal George O. Norwood G Company 2/7
Fire team leader assaulted enemy Machine gun nest

HM Samuel G. Orlando H&S Company 2/7 Posthumous Award
Corpsman who exposed himself to enemy fire on numerous
occasions to treat and save wounded Marines

Corporal Conrad A. Sipple G Company 2/4 Posthumous award
Exposed himself to enemy fire on four Occasions to assist
wounded Marines to safety

The Awards Process at the beginning of the Vietnam War

This was the beginning of a new war and determining the
requirements for awards had to be redefined or re-learned. The
witness to a heroic event usually was a rifleman who had no idea
how to write it up or determine what was heroic or not. The squad
leaders were in a better position to determine this if they survived the
action. I found that the front line troops set a very high bar for
awards for their peers. It was easier to write up the officers who were
mentioned in the After Action Reports and were awarded for their
leadership. Many of the officers will give credit to the grunts who
helped them win their awards and enable them to do what they did.
For the enlisted men, it was more of an individual effort, putting
themselves in harm's way to save another man or attack an
overwhelming force to save their unit from destruction.

At the beginning of the Vietnam War, no one knew how long this
war would last. Wars provide an opportunity for career military
personnel to improve their chances for promotion by earning medals,
especially combat awards. As a result, there was an obvious effort to
position certain officers and NCOs in posts where they could earn
medals and recognition. Some believe that this was the reason why
units were being committed in such a piecemeal fashion and
commanders were being rotated so quickly during this period.

Some awards were written up but for a number of reasons they
never went through. Many were downgraded or denied by

315

administrative staff who were never in combat but thought that a Staff Sergeant who did a good job running a PX deserved a Bronze Star over a private who gave his life trying to save a fallen comrade. Many times, we, the unit leaders, were the problem due to lack of proper documentation and follow through, especially if we were called out on another operation before we finished the paperwork from the previous one. In the weeks following Operation Utah there were several large battles, including Operations Texas, Indiana, Nevada, and Hot Springs that kept us busy. There were also instances where the witnesses were killed or transferred before the paperwork was done.

The company clerks were the ones who were tasked to type up the eye witness reports and chase up the paperwork and pass it on to battalion and regimental staff for endorsement before it was approved by division staff where they were far removed from the actual combat. Administrative staff were also very busy with other activities, especially during the build-up in 1965-1966. For the Marines, this involved the conversion from an amphibious assault organization to a protracted land warfare organization which required new facilities and supply chains. The Marine Corps was also busy transferring division headquarters from Okinawa where admin personnel were more permanent then in Vietnam where personnel were rotated every 13 months and were often called out on operations in addition to their day jobs. The Mix master program implemented as a way to rotate personnel also created confusion since the unit that initiated an award event might not be the one that processed the award. As a result, it was understandable that the processing of awards was often delayed or even lost in the shuffle during the beginning of the war. There is a two-year limit after the action occurs to submit an award nomination. However, with the rotation of personnel and units and the mixing of units during operations, if the awards were not processed within a month, it didn't happen.

After major joint battles with the ARVN forces, the South Vietnamese would ask for nominations for the Vietnamese Cross of Gallantry. These awards would not require any paperwork, so most commanders would ask the companies to select a few men to attend the ceremonies and receive the awards. Although the Vietnamese Cross of Gallantry is not a US award, I respect those who received it since the recipient was usually selected by their peers and was a result of action during combat. There was a limited number of these awards and as with any award, not everyone who deserved it received it. However, those who did should be proud that they were selected since it was usually done by their peers in combat and not by some administrator sitting up in division staff.

There is a process to still recognize an individual who deserves an award after the two-year deadline. It does require the involvement of a member of the United States Congress. Here are a few examples of how this was done.

Bronze Star Awards with Combat V Awarded 35 Years After Operation Utah

In Chapter 3, where I described the activity of Fox Company 2/7, I related the story of 1st Lieutenant Peter Amish, the Forward Air Controller who was wounded and exposed in a killing zone while looking for a landing zone for medevacs. Two radio operators tried to go to his rescue. First was Pfc. Thomas Wardrop III, who exposed himself, without hesitation and went to aid the wounded officer. Pfc. Wardrop was mortally wounded attempting to shield the wounded officer from the unrelenting fusillade. The second radio operator was Pfc. Frank Lopez who tried to reach Wardrop and Amish. Lieutenant Amish yelled at Pfc. Lopez to "Get out of here" and not expose himself to the deadly fire. Pfc. Lopez was mortally wounded as he reached Pfc. Waldrop and Lieutenant Amish and fell across their bodies.

In 1999, Lieutenant Amish heard from one of Pfc. Tom Waldrop's friends, Tom Miller, that he had visited with Tom Waldrop's parents and learned that there had never been any formal recognition of their son's actions on Operation Utah after Lieutenant Amish had been hit. Immediately following that conversation, Pete Amish wrote a letter to Tom's mother and then after hearing back from her they talked on the phone and set up a time to meet. At the same time, he made contact with Al Kehn who was working at Headquarters Marine Corps in the Awards Section and started the lengthy process of getting Bronze Star awards with Combat V approved for both Tom Waldrop and Frank Lopez.

It took almost two years, but with help from Al Kehn, Pete finally had the awards in hand and on Memorial Day weekend 2001, 35 years after Operation Utah, with his wife Lynn and four Marine veterans who had been in the same unit with Tom Waldrop and Frank Lopez; Tom Miller, Phil Cushman, Dave Zorn, and Jim Kisor, at his side, the Bronze Star awards were presented to the families of Frank and Tom.

On the Saturday of Memorial Day weekend, at a large church in the Detroit area, with several hundred attendees at a special Memorial Day service, Lieutenant Amish presented the Bronze Star award to three of Frank Lopez's aunts as his mother had died and his father had returned to Mexico. One of the Aunts, Flora Limon, had raised Frank, and the other two aunts had flown in from Los Angeles for the presentation. They then went to the cemetery where Frank was buried followed by a meal with Frank's extended family at a Mexican restaurant.

The very next day they drove to Huntington, Indiana to present the Bronze Star award to Tom's father where Tom was buried. It was a totally different setting, with just the five Marines and Pete's wife, and a Marine Color Guard from a nearby Reserve Unit. But it was equally as touching and equally important to the family and to each of the Marines there. They later gathered with Tom's father at his home and attended a church service at the church the family had attended. Tom's dad introduced the Marines during the service and explained why they were there, at the church where his son grew up, serving as an Altar Boy before joining the Marines. Tom Senior had not been back in the church since his son died 35 years ago.

Silver Star Awarded 40 years after Operation Utah

In 2005, Jim Lipori, who was a 2nd Lieutenant leading a Rifle Platoon in Mike Company 3/1 during Operation Utah attended a small reunion of members of his platoon. One of the Marines who attended the reunion was Danny Hernandez who had been attached to his platoon as a machine gunner. After Operation Utah, Jim had recommended Danny for a Silver Star for two extraordinary acts of heroism. As a result of his actions Danny was wounded in the back during his first act of risking his life, rescuing a severely wounded Marine who was stuck in a killing zone. He then assaulted a group of

NVA who were attacking the medevac area where many wounded were taking shelter. Danny stayed in the fight and refused to be med evacuated until he was wounded again in the head later that night. When he recovered from his wounds and returned to Mike Company, Lieutenant Lipori had been transferred to another unit. At the reunion, Lipori discovered that Danny had never even heard that he had been recommended for a Silver Star. Apparently the recommendation paperwork had either been lost or misplaced in the confusion of the many moves that 3/1 made in early 1966. Whatever the reason, Danny Hernandez never received the Silver Star he deserved. Lipori launched a two year effort to right this wrong even though this was over 40 years after the two year deadline for awards.

The Process for Late Award Nominations

According to Department of Defense regulation 1348.33, a recommendation for a medal or award has to be submitted within 2 years of the act or acts for which the medal or award is requested. Once that time period elapses, a much more stringent and complicated administrative process applies. The longer the elapsed time between the act or acts and the recommendation for a medal, the more stringent the process and the greater the scrutiny given to the recommendation and the evidence supporting it by military authorities. This process requires a request from a Member of Congress to the Secretary of the Navy (in the case of the Marine Corps).

DOD MANUAL OF MILITARY DECORATIONS, MEDALS AND AWARDS, and MARINE CORPS ORDER 1650.19 describes the administrative procedure needed to prepare and submit the recommendation.

1. A witness statement describing the reason for the delay in submitting the award.
2. Three statements of witnesses to the event
3. A completed form OP/NAV 1650.3—titled PERSONAL AWARD RECOMMENDATION
4. A written SUMMARY OF ACTION briefly describing the heroic act(s)

5. A PROPOSED CITATION FOR THE award MEDAL.

Most members of congress have a Veterans Affairs Liaison who can help in the process.

I was inspired by Jim Lupori's and Pete Amish's determination to obtain awards for their men and am working on a belated award for one of my men who was killed on Operation Utah. Since so much time has passed since Operation Utah, it is difficult to find eyewitnesses. Although it is difficult to get awards at this late date, it is hoped that this book will provide some help in obtaining some belated awards or at least provide some recognition for the contributions that have been made by the many unsung heroes, the Marines and corpsmen who fought in Operation Utah.

About the Author

Hubert Yoshida, was a 1st Lieutenant in charge of a Marine Rifle Platoon during Operation Utah. As a child he was interred in a prison camp for Japanese American citizens during World War II.

When his family was released from the internment camp, they returned to Watsonville, California, where they started with nothing, living in a converted garage while they began farming a small acreage of strawberries, which later grew into a sizable farm. He graduated from the University of California with a degree in Mathematics. Disturbed by the political situation at Berkeley and inspired by the words of President Kennedy, he applied for a commission in the US Marine Corps. Although initially rejected for Officer Candidate School, he enlisted in the Marine Corps, and later earned a commission in time to command a Rifle Platoon which he led to Vietnam in 1965.

After he returned from Vietnam he joined IBM and began a technical career in International business. Later he joined Hitachi Data Systems where he had the opportunity to visit the area in Vietnam where Operation Utah was fought. After he blogged about his visit, he was contacted by many people asking about relatives who were killed in Operation Utah. This inspired him to research Operation Utah and interview as many veterans as he could find to develop this book.

Hubert lives in Morgan Hill, California with his wife, Laura, and two children, Elizabeth and Michael. Thanks to his wife who endured the loneliness and uncertainty of being the wife of a combat Marine, he survived the war with no traumatic effects. The support of his family has enabled him to have a successful career in technology and retire as an Emeritus Chief Technology Officer for Hitachi Vantara. Although he is on partial disability from the effects of Agent Orange, he is thankful for the life he enjoys with family and friends and appreciates the sacrifices that were made by his comrades-in-arms.

Index

A

326